The Price of Smoking

Frank A. Sloan, Jan
Ostermann, Gabriel Picone,
Christopher Conover, and
Donald H. Taylor, Jr.

The MIT Press
Cambridge, Massachusetts
London, England

MIT Press books may be purchased at special quantity discounts for business or sales promotional use. For information, please e-mail special_sales@mitpress.mit.edu or write to Special Sales Department, The MIT Press, 5 Cambridge Center, Cambridge, MA 02142.

This book was set in Palatino on 3B2 by Asco Typesetters, Hong Kong, and was printed and bound in the United States of America.

Library of Congress Cataloging-in-Publication Data

The price of smoking / Frank A. Sloan ... [et al.].
    p.   cm.
  Includes bibliographical references and index.
  ISBN 0-262-19510-0 (hc. : alk. paper)
  1. Smoking—United States—Costs—Longitudinal studies. 2. Smoking—Health aspects—United States. 3. Smoking—Economic aspects—United States. I. Sloan, Frank A.
HV5760.P73   2004
362.29′6—dc22

                                                                        2004044921

10 9 8 7 6 5 4 3 2

Contents

Preface

Almost all smoking habits begin in either adolescence or young adulthood. Thereafter, some smokers decide to quit, often experiencing considerable hardship in doing so, as the descriptive title of a recent book, *Dying to Quit* (Brigham 1998) implies. Smoking is the leading cause of preventable death throughout the world. Although public policies focus on many risks to life and health far lower than smoking, the smoking habit has been not only tolerated, but historically, even encouraged in the form of public subsidies of cigarettes (Tate 2000).

This book provides a detailed analysis of the price of smoking, both in terms of the burden imposed on the smoker and his or her family and the burden imposed on other members of society. Private costs are those accruing to the individual smoker. In economic jargon, these are termed "internal costs." As a rule, economists have considered all costs to families as internal. The argument is that even if individual family members bear specific costs, through various processes, including intrafamily bargaining, these costs are distributed within the household in a way that maintains the family as a unit. For example, a husband may smoke but his nonsmoking wife engages in shopping sprees. Given the high rates of marriage dissolution at the end of the twentieth century and the effects of smoking on innocent children who clearly are ill positioned to bargain with parents, there is reason to question whether costs imposed by secondary smoke are really internal.

Costs of one's activity imposed on others are external costs. Such costs may reflect the adverse effects of an individual's activity (smoking, in our context) on survival and on health, as well as on others' financial status. The financial externalities reflect the impacts of the activity on payments made by government programs, such as Medicare, Medicaid, and Social Security, as well as payments made by taxpayers to these public programs. Also included are contractual arrangements among private parties such as private health insurance, life insurance, and private pension plans. The sum of private or internal cost and external cost is social cost.

In this book, we take a somewhat agnostic view about costs of smoking imposed on others within the same household, classifying such costs as "quasi-external" with external cost representing all other external cost. Social cost is thus the sum of three rather than two types of cost.

Economics defines a social optimum as the point at which marginal social cost equals marginal social benefit. If the marginal social cost (that is, in the context of this book) from adding another twenty-four-year-old to the pool of smokers is high, as we show it to be, then what is the marginal social benefit? Presumably, marginal benefit is reflected in the lift one gets from lighting up the first cigarette of the morning, relief from stress, appearing "cool" or "with it," having something to do with one's hands, and so on. Particularly in the state in which all but one of us live, North Carolina, some people may continue to argue that tobacco yields a community benefit by sustaining small farms and some local communities. Biological and psychological addiction may explain why some people continue to smoke, but there must be at least some of the above benefits that contribute to its starting.

We do not attempt to quantify the benefits of smoking in this book. At best, that would be a highly complex undertaking. Yet, as our results on cost imply, either such benefits are high or there is indeed a massive misallocation of resources.

At the time some of us wrote our last book on smoking (Sloan, Smith, and Taylor 2003), there were nearly seven hundred books in our Duke University library on the topic of smoking. Admittedly, Duke is located in the heart of tobacco country. But nevertheless, this is a lot of books. In the preface to the previous book, we asked "why another book?" The last book was on information, risk perception, and choices smokers make. One of our main findings was that, for many mature smokers, it takes an adverse health event, such as lung cancer or a heart attack, to induce them to quit smoking. Less severe personal health signals, such as beginning to have difficulty walking up a flight of stairs, are typically insufficient to motivate successful cessation.

In this book, we have a different focus. We quantify the private costs that a man or woman aged twenty-four who smokes at this age may be expected to incur over his or her lifetime, and quasi external and pure external costs such a person imposes on others, ranging from costs associated with secondary smoke for spouses or partners, to financial externalities involving private health insurance, life insurance, private pensions, Medicare, Medicaid, and Social Security.

As we discuss in chapter 3, not only have many books been written on smoking, but there have been many previous studies of the cost of smoking as well. Many of these studies have been published. Other studies have been conducted for specific purposes, such as for use in tobacco litigation. Most studies have used a cross-sectional approach. By contrast, our study is longitudinal. Compared to other research on the cost of smoking, we consider more effects and examine these effects in greater depth.

Our study is the first to quantify the effect of smoking on:

· Life years spent with disabilities. This cost is surprisingly small.

· Earnings over the life cycle. The loss due to smoking is considerable for men but virtually nil for women.

· Contributions and benefits from Social Security and Medicare using data on actual contributions to these public programs that sample persons actually made.

· Spouse mortality, morbidity, and disability. These effects are large, but, of course, not as large as the effects smokers impose on themselves.

· A comprehensive list of outcomes, holding other factors associated with smoking constant. We incorporated a comprehensive list of other factors that are likely to be correlated with smoking but that have been left out of previous studies, such as risk preferences and time horizon, problem and heavy drinking, and obesity. Accounting for these other factors reduces the estimated effects of smoking on various outcomes, but large effects remain.

This book has several different audiences. We hope our study will be of interest to researchers in the field of smoking and other health behaviors. Such persons should find our results interesting, and may want to use some material, such as the smokers' life table in chapter 4, in their own work. Also, the framework used in this book could be applied to other health behaviors, such as lack of exercise and excessive consumption of alcoholic beverages. Specialists in the field of tobacco control may want to use our estimates of the private and social cost of smoking in developing antismoking messages. For example, our finding that a twenty-four-year-old who smokes can expect to incur about \$140,000 in supporting his or her habit over the life cycle, which is equivalent to a cost per pack of nearly \$33, even considering that many such persons will eventually quit, should provide food for thought. State policymakers may be interested in our estimates for purposes of setting cigarette excise taxes. Depending on whether or not the quasi-external costs are included, external cost amounts to \$6.88 (included) or \$1.44 per pack (excluded). Even the latter estimate substantially exceeds excise taxes on cigarettes currently.

Some state and federal policymakers might not be happy with our estimates of the effects of smoking on Medicare and Medicaid, which are much lower than have been alleged. Finally, our results may be useful for parties involved in litigation, including the attorneys who represent these parties.

Acknowledgments

This study was supported in part by a grant from the National Institute on Aging, "The Private and Social Cost of Smoking" (Grant 1R01-AG-16816).

Our primary data source was the Health and Retirement Study (HRS), a nationally representative survey of adults in late middle age. This study was conducted by the Institute of Social Research (ISR) Survey Research Center at the University of Michigan and funded by the National Institute on Aging. We are very grateful for the survey data. In particular, Cathy Liebowitz of ISR was helpful in processing our many requests. We also thank the respondents to the HRS for their help. It is a lengthy survey, with many questions of a personal nature. One of us participated in a HRS pretest, which lasted two hours and nine minutes. He was only surveyed once, but HRS respondents are surveyed repeatedly.

Having access to some restricted-use data sets was very important for this study, especially a file we used to compute contributions by HRS respondents to Social Security (back as far as 1951) and to Medicare (back to the program's inception in 1966). Having these data allowed us to compare contributions by smoking status as well as earnings subject to Social Security and Medicare payroll taxes. In general, inferences about earnings over the life course are made from cross sections. Using this restricted use file, we were able to monitor actual taxable earnings over time.

Several persons participated in bibliographic work for this study: Khuwailah Beyah, Emily Carlisle, and Anne Fletcher, all on the staff of Duke University's Center for Health Policy, Law, and Management. Emily Carlisle edited several versions of the manuscript. We take responsibility for any lack of clarity that remains.

1   Tabulating the Cost of Smoking

Smoking and the Public's Health

Cigarette smoking is the number one preventable cause of premature death. Smoking is a major source of mortality and morbidity in the United States and in other countries, causing various forms of cancer, heart attacks, chronic obstructive pulmonary disease (COPD), and stroke. Yet almost fifty million Americans smoke (Ho 1998). Mortality from certain smoking-related diseases, such as lung cancer, has risen over the past few decades at the same time as mortality from some other causes has declined. Trends in morbidity and resource costs attributable to smoking are more difficult to monitor, but they plausibly parallel mortality trends.

Compared to the rest of the world, the United States has made considerable progress in reducing the magnitude of the burden imposed by smoking, but still has a long way to go (Jones 1996). The good news is that by 2000, per capita cigarette consumption among adults was only half the peak reached in 1963 (Wray et al. 1998). The bad news is that although seventy percent of smokers say they want to quit and thirty-four percent of smokers make an attempt to quit in any given year (Taylor et al. 2002), only 2.5 percent of U.S. smokers succeed in quitting each year (Miller et al. 1997). With fifty-one million Americans who still smoke, this means only about 1.3 million quit smoking annually.

Particularly troublesome is that even as youth perceptions of the risk of smoking and youth disapproval of heavy smoking rose during the latter half of the 1990s, heavy cigarette use generally rose among high school seniors during this same period (Rice et al. 1986). The percent of twelfth graders who said that they smoked increased 1991 through 1997, then declined through 2000 (Sterling, Rosenbaum, and Weinkam

1993, p. 178). As more than three-quarters of smokers begin smoking before age 19 (Centers for Disease Control and Prevention 1997) and many begin their habits in their early teens (Leu 1984; Manning et al. 1989), trends among minors in particular merit monitoring.

Smoking Benefits and Costs and Public Policy

Smoking and smoking policy have been analyzed from a number of alternative but partially complementary perspectives. From a medical standpoint, smoking is one of the most hazardous health behaviors. Physicians routinely counsel their patients who smoke to quit. Practice guidelines for smoking cessation exist and have been widely disseminated. Similarly, from the vantage point of public health, smoking is the major cause of mortality and an important source of morbidity and long-term disability. Such concerns have led public expenditures on tobacco control programs, restrictions on access to cigarettes, especially to youths, bans on advertising of tobacco products, and increased excise taxes on cigarettes. To the extent that smoking is viewed as an absolute "bad," it seems unnecessary to quantify costs attributable to tobacco consumption.

An alternative view, shared by most economists, is that people are the best judges of the goods and services they consume. This view is incorporated in the doctrine of "consumer sovereignty." In determining what and how much of each good and service to consume, people weigh benefits accruing to them personally with the costs. Both the benefits and costs are private. Costs include the price of the good or service, but also later consequences, such as effects on health in later life. At the same time, consumption contributes to the person's utility or well-being. In the context of cigarette consumption, people smoke because they enjoy it, for relief of stress, to display their maturity or sexuality, to satisfy an addiction, and for other reasons.

If one accepts the doctrine of consumer sovereignty, only those benefits and costs from the person's consumption that are external to the individual are relevant for public policy decisions. There are few external benefits of tobacco consumption. Some might list employment opportunities in tobacco growing, manufacturing, and sales as external benefits, at least in the short run until such resources can be allocated to alternative uses. There are two major types of external cost—(1) adverse health effects and discomfort that smoking imposes on others and (2) the financial burdens from smoking-attributable illnesses that are borne by others in addition to the smoker. A third, somewhat more controversial external cost, is loss in well-being that a nonsmoker suffers from just knowing that others smoke. This third type of external cost is inconsistent with consumer sovereignty. Its existence presupposes that smokers should know better or that they are simply too addicted to quit.

Social benefit is the sum of private benefits to each consumer of the product plus the external benefit. Likewise, social cost represents the sum of private costs incurred by individual consumers as well as the external cost.

In the past, based on an assumption of consumer sovereignty, economic studies of the cost of smoking have focused on its external cost. The fact that people decide to smoke suggests that, at the margin, private benefits cover private cost. Knowing the external cost is useful for determining optimal levels of excise taxes on tobacco products.

The assumption that people are sovereign consumers of tobacco product is likely to be violated under several conditions. First, consumer sovereignty presumes people know the private benefits and costs of the goods and services that they consume. But smoking imposes costs on the smoker that are not likely to be anticipated, particularly since much of such cost occurs late in the life cycle—many decades after the smoking habit is typically initiated. A value in documenting the private cost of smoking is its use in informing adolescents and young adults about costs they are likely to face as they age.

A second circumstance under which consumer sovereignty is violated is that consumers may lack self-control over their consumption decisions. Financial call-in radio and television programs often receive calls from people who would like to control their credit card debt but cannot. Others say that they want to lose weight and sometimes succeed, but only temporarily. Heavy drinkers or smokers may say that they want to quit, but they experience problems in follow-through. Such self-control problems are inconsistent with consumer sovereignty (Manning et al. 1991; Harris 1997a). By discouraging consumption, excise taxes and smoking bans are devices that can help smokers deal with their self-control problems. Under such circumstances, internal or private costs as well as external costs are relevant to setting the optimal level of the excise tax and for computing the benefit of a public tobacco control program.

In general, economists consider costs borne by the household to be private. Household and individual decision making are viewed as virtually interchangeable. In the microeconomics of household behavior, the distinction has largely been a matter of mathematical notation. Implicitly at least, every family member is assumed to have identical preferences. Or, at a minimum, a smoker is presumed to have incorporated all preferences of other family members in decisions about how much to smoke.

In the past two decades, economists have begun to model interactions among household members, especially between spouses (see chapter 10). This research is motivated by the notion that spouses' preferences differ. Bargains are struck that involve trades between spouses regarding consumption of commodities from which they may derive different levels of utility (or lack of utility). There is an outside option of dissolving the marriage, but many couples will remain married having resolved their differences through bargaining. In the context of smoking, for example, a husband may continue to smoke, and this is a source of aggravation to his wife. In trade, the two may agree that the wife can take a trip to Hawaii with a girlfriend. To the extent that this bargaining process within the household market functions well, health and aggravation effects of smoking on the spouse, as well as the financial burdens of smoking shared by both spouses, may appropriately be viewed as internal.

An alternative viewpoint is that, in the case of smoking, costs borne by household members other than the smoker should be viewed as external. Maternal smoking has potential adverse effects on offspring, and youngsters with smoking-related health problems sometimes become adults with such problems. Persons have no bargaining power before birth or as infants or young children.

Even when bargaining power is likely to be more equal, smoking by one spouse may adversely affect the health of the other spouse (chapters 3 and 10), and, in the United States and in many other high-income countries, a high percentage of marriages dissolve. Then at least some of the financial burden generally absorbed by households as between spouses, may be shared by others. Also, some spouses, such as wives with low earnings potential, may have few options outside of the current marriage. In such cases, acceptance of the results of household bargaining may violate social norms. In this study, we will take an agnostic view about how to count the cost that smoking by one spouse imposes on the other spouse. To distinguish these costs from other private costs, we will refer to them as "quasi-external" costs and identity them in a separate category.

Governments' Role in Markets for Tobacco Products

For a good or service in which the consensus is that consumption has no important externalities, there is no role for government intervention. In fact, in most markets, governments play at most a minor role. But when these circumstances do not hold, government intervention is warranted.

First, to deal with externalities, one appropriate government response is to levy a tax on use, in effect marginally raising cost to provide a disincentive for consumption of the product. Another policy is to ban consumption especially in certain locations, such as schools, workplaces, and places where people congregate.

Apart from concern about adverse health effects on nonsmokers, there is concern that nonsmokers pay for the smoking-attributable cost in the form of higher insurance premiums, contributions to social insurance programs, such as Social Security, and higher taxes to support programs such as Medicaid (see Harris 1997; Max 1997a,b,c). But especially considering the cigarette excise taxes smokers pay as well as payments from the Master Settlement Agreement (MSA) between states and major tobacco companies (which have been shifted forward to consumers in the form of higher product prices), whether nonsmokers subsidize smokers or the reverse is no longer clear.

Second, governments may intervene to correct distortions in information flows. Decades ago, tobacco manufacturers advertised that "more physicians smoke Camels than any other cigarette," and "you can't help inhaling, but you *can help your throat*! Call for Philip Morris."[1] Such messages conveyed the idea that smoking was not harmful to one's health. Such advertisements may seem amusing, but five decades or so ago, they were both "informative" and reassuring to readers. By contrast, in certain sectors, most notably pharmaceuticals, the federal government only permits companies to make those claims that are substantiated by evidence from randomized clinical trials. In such cases, the government response is information regulation, rather than taxation (see, e.g., Miller et al. 1997).

The empirical evidence on advertising as a determinant of smoking has been debated and investigated at length. In brief, the empirical evidence is mixed (see e.g., Miller, Ernst, and Collin 1999; Rubin 1997), in spite of frequent advertising suggesting that smoking the advertised product yields benefits and is safe. Complicating the picture is that information about the underlying risk has not been constant but rather has evolved during the course of the twentieth century. During the first half of the century, although harm from smoking was suspected, there was a paucity of empirical evidence, much analogous to information on the health effects of cell phone use today.

An important characteristic of tobacco consumption is the long latency period between the time of initiation and the onset of adverse events. Relatively few adverse health events occur before late middle age. To illustrate, at age 35, the cumulative probability of survival is the same for those who have never smoked and smokers. At age 45, the ratio of such probabilities, those who have never smoked to smokers, is 1.02 for males and 1.00 for females. The lower ratio for females may reflect an average higher age of onset of the smoking habit than males. At age 55, the corresponding ratios are 1.06 for males and 1.02 for females, and at age 65, the ratios are 1.18 and 1.08, respectively. By age 85, the ratios are 2.11 for males and 1.57 for females (Rice, Kelman, and Durmeyer 1990, p. 91). Excess morbidity and consequently elevated cost occurs earlier, however, for some smoking-related diseases such as lung cancer; for this disease, the lag between initial treatment and death is less than a year on average (Hartunian, Smart, and Thompson 1980; Gold, Gold, and Weinstein 1996).

The third kind of justification for government intervention occurs when assumptions underlying the doctrine of consumer sovereignty are violated. But in the context of smoking, people may be ill informed about the underlying risks, myopic (not forward-looking), barred from acting by their underlying addictions or other reasons, or simply lacking in self-control over consumption decisions (Freeman 2003; Diamond and Hausman 1994). Under such circumstances, a tax on use could be implemented to discourage consumption, especially if smoking cessation aids marketed by the private sector are viewed as insufficient to assist smokers with their problems of self-control. A government ban on sale of the product as occurred during national prohibition of manufacture and sale of alcohol during the 1920s and early 1930s, may also be justified on this basis.

The argument is that people who know that they will have trouble in the future with self-control may actually favor externally imposed controls over their decisions. In the context of public assistance, a time-inconsistent potential recipient may actually favor statutory time limits on eligibility for welfare. In the context of smoking, a smoker may be better off with an increase in the state excise tax. Under standard models, smoker well-being clearly is worsened by a tax increase of this sort (Diamond and Hausman 1994).

Equity and Smoking Policy

Another goal of public policy is fairness. The equity principle relates to the just distribution of the burden of smoking based on smoking status or some other basis such as income. Equity is a much less studied aspect of tobacco control policy.

The equity principle has both "horizontal" and "vertical" dimensions. All other things equal, horizontal equity requires that people in equal circumstances (e.g., with equal incomes) pay the same tax. There is no consensus on what constitutes vertical equity, how much tax an affluent person pays relative to a less affluent person, except that it is generally undesirable for those with low incomes to bear a higher relative tax than those with higher incomes. Cigarette taxes are well known for being regressive in their impact, in part because the odds of smoking among poor adults are three-fifths higher than among non-poor adults (Kunreuther, Novemsky, and Kahneman 2001). Moreover, in contrast to the assumption underlying traditional analyses (that prices rise by the same amount as excise taxes), for various reasons cigarette manufacturers may use excise tax increases as an opportunity to raise retail prices by more than the increase in tax rates (Warner et al. 1995; Chaloupka et al. 2000). Empirical evidence supports this view. Such "overshifting" therefore worsens any regressive impacts of such taxes. On the other hand, Cutler et al. (2002) have argued that although the poor pay a higher fraction of their income in cigarette excise taxes, as smokers they also benefit disproportionately from the reduction in mortality and morbidity brought about by the drop in consumption that excise taxes cause. Finally, concerns about equity also motivate other policy interventions, such as inclusion of smoking cessation programs under Medicaid.

The Relationship of the Private and Social Cost of Smoking to Public Policy: Four Examples

Public policy decision makers cannot properly gauge the extent to which policy contributes either to efficiency or equity without accurate estimates of the costs of smoking. We agree with Meier and Licari

(1997) that rather than guiding public policy, estimates of smoking-attributable cost often have been developed by advocates of a particular policy position, not as a guide to appropriate policy but rather as support for a position developed independently of the estimates. Thus, rather than serve the analytic purpose of guiding public policy in setting taxes, determining appropriate amounts of compensation in tort litigation, and assessing social returns from public programs that discourage initiation or encourage cessation, the estimates are in effect weapons, either to attack adversaries who oppose one's position or to be used in self-defense. Even though an extensive literature covers the costs of smoking (see chapter 3), we began this study without any preconceived notions of what the costs might be.

Tobacco policy relies on a combination of information, incentives ("carrots"), and regulations ("sticks") on both the demand and supply sides of the market to steer it toward an efficient level of tobacco consumption. Although the principal goal of smoking control efforts is to improve health, which individuals' health might be improved depends critically on the policy instrument selected. This in turn depends on the rationale for intervention. Of all those harmed by smoking, the victims most in need of public protection arguably are children; indeed, the public health community and economists appear to have consistent views on this (Chaloupka et al. 2000; MacKensie, Bartecchi, and Schrier 1994). The rationale for focusing on children stems from concern about the external effects of smoking on infant health and development and on children who grow up in a home in which adults smoke, as well as the notion that, in the context of smoking, the necessary conditions for relying on consumer sovereignty probably do not apply in the case of children and adolescents. However, interventions that target only children and adolescents are unlikely to be effective in isolation; some of the most potent interventions, such as cigarette taxes, unavoidably will reduce adult consumption as well (U.S. Department of Treasury 1998; Harris 1993). Also, parents have a major influence on the smoking behavior of their children (Passell 1993; Gravelle and Zimmerman 1994).

Volumes have been written about U.S. tobacco policy (see e.g., the many reports of the U.S. surgeon general; Tollison 1994; National Center for Health Statistics 2001; and many others). Rather than rehash what is already known about the extent and effectiveness of various policies, we focus here on the extent to which cost estimates either have been used to develop or might be needed to improve current policy. Some relevant policy applications are tobacco excise taxes, smoking cessations aids, tobacco litigation and allocation of tobacco settlement funds, and forecasting contributions for and expenditures on major social insurance programs, especially Social Security and Medicare.

Tobacco Taxes

Tobacco taxes are an extremely potent policy instrument. Extensive analysis has revealed a typical aggregate demand elasticity of −0.3 to −0.5 and further has suggested that the participation price elasticity is roughly half the demand elasticity (Orzechowski and Walker 2002; U.S. Department of Health and Human Services 2000a; Rigotti 2002). Many existing studies of the impact of taxes on demand for cigarettes have not taken into account that states may raise excise taxes on cigarettes when demand for this product is high ("endogeneity" of taxes). The handful of studies that correct for endogeneity show that tobacco taxes have roughly double the impact on demand than was found previously in studies that did not make this correction (Silagy et al. 1998; Ranson et al. 2000). Evidence is mixed on whether prices influence the probability of initiating smoking or quitting (U.S. Department of Health and Human Services 2000a).

Tobacco taxes have been the subject of extensive research and discussion regarding how to determine the optimal level.[2] The conceptual task of setting the optimal cigarette excise tax rate is quite complex. As noted above, the optimal tax would force the potential smoker to consider the cost of all consequences smoking imposes on others. To the extent that smokers are irrational and myopic, the optimal tax would reflect private costs of smoking as well. Thus, to determine the optimal rate, one needs to both understand choices people make about smoking as well as quantify the external and perhaps the private costs of smoking. Private costs far exceed the external costs of smoking. Thus, one's assessment of the extent that smokers are rational and forward-looking or irrational and myopic has an important bearing on what the socially optimal excise tax should be. Equity considerations add further complications, because an economically efficient tax may be viewed as inequitable.

As will be discussed in more detail in chapter 3, the general consensus from studies as of the mid-1990s was that, using a three percent discount rate, smokers generally more than "paid their own way" when only financial costs (such as medical care, Social Security, and retirement) were taken into account, that is, smokers end up subsidizing nonsmokers by nearly 25 cents a pack because any higher medical costs experienced by smokers are more than offset by the reduction in retirement and Social Security payments that result from their earlier deaths (updated figures from Hu et al. 2000, reported in Nielsen and Fiore 2000, and Viscusi 1999). This conclusion was based on an assumption that smokers should pay for costs imposed on others outside their households and not costs imposed on other family members or purely internal costs.

Even when intermediate estimates of loss of life from lung cancer and heart disease attributable to environmental tobacco smoke (ETS) were taken into account, smokers subsidized nonsmokers by 9 to 11 cents a pack (Cutler et al. 2002). Others concluded that costs of maternal smoking alone amount to 42 to 72 cents per pack (Price and Dake 1999), while others placed this cost as high as $4.10 per pack in 1990 (Wilson 1999). By far, the largest cost stems from the average loss of years of life for smokers—an amount equivalent to $22 per pack undiscounted and $6.63 per pack when discounted at five percent, costs that become relevant for public policy when assumptions underlying consumer sovereignty are violated.[3]

According to Cutler et al. (2002), smokers lose an estimated two hours of life expectancy per pack—a loss whose undiscounted value amounts to $22 per pack. At issue is whether smokers obtain $22 worth of pleasure from smoking a pack or whether they instead have underestimated the risks associated with smoking. If they do not, excise taxes on cigarettes should be much higher than they are now.

A skeptic of the view that excise taxes are too low is W. Kip Viscusi, a professor at Harvard Law School. Viscusi (Sims 1994) estimated that, as of the mid-1980s, state excise taxes' deterrent effect was equivalent to the effect of a smoker's believing that his or her lifetime risk of getting lung cancer from smoking was anywhere from 17 percent (assuming an elasticity of −0.4) to 51 percent (assuming an elasticity of −1.4, a figure sometimes cited for teenagers). The actual lifetime risk of lung cancer for smokers was only five to 10 percent; moreover, smokers responding to a survey he described assessed this risk at 37 percent on average. Thus, state cigarette taxes inflated an already exaggerated risk by roughly 50 to more than 100 percent. In short, excise taxes more than compensated for any health information gaps that might lead smokers to erroneously continue their behavior.

Previous studies generally concluded that overall, smokers pay more in the form of excise taxes than the losses they generate. Yet excise taxes are rising in most nations, as are prices of cigarettes. Obviously, public policymakers do not seem to be paying much attention to such calculations. Should they? What does our empirical analysis imply for resolving disputes of losses allegedly due to smoking via tort claims? Our results likely will have major implications for tort claims currently pursued by various parties including state Medicaid programs. It is important to compare the evidence with the parties' arguments.

Under the best of circumstances, objective analysis is only one input into the policy decision-making process. Another consideration is politics. For example, although U.S. Public Health Service (PHS) scientists had concluded as early as 1957 that lung cancer was caused by smoking, the PHS rejected tobacco-related public health actions, such as placing warning labels on cigarettes. One possible reason was the prospect of loss of congressional support and funding if the PHS took a more aggressive stance (Watson et al. 1995).[4]

Smoking Cessation Aids

More than two-thirds of current smokers report wanting to quit, but only 2.5 percent actually quit in a typical year (Oster 1996). Smoking behavior for motivated individuals can be influenced by subsidizing activities related to smoking cessation, including physician advice, counseling, and pharmacotherapy. Nicotine replacement therapy (NRT) takes various forms (chewing gum, transdermal patches, nasal spray, and vapor inhalers), and has been demonstrated in numerous studies to increase a smoker's chances of quitting (Hopkins and Lynch 1997). Such products were sold only by prescription until 1996, but today most sales are over-the-counter (Harris 1997a).[5]

If smokers paid for such help in full and we could fully rely on consumer sovereignty in this context, an explicit calculation of the benefits of quitting by someone other than the smoker would be unnecessary. But health insurers do consider covering such help, and individual smokers may be ill informed about the benefits of quitting. Thus, quantitative estimates of the benefits to be derived from smoking cessation are useful. In the discussion that follows, we intend to emphasize applications of the calculations rather than the results of past studies. As reported in later chapters, we have developed our own estimates for many effects of smoking.

Smoking cessation is particularly important for Medicaid because the rate of smoking is roughly 50 percent higher among Medicaid recipients than the general population (Harris 1997). Although the U.S. Centers for Medicare and Medicaid Services (CMS), the agency that runs the Medicare and Medicare programs, could in principle either mandate or exclude Medicaid coverage for clinical services for smoking cessation or NRT, to date it has done neither—leaving it to individual states to decide whether such services should be covered for smokers generally or particular subgroups (e.g., pregnant women).

Likewise, Medicare could elect to make such services covered under Medicare, but to date has not done so. Such services are optionally covered by some of the plans offered under the Federal Employees Health Benefits Plan (FEHBP); the fee-for-service plans generally cover up to $100 per member per lifetime toward the cost of enrollment in one smoking cessation program.[6]

Although employers generally may be reluctant to interfere with private activities of workers, they may have a financial stake in altering behaviors affecting a worker's own productivity and that of others. Kristein (Max 1997a) estimated that a typical smoker imposed a cost of $336 to $601 on the employer, taking into account the effects on excess health insurance costs, higher absenteeism, productivity losses while working, excess workers' compensation costs, increased occupational health costs, higher life insurance costs, and fire losses. Roughly half of this was borne in the short term (1–3 years) and the balance were longer-term costs that could be fully "recaptured" only if the employee remained with the same employer for 10 to 15 years. Kristein showed that under various assumptions, the rate of return on a smoking cessation program could range from 25 to 100 percent. Max (1997b) used a simulation analysis for a large manufacturing firm, showing that a work site smoking cessation program will generate financial returns exceeding the program's cost, taking into account returns in the areas of medical care, absenteeism, on-the-job productivity, and life insurance.[7]

In these applications, the desirability of paying for smoking cessation services depends on which costs and benefits are included. An employer will want to consider as benefits costs averted that are not borne by the employee as well as savings attributable to reduced employee turnover, assuming that employees value the benefit. In any case, the calculation involves private costs and benefits. For Medicaid and Medicare, the ideal calculation is more complex. In a narrow sense, one would cover a smoking cessation service if the savings in outlays for other care, appropriately discounted, would cover the cost of offering the service. Cost offsets, however, constitute too narrow a view of the benefit. Savings in nonmedical costs, such as work disability, are also an appropriate part of the benefit calculation.

Tobacco Litigation and the Tobacco Settlement

In recent years, private and public parties have sued tobacco companies (Max 1997c; Miller 1997a,b; Oster 1997a). Two parts are essential to a tort claim: establishing liability and determining damages. Liability depends on a finding of harm to the defendant, an action or inaction on the part of the defendant causing the harm, and a finding of failure to exercise due care, that is, negligence. Estimates of the cost of smoking are directly relevant for establishing the amount of damages. As far as determination of liability is concerned, studies of the cost of smoking establish that damage occurred. Also, for damages to be attributable to smoking, it is necessary to establish causation.[8] In litigation with individual smokers as plaintiffs, it is not only required that smoking caused the loss, but that the tobacco manufacturers were at least partly responsible for the fact that the person smoked by deceiving people about the benefits and especially the private cost of smoking. There is controversy about whether smokers were misled by cigarette company advertising. The cost studies do not take a position on this issue.

Viscusi (Oster 1997b) in particular has persuasively argued that the settlements in the late 1990s between the states' attorneys general and the major cigarette manufacturers, the most important of which being the Master Settlement Agreement (MSA) between forty-six states' attorneys general and the major cigarette manufacturers (MSA), were not based on careful and detailed assessments of smoking-attributable cost. Both he and we argue that if compensation was not based on such assessments, it should have been. As the door on future tobacco litigation is not closed (only closed for the states and even then it is useful to learn from past experience), there is room for the use of such assessments in resolving ongoing and future litigation. And rather than serve as a bad example of damage determination for litigation in other areas, such as against gun manufacturers and fast food restaurants, the opportunity for a midcourse correction still remains.[9]

The relevance of estimates of the cost of smoking for establishing damages, conditional on a conclusion that the defendant is liable, is clear. In contrast to much other public policy relating to tobacco control, cost estimates played a central role in determining the final amount of the settlement. The heart of the settlement are annual payments designed to compensate states for Medicaid damages. A number of different studies were developed, many of which were used on both sides of the litigation process.[10] Some retrospective analyses of the settlement have been done using state data: Schumacher 1996 (Massachusetts); and Harrison 1998a (Massachusetts). The standard method used in nearly all of these studies was to estimate the smoking-attributable fraction of Medicaid expenditures based on the excess medical costs of smokers compared to nonsmokers at a slice in time. Some of the more sophisticated models also accounted for the impact of parental smoking on medical costs for children (e.g., Harrison 1998b). One retrospective analysis concluded that the overall savings to Medicaid that can be expected as a result of smoking reductions through the year 2025 will amount to only about one percent of all Medicaid spending attributable to smoking during that period (Harrison 1999).

Proposed and actual settlements between tobacco manufacturers and the states have been vociferously criticized on legal grounds (Hanson and Logue 1998; Levy 1998a,b) and on antitrust grounds, on the view that they have facilitated collusion among the companies to raise prices, ultimately benefiting plaintiffs (states), lawyers, and defendants at the expense of consumers (Federal Trade Commission 1997; Bulow and Klemperer 1998). Viscusi (1999, 2002) sharply criticized the approach used in the MSA, arguing that by focusing only on short-term medical cost differences between smokers and nonsmokers, this settlement does not account for the substantial savings states receive in their nursing home and pension costs due to the reduced life expectancy of smokers. His calculations showed that literally every state saves money on smokers; moreover, even if one restricts the analysis to pure medical losses (leaving aside nursing home and pension losses), most states will receive from the MSA more (in some cases 2.9 times as much) than their actual medical losses.

Yet others have criticized the MSA on grounds that it is not at all clear what the payment is intended to cover (e.g., a payment for past harms vs. a payment for future expected harms) and on grounds that the implicit excise taxes that will result from the settlement are too low to fully account for externalities arising from addiction and inaccurate personal risk perceptions among smokers (see Hanson and Logue 1998 for a discussion of the proposal settlement that preceded the MSA). These authors have proposed a comprehensive alternative to the settlement—a smokers' compensation system—that purportedly would create incentives for tobacco manufacturers to reduce the harms associated with tobacco rather than seek ways to evade the letter and spirit of the settlement (Hanson, Logue, and Zamore 1998). We will eventually find out whether the MSA becomes an enduring feature of the tobacco regulation landscape or is ultimately swept away by alternative approaches.

Future Solvency of Social Security and Medicare: Forecasting Future Contributions and Expenditures

Ironically, although promoting good health habits such as smoking cessation may be good for Americans' health, this may be bad for Social Security's and Medicare's future financial health, as will be apparent from results we present in this book. This does not mean that promoting health is not a desirable public policy objective, but rather that this objective comes at a cost. Having estimates of impacts of smoking on cash flows accruing to Social Security and Medicare are important for documenting the trade-off.

Goals of This Book

This book has three objectives: (1) to calculate the cost of smoking updating previous estimates using a new data set, which allowed us to follow smokers and nonsmokers longitudinally and to assess some types of cost that have not been analyzed in detail before; (2) to analyze the consequences of smoking from standpoints such as the effect on morbidity, functional states, and other health outcomes; and (3) to tally the cost of smoking, identifying the major contributors to the private and social cost of smoking.

Improved Estimates of Private and Social Costs of Smoking over the Life Cycle

The primary purpose of our study is to provide a comprehensive analysis of the cost of smoking and incidence of such cost within the context of a rigorous normative framework. The magnitude of smoking-related costs is relevant not only for guiding the wide range of current policies aimed at smoking, but also for improving management of public programs that cover a growing share of the U.S. population, for example, pregnant women, children, the aged, the blind, the disabled, and single parents under Medicaid, the elderly and disabled under Medicare, and federal employees, retirees, and their dependents.

We evaluate private and social costs of smoking for men and women who smoke at age 24. Many of the smokers will quit before they die, many long before this, a factor accounted for in our analysis. But, especially for those persons who quit after smoking for many years, and those who never quit, health and financial consequences are long lasting if not permanent. We selected age 24 as the base year to focus on adult smoking. Many teenagers experiment with cigarettes, but their smoking habits do not extend into adulthood.

Because (1) most smoking-related disease begins after age 50 (see chapter 4) and (2) we have a longitudinal data set containing detailed information on smoking behavior, health, and utilization of personal health services of both spouses for married persons, we focus much of our analysis of the cost of smoking to the over-50 age group. As explained above, most adverse health effects from smoking, including excess mortality, occurs after age 50. Earlier studies of the cost of smoking were conducted before these data became available. By combining our new results with a synthesis of past work, we develop a comprehensive estimate of the total private and social costs of smoking, showing how these costs are distributed among the smoker, the smoker's family, and the rest of society.

Because tobacco products are legal goods, the ultimate decision maker about tobacco consumption is the individual. Informing people about the consequences of their choices is a public role when such choices involve elevated probabilities of adverse consequences to the user. Estimates of the internal costs of smoking are useful also to employers who self-insure, insurance companies, and managed care companies, to determine, for example, the cost-effectiveness of smoking cessation benefits.

The vast majority of information programs indicate only that the activity is harmful to the user. Examples are warnings that the use of alcohol carries health risks to unborn children and various messages that "smoking is bad for you." Our estimates of the private costs of smoking to a 24-year smoker have a shock value and should be useful for antismoking public health campaigns.

One of the most influential prior studies of smoking-attributable cost is by Manning et al. (1989, 1991) with estimates updated by Viscusi (1999). This research was based on short longitudinal databases for a three to five year period, the Rand Health Insurance Experiment (HIE) and a single cross section, the National Health Interview Survey (NHIS). We also use the NHIS, but more importantly, we use a panel data set spanning 1992 to 2000, the Health and Retirement Study (HRS). The HRS not only allows us to follow individuals' consumption and income over time, but to assess the effects of cigarette consumption on utilization of personal health care services over time. Since Social Security records have been merged with data from the HRS, we are able to study the effect of smoking on contributions to and benefits from the Social Security program. The Rand HIE excluded persons over age 62 and ran for 3 to 5 years in six localities. By contrast, HRS data are national and include persons into their 90s.

Past calculations have been too narrow in another sense, namely that they have disregarded the nonpecuniary losses from smoking. Such losses stem from pain and suffering, lack of independence in one's activities of daily living, or both, as a consequence of poor health; also included in such losses is the premature death or disability of relatives and friends.

Much of the previous analysis has disregarded distributional consequences. A practical impediment to raising excise taxes on tobacco products has been the regressiveness of such taxes. The incidence of the burden of smoking and policies aimed at reducing the prevalence of smoking is not at all well documented. Distributional concerns address how the burden of smoking and related policies is borne by various segments of the population, in particular smokers and nonsmokers. Such analysis is complicated because smoking affects not only mortality but also many other consumption and saving decisions, including the purchase of insurance (health, life, and disability), contributions to and benefits from pension plans, sick leave, and utilization of personal health services. Past researchers were more limited by lack of sufficiently detailed data than were we.

Better Estimates of Effect of Smoking on Health

Most past studies of smoking's effects on health have been based on small clinical samples or longitudinal data from a particular locality, such as the Bay Area, California, or Framingham, Massachusetts. The HRS tracks survival, numerous dimensions of physical functioning, as well as morbidity. A very unique feature of the HRS that we exploit is that identical data are collected on both spouses. This includes smoking behavior and many other factors.

Expanding the Tally of the Cost of Smoking

Given our data, we are able to study more impacts in greater depth than has been done in previous research. We are not only able to show that the total cost of smoking is considerable but to quantify the major components of such cost.

Chapter Overview

Chapter 2 has two objectives: (1) to provide a conceptual framework for measuring the private and social cost of smoking; and (2) to describe the databases used in our study. We argue that the appropriate framework is longitudinal and that cross-sectional studies can yield misleading findings, except under a very limited set of conditions. Although our results are not qualitatively different from previous studies that have used a longitudinal approach, our analysis is much more detailed and comprehensive in important respects and based on data not previously available. In our study, we ask what is the present value of loss over the life cycle associated with an individual's being a smoker at age 24. Few people initiate smoking after this date. Persons who permanently quit before reaching the age of 24 do not generally experience harmful effects from smoking (Sloan, Smith, and Taylor 2003). We summarize the major databases used in our analysis, including (a) the 1998 National Health Interview Survey (NHIS), (b) three waves of Asset and Health Dynamics of the Oldest Old (AHEAD, 1993, 1995, 1998, and 2000), and (c) five waves of the Health and Retirement Study (HRS, 1992, 1994, 1996, 1998, and 2000). In related work on mortality, we have used the Cancer Prevention Study 2 to assess the impact of smoking cessation on longevity of older persons (Taylor et al. 2002; Hasselblad et al. 2003). These results are used here for comparative purposes.

Chapter 3 discusses previous studies of the cost of smoking. Studies vary considerably in the scope of impacts evaluated, the data used, and crucially, the underlying methodology. As discussed in length in that chapter, one approach addresses the question, "in a year, how much more is spent because people smoke?" We term this the cross-sectional approach. Others have called this a "prevalence" approach because it is based on the number of smokers alive in a given year. This methodology is mainly appropriate for informing a policymaker about how much will be spent on smoking-related problems during a fixed time period, such as a year, although such studies have been used inappropriately for more general purposes.

The other approach asks the question, "If we were able to influence a person not to smoke, what would be the savings over the person's lifetime?" In our terminology, this is the life cycle approach. This is sometimes called the "incidence" or "longitudinal" approach in that it reflects impacts of persons who become smokers at a point in time, such as a year.

We argue in chapter 3 that the longitudinal approach is the conceptually superior method, but this is controversial, especially to parties that stand to benefit from having a large estimate: our approach typically yields answers that imply much lower smoking-attributable loss. Intuitively, it relies on the notion that a dead smoker does not require medical care or income support. To illustrate the tenor of the controversy, we reproduce a quotation from the state of Mississippi in box 1.1. After reading this, we suspect that all readers will agree that the subject is controversial. We will address the merits of the argument in chapter 3.

Box 1.1
Critique of Longitudinal Approach

"A credit to the cigarette industry for any monetary savings in elderly health care, as well as other savings resulting in the premature deaths of smokers, is utterly repugnant to a civilized society and must be rejected on grounds of public policy.... The contention of entitlement to an 'elderly death' credit is, on the face, void as against public policy. That policy and basic human decency preclude the defendants from putting forth the perverse and depraved argument that by killing Mississippians prematurely, they provide an economic benefit to the State. No court of equity should countenance, condone, or sanction such base, evil, and corrupt arguments.... The defendants' argument is indeed ghoulish. They are merchants of death. Seeking a credit for a purported economic benefit for early death is akin to robbing the graves of the Mississippi smokers who died from tobacco-related illnesses. No court of law or equity should entertain such a defense or counterclaim. It is offensive to human decency, an affront to justice, uncharacteristic of civilized society, and unquestionably contrary to public policy." Litigation *Memorandum*, State of Mississippi. Cited in Viscusi (2002, p. 87).

Chapters 4 through 10 implement the analytic approach described in chapter 2. In chapter 4, we present estimates of smoking-attributable mortality. The life table described in this chapter was used throughout our empirical analysis. In estimating smoking-attributable mortality, it is essential to compare mortality experience of actual smokers with what they would have experienced if they did not smoke. We term the latter "nonsmoking smokers." Such persons are as close to smokers as our data allow us to make them. The only difference between actual smokers and nonsmoking smokers is that the latter did not smoke at age 24 and did not initiate the habit thereafter. Adjusting for factors that may affect mortality other than smoking but are correlated with smoking is important. These other factors include other health behaviors, such as excess alcohol consumption, educational attainment, risk and time preference (degree of risk tolerance and impatience for present versus future returns, respectively), and demographic characteristics. The difference between survival of smokers and nonsmoking smokers is less than that between smokers and nonsmokers, but considerable nonetheless. Our study's data permitted a much more comprehensive adjustment for the nonsmoking smoker than was possible heretofore.

A key question of our study involves a comparison of contributions smokers make to various funds, including Social Security, pensions, health insurance, and other insurance relative to the benefits they receive. In chapter 5, we assess the impact of smoking on expenditures on personal health services over the life cycle—between the ages of 24 and 50, 51 and 64, and 65 and over. We find that smoking increases expenditures incurred by persons aged 24–50, but decreases expenditures at later age, largely because smoking reduces the probability of survival. Smoking-attributable cost to such public programs as Medicaid remain considerable, but only at a point in time, not over the life cycle. The impact of smoking on Medicaid expenditures was far less than implied by the compensation states received from the MSA. Effects on contributions to health insurance plans are complex, but overall the effect of smoking is to decrease such contributions.

In chapter 6, which presents results on the influence of smoking on contributions to and payments from Social Security Old Age and Survivors Insurance (OASI) and Social Security Disability Insurance (SSDI), we present new evidence on earnings and individuals' contributions to Social Security and Medicare trust funds, based on files for the years 1951 to 1991 that have been linked to HRS respondents. We show how smoking affects lifetime contributions made by workers to these public programs. This analysis marks the first time *actual* contributions to these public programs and actual taxable earnings of smokers and nonsmokers and taxable earnings have been compared. As with Medicare, the effect of smoking is to reduce expenditures on Social Security's net spending (i.e., payments minus contributions). Somewhat surprisingly, we found considerable earnings loss attributable to smoking for men (nearly $40,000 over the life course), but trivial effects for women. In the context of smoking, since longevity and smoking patterns differ by gender, it is essential to perform separate calculations for men and women.

Chapter 7 presents a parallel analysis for private pensions. In the United States, private pensions may be defined benefit or defined contribution plans. Under defined benefit, the employer guarantees the employee a fixed payment based on a formula including such factors as years of service and earnings. Smokers may lose in such plans by dying earlier than nonsmokers, but smoking also affects lifetime contributions to private pension plans. By contrast, for defined contribution plans, no transfer is made between nonsmokers and smokers because the amount the employee receives after retiring or as a death benefit depends on the amount contributed to the employee's account as well as the return on these contributions. Data from the HRS provide valuable detail on characteristics of individual respondents' pension plans, offering a unique opportunity to study the impact of smoking on, as it turns out, cross subsidies from smokers to nonsmokers.

In chapter 8, we study the influence of smoking on life insurance. If life insurers imposed actuarially fair surcharges (compensating for the amount an insurer expects to pay on behalf of an insured person at the time the premium is paid) to reflect the reduction in life expectancy from smoking, there would be no transfer. However, as seen in this chapter, at least historically, this has not been the case. Thus, in the context of life insurance, smokers benefited at the expense of nonsmokers.

Chapter 9 assesses the influence of smoking on morbidity, disability, and on work loss. That smoking affects morbidity and disability as well as mortality is not surprising. What *is* new, important, and surprising is that smoking has such a small impact on years spent with major disabilities. In prior research, some of us had found that smokers found information about the effects of smoking on disability more salient than those on survival (Sloan, Smith, and Taylor 2003). Here, we find that although smokers become disabled sooner on their way to a sooner death, they do not spend much more time with a major disabling condition. To the extent that smokers discount the future at moderate rates, having disability sooner rather than later should matter. However, if smokers are very shortsighted, they may not care at 24 if disability is xx years in the future or $xx + y$ years away. We quantify losses from disability in dollar terms, based in part on some previous research one of us conducted on willingness to pay to avoid limitations in activities of daily living among the elderly. Putting a dollar value on death and disability is controversial (see, e.g., box 1.1), but it is done by all private and public parties, implicitly through actions and decisions that people make. Of course, one can argue with the values used, but we provide a transparent method for plugging in alternative assumptions.

In chapter 10 we turn to the effects of smoking on the health of spouses and partners within the same household. Our database, the HRS, is unique in providing identical information on both husband and wife. Thus, not only do we know how much and for how long each has smoked, but we know a lot of each person's characteristics, particularly their health and functional status. With this information, we are able to produce new estimates of the mortality and disability cost a smoking spouse imposes on his or her partner. For smoking men, such cost is about $30,000. For smoking women, the cost is about half as large. In this study, we provide no new information about the effect of environmental tobacco smoke on children. For this, we rely entirely on the literature review presented in chapter 3.

Chapter 11, our concluding chapter, provides an opportunity for a net assessment. Having assembled the various pieces of the puzzle, we are able to state from a global social perspective whether smokers "pay their own way." The bottom line is that women who smoke at 24 generate a social cost with a present value of $106,000 ($86,000 private) in year 2000 dollars. For men, the present value is twice as large, $220,000 ($183,000 private). If men who smoke in early adulthood face a future cost of $183,000 attributable to their smoking habit, we can only wonder why they smoke. We ask but do not answer this fundamental question. Just to respond that people smoke because they are addicted is one answer, but not a very satisfying one. After all, many smokers quit. Finally, we assess how well current policies measure up in light of this net social burden and offer guidance for future research and policy directions.

2

Approaches for Assessing the Cost of Smoking

This chapter provides the conceptual basis for our analysis of the cost of smoking and, interpreting the previous literature on smoking costs, presents our analytic approach and describes the data used in our study.

Alternative Frameworks

Choosing the Right Analytical Approach: Cross-Sectional Analysis versus the Life Cycle Approach

The cost of smoking can be measured either over the life cycle of the smoker or for a single period, such as a year. At a single point in time, smoking may increase various dimensions of cost, but higher mortality attributable to smoking has opposite impacts on cost over a lifetime. Consider, for example, expenditures on medical care. Higher medical care use increases lifetime expenditures associated with smoking. Offsetting this increase, at least in part, is the decrease in survival of smokers relative to nonsmokers. Deaths from any cause are highly regrettable. But from the vantage point of cash flows, deaths reduce the financial obligations of some medical and retirement plans.

Patterns in medical care use by smokers and nonsmokers in any year as well as over the life cycle are affected by various demand determinants, including health status, price of health services, state of the underlying technology for diagnosing and treating disease, care standards, and other factors. None of these factors can be known with any degree of certainty at the time smoking is initiated. Both mortality and cost per year are partly affected by cessation, which occurs throughout the life cycle and, for many individuals, occurs only after a major adverse health event, such as a heart attack, has been experienced (Ho 1998; Jones 1996; Wray et al. 1998; Taylor et al. 2002). Two frameworks underlie most current estimates of smoking cost. One approach gauges cost attributable to smoking at a single point in time, such as a year. At issue is the extra cost imposed by smoking during that period. This *cross-sectional approach* takes the population alive during the period and the fraction of the population by smoking status as givens. The cost of smoking is then evaluated based on this population's use of health services and the distribution of the population by source of payment for such services. This approach has been used to gauge the aggregate burden of illness on society in a cross-sectional slice in time in general and the cost of smoking to a public program, such as Medicaid, for a specific period of time, such as a year, in particular.

By contrast, the *life cycle approach* gauges the present value of the cost of adding a smoker to society. In any time period, such as a year, a certain number of people initiate the smoking habit. The life cycle approach assesses the net social cost of this additional smoker. The approach recognizes that each time a person begins the smoking habit, there are downstream implications for resource use—for the smoker, for the smoker's family, and others in society. The life cycle approach provides a forward-looking view of an illness's burden. This method conceptually links the cause (smoking) with the effect (future medical expense) much more directly (see e.g., Miller et al. 1997). Under this approach, one calculates the net present value of all lifetime costs for all individuals who become newly diagnosed (or initiate a new behavior) in the base year. This essentially entails determining such costs for a typical individual and multiplying by the number of new cases expected that year.

The life cycle approach is advantageous in some important public policy applications, such as for determining the optimal level of excise taxes on cigarettes. This approach allows one to identify the cash flows associated with another person's starting the habit as well as the cash flows from quitting or continuing to smoke but reducing one's level of cigarette consumption. Life cycle estimates also have direct applications in evaluating tobacco control programs to discourage initiation. The cross-sectional approach has the advantage of simplicity and greater ease of application with available data. Only information from a single survey (cross section) is required. Making assumptions about future behavior and survival rates is unnecessary.

Overall, the arguments for using a life cycle approach, which we use in this study, are far more compelling. Individuals, families, and societies make decisions in a multiperiod context, whether they explicitly think in these terms or not. The decision to initiate and quit the smoking habit is inherently a multiperiod choice. Some costs and benefits accrue immediately, but much of the cost is delayed. For example, other family members bear the cost of increased expenditures on cigarettes, leaving less money for consumption of other goods and services, not only currently, but, given the addictive nature of tobacco consumption, in many later periods. And, like smokers, nonsmoking family members may suffer adverse health effects subsequently. Especially because smoking affects health and survival, it affects a number of household decisions over the life cycle. For public entitlement programs, expenditures across periods are linked. Given the latency period, a person who begins to smoke today will affect expenditures of public funds in distant future years. The habit will also affect the future stream of contributions by individuals to such public programs. In recent years, longitudinal data have become available that permit empirical analysis of the downstream effects of such behaviors as smoking.

Implementing the Cross-Sectional Approach

Although we do not use it in our study, the cross-sectional approach has been used in the vast majority of hundreds of past studies (see chapter 3).[1] For this reason, we describe the method here.

In this approach, one estimates the value of resources used (expenditures) and lost (productivity losses) and the total output lost as a result of illness or premature death to obtain the value foregone (Rice et al. 1986). Such studies have been designed to demonstrate the aggregate economic burden imposed on society attributable to a specific diagnosis (e.g., depression), group of diagnoses (e.g., mental illness) or behavior (e.g., drug abuse).

In analyzing a particular cross section, most often done in the context of spending on personal health care services, the researcher typically finds a smoking-attributable fraction (SAF), that is, the increase in expenditures on personal health services attributable to smoking. The studies generally rely on methods to determine the share of costs (or deaths) that can be attributed to smoking, using a standard attributable risk formula:

$$SAF = [p_0 + p_1(RR_1) + p_2(RR_2)] - 1)/[p_0 + p_1(RR_1) + p_2(RR_2)] \quad (2.1)$$

where p_0 = prevalence of never smokers in the population, p_1 = prevalence of current smokers, p_2 = prevalence of former smokers, RR_1 = relative risk for current smokers relative to never smokers, and RR_2 = relative risk for former smokers relative to never smokers. The relative risk may be defined in terms of the use of a particular service, such as a hospital stay or a physician visit during a time period.

The SAF reflects the RR terms in equation (2.1). To estimate the RRs, explanatory variables other than those for smoking behavior are included to control for other determinants of spending. Once the SAF has been estimated, the SAF then is applied to other data on expenditures, such as for Medicaid in a given state in a particular year, to derive the cost of smoking for that payer.[2]

An alternative method used in several recent cross-sectional studies is to compute SAFs directly by examining all resources used by smokers compared to nonsmokers and using regression analysis to predict relative use. This approach can take all differences in health costs between smokers and nonsmokers into account, even for diseases not known to be related to smoking, as well as differences between smokers and nonsmokers in terms of lifestyle, sociodemographic characteristics, comorbidities, and even access to personal health services. Because these studies traditionally have been conducted from a social perspective, no distinction is drawn between costs presumed to be internal to the smoker, that is, taken into account when making a smoking decision, and external costs borne by nonsmokers.

However, as explained in chapter 1, for purposes of policy making, this distinction is quite important. Moreover, some costs generated internally (e.g., a smoker's medical costs) may be financed externally, as in the case of medical expenses covered through health insurance, government programs, or sick leave borne by a worker's employer.

To obtain the SAF, one needs only a single cross section of data on individuals, with data on expenditures and determinants of such expenditures, including smoking behavior. The SAF is then readily applied to databases publicly available from insurers. The approach generally includes all medical costs, including in some studies, costs associated with receipt of medical care, such as from transportation to the health facility, and morbidity losses that occur in a base year for all those living with a disease (or engaged in some unhealthy behavior) that year. To account for mortality losses, this approach generally adds the net present value of future lifetime earnings foregone for all individuals who died of the disease in the base year. In the case of diseases, such figures are readily available through vital statistics databases, but in the case of smoking, an extra step is required to determine the SAF of costs for different causes.

However, cross-sectional estimates do not measure the net reduction in gross domestic product (GDP) from a disease, because the lion's share of the mortality losses will not adversely affect GDP until many years in the future. A more serious limitation is that a cross-sectional estimate provides little guidance to policymakers about how much would be saved were a disease, condition, or behavior either eliminated or appreciably reduced. Outlays from an insurer, for example Medicaid, depend on the number of enrollees and outlays per enrollee. To the extent that smoking results in premature deaths of persons who would otherwise have been enrollees, expenditures are correspondingly diminished. The mortality losses reflect the effects of years or decades—costs that by definition cannot be averted even if the disease were eradicated tomorrow. Also, persons who survive change insurers. The cost of smoking may have more to do with numbers of people enrolled in a particular program than with spending attributable to smoking, conditional on the number of persons covered by the program.

Three other criticisms have been leveled at the cross-sectional approach. First, early studies used disease-specific SAFs from mortality data and applied these to estimates of the medical costs of various illnesses to approximate the share of these direct costs likely to be attributable to cigarette smoking. This ran the danger of either under- or over-estimating the true fraction of expenditures related to smoking, depending on whether smokers with disease x had higher or lower average expenditures compared to nonsmokers with the same disease. Later studies avoid this simplification.

Second, many studies have relied on relative risks that are very low.[3] Such low relative risk may be insufficiently reliable to permit an inference that the factor actually caused the disease. Third, the cross-sectional method, as applied by some public agencies for calculating attributable risks, does not adequately control for confounding variables. Sterling, Rosenbaum, and Weinkam (1993) showed that adjusting for differences in income and alcohol consumption alone lowered the estimated number of smoking-attributable deaths reported in the

1989 surgeon general's report by 26 percent. Others have reported little change in smoking-attributable mortality estimates even after adjustment for confounders (Centers for Disease Control and Prevention 1997).

Irrespective of approach, one wants to know the resource use patterns of persons who, except for their smoking behavior, are identical to smokers. Leu (1984) was the first to use the term "nonsmoking smoker," which also could be termed a "counterfactual never smoker." Conceptually, the nonsmoking smoker is identical to the actual smoker, except that he or she does not smoke. Once we know a value for the nonsmoking smoker, the effect of smoking is computed as the difference between the value for the actual smoker and the corresponding value for the nonsmoking smoker. This concept has been used subsequently by others, such as by Manning et al. (1989, 1991). Earlier than Leu (and unfortunately, also later), much past smoking cost research had focused on comparing the crude cost or expenditure differences between smokers and nonsmokers, attributing the entire difference to smoking. Smokers might not only engage in different behaviors from nonsmokers, but they may also differ in other important ways that bear on both their survival and on their patterns of resource use. Without controlling for these differences in taste for unhealthy/risky behavior, previous estimates of the cost of smoking inadvertently attributed excess expenditures to smoking that more properly were attributable to other unhealthy behaviors among smokers. Using this method for correcting for the influence of other factors, smokers are not compared to actual nonsmokers but to hypothetical "nonsmoking smokers," whose demographic, socioeconomic, and lifestyle characteristics matched those of smokers in all respects except for smoking status.

The cross-sectional approach has been widely used in studies by experts for plaintiffs in tobacco litigation (see e.g., Harris 1997; Max 1997a,b,c). The general methodology is to derive smoking-attributable fractions for particular health services, such as for hospital care, and apply these fractions to data on expenditures. The SAFs consistently have implied excess spending on behalf of smokers (see e.g., Miller et al. 1997; Miller, Ernst, and Collin 1999) and therefore are favorable to plaintiffs in such litigation. Smoking-related cost is always a positive amount since there is no saving occurring from premature mortality. These studies have been criticized by experts for the defense on grounds that they underadjust for behaviors other than smoking and fail to account for premature death due to smoking (see e.g., Rubin 1997). As indicated in chapter 1, how one deals with smoking-attributable mortality has been a very contentious issue.

Implementing the Life Cycle Approach

Although, as we have argued, the life cycle approach is conceptually preferable, the practical difficulties in making such lifetime calculations are daunting, as it requires predictions about the probable course of illness and its many alternative paths, duration, survival rates, the likely onset and patterns of medical care, and the effects of a disease on employment (Rice, Kelman, and Durmeyer 1990). These difficulties have limited the application of this approach to relatively few diseases (see, e.g., Hartunian, Smart, and Thompson 1980). Only a handful of smoking cost studies have used the life cycle approach;[4] most have used an individual smoker perspective or express their findings in terms of the cost per pack of cigarettes (to facilitate comparisons with existing excise taxes). But as we shall see, estimates of the lifetime costs of smoking play a critical role in our understanding of whether smoking is a net cost or benefit to society.

Valuing Loss: The Human-Capital Approach versus Willingness-to-Pay

For losses such as excess expenditures on medical care, one can use market data to compute the loss. For the loss from morbidity and premature mortality, however, market data are lacking. Thus, losses must be imputed in some other way. Two approaches for making such imputations are in widespread use, the human-capital and willingness-to-pay approaches.

Human Capital

In the human-capital approach, one simply equates the value of a life to the discounted stream of foregone earnings resulting from a premature death. A positive feature of this approach is that it recognizes the cost of lost market productivity. But people do not live for market output alone. Also, the approach assigns a zero value to persons who are unable to work because of age or a disability due some other cause—in our context, some cause other than smoking. Because men tend to earn more than women, and whites more than blacks, the approach yields the result that white males' lives are more valuable than others. People are not machines—the total cost of a cough is both more than and different from the value of the time lost in market work. In economic jargon, the human capital framework disregards the value of consumption benefits from improved health and longevity—that is, benefits valued by people in utility terms. In our study, we compute lost earnings attributable to smoking (see chapter 6), but do not equate such loss to the value of life. Life and good quality of life have more value than is reflected in returns from market work.

We will use a willingness-to-pay approach to value loss from disability (chapters 9 and 10) and estimates of the value of a life year roughly derived from studies that base values on personal decisions (chapters 4 and 10).

Willingness-to-Pay (WTP) Approach

The WTP method provides quantification of the nonpecuniary benefits that the human-capital approach ignores (Gold, Gold, and Weinstein 1996). Researchers attempt to uncover preferences for nonmarket goods, either by observing behavior—the revealed-preference method—or by eliciting preferences directly (Freeman 2003). Nonmarket goods include consumption by persons other than the person who purchases the good, such as person B's decreased probability of contracting an infectious disease when person A is vaccinated, as well as public goods, such as national defense and biomedical research. In the revealed-preference approach, one infers the value of life from observed behavior. For example, suppose two jobs are available and differ only in the probability of being killed on the job. One can infer a value of life from the compensating wage differential. The key in empirical analysis is to hold other relevant job characteristics constant, a feat more easily said than done, although some studies do credible work on this.

WTP might also be found through surveys of WTP for a reduction in the probability of dying—generally called the contingent-valuation method, as values are elicited from respondents based on assumptions about the probabilities of bad outcomes specified in the survey. Respondents are asked, for example, how much they are willing to pay for a reduction in a risk of harm. Contingent-valuation approaches have been refined over the years, but the approach has been controversial (see, e.g., Diamond and Hausman 1994). Criticism centers on the difficulty in eliciting accurate valuations from people (see, e.g., Diamond and Hausman 1994), but methods for eliciting values are being continuously refined (see, e.g., Kunreuther, Novemsky, and Kahneman 2001; Krupnick et al. 2002; Freeman 2003).

Another objection is that the rich may be willing to pay more for some outcomes on average, such as improved survival or reduced disability. For this reason, allocations based on WTP may give disproportionate weight to the preferences of persons with high incomes. But as Pauly (1995) has noted, it is possible to adjust for this pattern statistically.

Some experts prefer to derive all values from actual decisions rather than statements of value elicited from surveys. However, for certain phenomena, such as various types of disability, especially for nonworking persons, such measures are simply unavailable. To not use values from WTP would be to commit a worse error, that is, implicitly assigning a value of zero dollars to outcomes that people plausibly value. In our analysis, we will use a value of a life year derived from the revealed-preference approach to obtain a monetary estimate of life years lost due to smoking (chapters 4 and 10) and an estimate from a contingent valuation study to value life years spent with disability (chapters 9 and 10).

Data Sources Used in Our Study

We used several data sources in this study. Almost ideally, we would have panel data over the person's entire lifetime. We say "almost" because the date of onset of young adulthood would be a long time ago if we insisted on using data from a birth year in which we observed dates of death for everyone in the sample. We had access to excellent panel data sets for persons over age 50. Panel data on persons younger than this are not nearly as good for our purposes. Fewer health questions are asked. Also, smoking behavior tends to be measured inconsistently. For this reason, we used a single cross section to fill gaps, mainly in age groups covered, in the panel data. The three principal data sources we used are the Health and Retirement Study (HRS), the Assets and Health Dynamics Among the Oldest Old (AHEAD), and the 1998 National Health Interview Survey (NHIS).

Health and Retirement Study

The HRS is a national panel survey conducted by the University of Michigan's Institute for Social Research (see Juster and Suzman 1995). Persons eligible for the survey were born between the years 1931 and 1941; they were between the ages of 51 and 61 in the year in which baseline interviews were conducted, 1992. Spouses of sample persons were also included and could be of any age. They were administered survey questionnaires identical to those for the sample persons. The survey has been conducted every two years since 1992, with each respondent surveyed in person at baseline and subsequently by telephone. By 2002, five waves of the HRS had been released, at least in preliminary form: 1992, 1994, 1996, 1998, and 2000. We used data from the first five waves in this study with one exception: in the analysis of mortality, we only used four waves, because the data on deaths after 1998 had not been released in time for this study.

The HRS is uniquely suited for our study in several respects. First, the HRS asked individuals about their smoking behavior, including questions about smoking prior to the baseline interview. In each wave, the survey asked whether the person currently smoked, and, conditional on smoking, the amount smoked. The survey did not ask about the type or brand of cigarette smoked or about smoking habits, for example, extent the person inhaled. Second, the HRS is a longitudinal database. That is, the same individual is asked many of the same questions periodically over time. Having a panel allows the researcher to investigate the impact of a decision on outcomes that occur subsequently. This helps with inferences about causal effects. Third, the HRS is unique in eliciting detailed health and financial information. Most surveys offer detailed information on *either* health and health care *or* on household finances. No panel data set offers as much information on both for a period as long as eight years. The information on health is especially detailed. It includes specific diagnoses, such as cancer, heart attack, and stroke, the onset of which can be dated within a two-year time window, and numerous measures of disability. Dates of death are recorded, and deaths are distinguished from attrition. Because identical data were obtained on the sample person and spouse, one could examine the effect of smoking on the health of one's spouse. The collection of detailed financial information, including data on income, assets, and employment, was, at least initially, motivated by the objective to study retirement decisions (the "retirement" part of the HRS).

Assets and Health Dynamics among the Oldest Old

AHEAD, conducted in 1993 and 1995, focused on persons who were aged 70 and over in 1993. In 1998, AHEAD and HRS merged into a single survey to be conducted every two years indefinitely. At AHEAD wave 1, 8,222 persons were interviewed. This survey is nationally representative of persons aged 70 and over and their spouses who could be of any age. Thus, all persons under age 70 were spouses of persons originally selected for interviews. Both spouses received the same interviews.[5] AHEAD and HRS are very similar, but because of its initial focus on a much older age cohort, AHEAD did not contain information on problem drinking, risk preferences, financial-planning horizon, or quitting age for former smokers. The latter was assumed to be age 55 in our analyses (see chapter 5 for explanation).

National Health Interview Survey

The National Health Interview Survey (NHIS) is an annual survey, designed as a repeated cross section on a nationally representative probability sample of the civilian noninstitutionalized population of the United States. The survey is conducted by the National Center for Health Statistics of the U.S. Centers for Disease Control. Each week, personnel of the U.S. Bureau of the Census administer face-to-face interviews in a sample of households and obtain information about the health and other characteristics of each member of the household.

The 1998 NHIS public-use data set contained information on 38,773 families, covering 98,785 persons, including 32,440 sample adults, one from each family. Sample adults answered detailed questions about health and health behaviors, including smoking status. This sample of adults was used to estimate the effect of smoking on various health outcomes, health care utilization, work loss in the 24-to-50 age group, as well as overall smoking rates by age, and the family income distribution by smoking status for all ages. Covariates included in this data set and used throughout the book included the following: smoking status, alcohol consumption, body mass index (BMI), race, education, marital status, and age (further description below). Unlike the HRS, the NHIS contained no measures of a history of problem drinking; nor did the survey include variables describing risk preferences or respondents' financial-planning horizons.

Our Analytic Approach

Questions Addressed

In this study, we used the life cycle approach to address two fundamental questions. First, if individuals had not begun to smoke, what would have been the effect on resource use? Second, to what extent are nonsmokers harmed or benefited by smoking? Although this may seem implausible at first glance, nonsmokers may benefit to the extent that smokers make greater net financial contributions to Social Security, Medicare, or private life insurance plans, or that they pay more in taxes than the extra resource burdens they impose on others.

Choice of Age 24 as Reference Age

We took age 24 as the age at which we computed lifetime cost. The vast majority of persons initiate the smoking habit before then (Gruber and Zinman 2001), but many young persons quit after smoking for a relatively short time. Early quitting is associated with few if any adverse health effects. In fact, people who quit 15 or more years before the HRS interview reported health and functional status (ability to perform personal and other tasks around the home) more nearly resembling never smokers than any other group of smokers (Sloan, Smith, and Taylor 2003).

Analytic Steps

To develop measures of the present value of cash flows attributable to smoking at age 24 in 2000 dollars, in general terms, we performed the following analytic steps. First, we isolated the effect of smoking from many other factors that potentially affect outcomes using regression analysis. Second, we estimated the outcomes that would have occurred had the person not smoked, employing the concept of the nonsmoking smoker described above. We attributed the difference in the predicted actual value and the predicted value for the nonsmoking smoker to smoking. Third, we accounted for smoking-attributable mortality and propensities to quit smoking over the life cycle. Finally, we discounted cash flows back to age 24.

Accounting for Determinants of Outcomes Other than Smoking

Whenever feasible, we used the following consistent set of covariates. To account for the effects of smoking, the key explanatory variables were binary variables indicating whether the individual was a current smoker (defined as persons who smoked at the time of the survey or who said they had quit smoking less than five years before the survey), or a former smoker (who had quit five or more years previously), with never smokers being the omitted reference group in each case. We combined persons who quit within the past five years with current smokers because (1) such persons are much more likely to relapse, and (2) short-term quitting is often motivated by an adverse health event (Moore and Hughes 2001; Taylor et al. 2002). In fact, in preliminary analysis, we found that persons who had quit smoking less than five years before the survey consumed more medical care services on average than did current smokers.[6] All analyses were separated by gender to allow for differential effects of smoking on men and women.

In our basic equation specification, in addition to variables for current and former smoking, we controlled for alcohol consumption (abstainer, light/moderate drinker, heavy drinker), having a history of problem drinking, age, body mass index or BMI (25–29.9, 30+), gender (male), ethnicity (white), marital status (married), education (less than high school education, college degree, with high school or some college, the omitted reference group), risk tolerance, and financial-planning horizon (less than 1 year, more than 10 years, with horizons of 1–10 years, the omitted reference group). In analyses for individual chapters, we retained this specification as often as possible. When data sets did not contain all these variables, the specification was adjusted accordingly. All analyses were weighted to ensure that estimates are nationally representative of the respective cohort from which the samples were drawn, and we adjusted for repeated observations on the same individuals or sample-design-related clustering within geographic areas, as necessary.

The HRS obtained data on alcohol consumption at each wave. We defined variables for abstainers (no consumption), heavy drinking (three or more drinks daily), with the remaining group being light-to-moderate drinkers.

We measured problem drinking with a binary variable based on the CAGE instrument for clinical assessment of alcohol disorders. The instrument asks four questions: Have you ever felt that you should *cut down* (C) on your drinking? Have people *annoyed* (A) you by criticizing your drinking? Have you ever felt bad or *guilty* (G) about drinking? Have you ever had a drink first thing in the morning (*eye opener*, E)? The CAGE instrument has been found to be a valid indicator of alcohol problems (Fink et al. 2002; Hearne, Connolly, and Sheehan 2002).[7] It picks up extreme rather than early cases (Edwards, Marshall, and Cook 1997, p. 197). The HRS asked the CAGE questions only at the baseline interview. The survey did not ask when the person had experienced problems with alcohol use. We set a binary variable for "problem drinker" to one if the respondent gave affirmative answers to two or more of these questions. A person with a BMI between 25 and 30 is generally considered to be overweight. A person with a BMI over 30 is considered to be obese. We used the measure of risk tolerance described by Barsky et al. (1997) and included it in the HRS. At wave 1, every individual was asked to choose among four different gambles on lifetime incomes based on the following questions:

Suppose that you are the only income earner in the family, and you have a good job. . . . You are given the opportunity to take a new and equally good job, with a 50–50 chance that it will double your income and a 50–50 chance that it will reduce your income by a third. Would you take the new job?

If the answer was "no," the interviewer asked:

Suppose the chances were 50–50 that it would double your income and 50–50 that it would cut your income by 20 percent. Would you still take the new job?

If the answer to the first questions was "yes," the interviewer asked:

Suppose the chances were 50–50 that it would double your income and 50–50 that it would cut your income by half. Would you still take the new job?

From the answers, Barsky et al. (1997) separated individuals into four risk-preference categories. Each group corresponded to a range of risk preferences. The first group (the more risk averse) had a lower bound for relative risk aversion of 3.76, the second had an upper bound of 3.76 and a lower bound of 2, the third had an upper bound of 2 and a lower bound of 1, and the fourth group had an upper bound of 1 and a lower bound of 0. In our empirical work, we used the reciprocal of relative risk aversion. The average risk tolerance for the first group conditional on survey response was 0.15, for the second 0.28, for the third 0.35, and for the fourth 0.57 (ibid.).

The questions used to construct the HRS measure of risk aversion were related to financial risks. Individuals may respond differently to health risks. A large literature in psychology covers this topic, and the issue has not been settled. However, Barsky et al. found that the HRS measure of risk tolerance predicted risky behaviors including smoking, drinking, and not having insurance, rejecting the null hypothesis that risk tolerance is not correlated with health behaviors.

Time preference, which reflects the amount of compensation an individual requires to defer consumption from the present, plays a crucial role on the demand of preventive care. An individual who is less present oriented (has a low discount rate) is likely to invest more in health. Farrell and Fuchs (1982) claimed that the differences in time preferences explain differential investments in health and the positive relationship between education and health investments. Becker and Mulligan (1997) challenged this view and claim reverse causation, that differences in health cause differences in time preference.

Similar to the risk tolerance questions, Barsky et al. developed a question to calculate the rate of time preference and the elasticity of intertemporal substitution of individuals. Unfortunately, this question was only asked of a small subset of the sample. Instead, the HRS asked all individuals a question about their financial planning horizon. We used the answer to this question as a proxy for their rate of time preference. In its first wave, the HRS asked all individuals:

In deciding how much of their (family) income to spend or save, people are likely to think about different financial planning periods. In planning your (family's) saving and spending, which of the time periods listed in the booklet is most important to you [and your (husband/wife/partner)]?

If the individual's answer was less than a year, we considered the person to have had a short time horizon. At the other extreme were individuals with a long time horizon of greater than ten years. The omitted reference group is individuals with a financial horizon between one year and ten years.

As with our measure for risk tolerance, individuals' financial-planning horizons may be independent of their health rates of discount. However, the ultimate test of the usefulness of this measure would be whether it helps to explain behavior such as cancer screening.[8] The relationship between schooling and health has been widely studied.[9] Most of this literature has found a positive relationship between schooling and preventive behaviors, possibly due to a positive correlation between education and health knowledge or because more education improves the efficiency with which an individual produces health.

Finally, we did not include health status measures in our empirical specification, because health is determined in part by smoking. We excluded household income for the same reason. The risk tolerance and time horizon variables were available only in the HRS.

Specific Analytic Steps for Deriving Costs for a 24-Year-Old Smoker Over the Life Course

Overview

To estimate various costs attributable to smoking, we performed these analytic steps: (1) compute transition probabilities of smoking cessation at each age; (2) perform regression analysis to determine the probability of death within a two-year time span using HRS panel data, 1992–1998, to compute relative risk of death by smoking status and the share of smoker deaths at each age not attributable to smoking—the nonsmoking smoker calculation; (3) compute life tables by gender from ages 24–100 by smoking status at age 24; (4) estimate costs attributable to smoking, conditional on surviving to a given year; and (5) compute expected cost by smoking status by multiplying survival probabilities by the estimates conditional on survival from the fourth step; (6) compute smoking-attributable cost that is the difference between expected values for actual and nonsmoking smokers.

Step 1: Calculating Transition Probabilities of Smoking Cessation

Assuming that no one starts smoking after age 24, the only smoking transition probability we needed to quantify was for the probability of smoking cessation. Most persons who smoked at age 24 quit before death. Since quitting potentially affects all of the dependent variables we studied, we needed to estimate the transition probabilities of smoking cessation.

We used data from the HRS to compute probabilities of quitting at each year of age between 24 and 68. We needed to project quit rates up to age 100, our assumed terminal age. To do this, we regressed a binary (0–1) variable for smoking status (smoke, no smoke) on age, age square, and age cubed. We then predicted quit rates by age and gender (fig. 2.1, the darker curve representing predicted values).

The quit rates we estimated are plausibly higher than rates we would have calculated from a younger birth cohort. Since the mid twentieth century, there has been a secular decline in smoking rates in general and in initiation of smoking in particular (Sloan, Smith, and Taylor 2002). Starting from a lower base rate at age 24 must lead to a lower rate of quitting for adults born after the HRS cohort. In sum, by relying on quit rates reported by persons aged 50+ who responded to the HRS during 1992 to 2000, we may have overestimated rates of quitting among person who are age 24 today.

Step 2: Compute Share of Excess Smoker Deaths Not Attributable to Smoking

We used logit analysis, a type of regression analysis used when the dependent variable takes either a one or zero value, to estimate the effects of smoking status and other factors on the probability of dying within a two-year interval. Smoking status was measured at the beginning of the two-year interval. Other explanatory variables were those in the basic equation specification described above.[10]

Step 3: Compute Life Tables by Smoking Status at Age 24

The second transition probability was for survival. Life tables, which give probabilities of dying at each year of age, came from http://www.LifeExpectancy.com, a web site maintained by David Strauss and Robert Shavelle, who used data from Richards and Abele (1999) to compute excess death rates for smoking status separately by age, sex, race, and education. Their estimates were based on mortality data from the Cancer Prevention Study II (CPS-II) cohort.[11] We applied the smoking cessation rates described above to develop a life table for typical 24-year-old smokers by gender, accounting for quit rates, as well as for nonsmoking smokers, using relative risks from the regression analysis from step 2 (see chapter 4).

By using the life table, we could account for loss to the HRS and AHEAD baseline samples, and NHIS due to smoking. A problem with any single cross section and the HRS panel, which starts with persons in late middle age, is that they do not include persons who died before

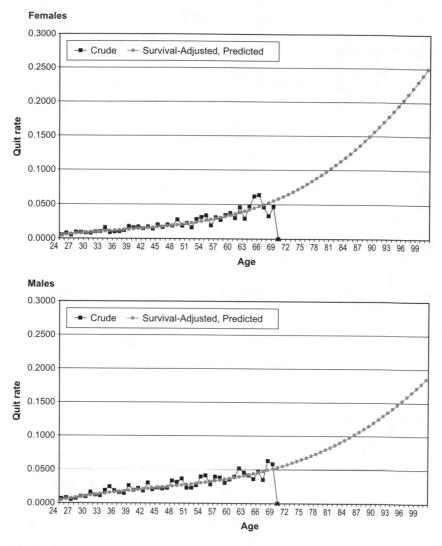

Figure 2.1
Actual and predicted quit rates by age and gender, HRS.

the survey date. By using the life tables, we could take these omissions into account.

Step 4: Compute Costs (or Other Dependent Variable) Attributable to Smoking from NHIS and the HRS/AHEAD Panels

Using various forms of regression analysis, we computed the various costs attributable to smoking, based on a common equation specification as the data would allow. From the parameter estimates, which are used to gauge the effect of a change in an independent variable on the dependent variable, we generated predictions of cost by gender and smoking status. Predictions for the 24–50 age range came from analyses based on the 1998 NHIS, for persons aged 51–62 from HRS, and for persons aged 65+ from AHEAD.

Step 5: Compute Expected Values and Amounts Attributable to Smoking

With survival and smoking cessation transition probabilities for persons aged 24–100 by gender and predicted values of various outcomes (e.g., use of health services, work days lost), we computed *expected values* of these outcomes.

Step 6: Discount

We discounted cash flows to age 24 using a real discount rate of three percent. This real discount rate is approximately the long-term rate of return on financial assets (Ibbotson and Sinquefeld 1976) and the one recommended for use in cost effectiveness analysis by the U.S. Panel on Cost Effectiveness Analysis (Gold et al. 1996). Health discount rates may be considerably higher (see Moore and Viscusi 1990a,b), but, in this context, the appropriate discount rate is the social discount rate applicable to resource decisions in general. After all, money not spent on personal health services might be allocated to bridges, food programs for the hungry, and myriad other uses. Some might argue that the three percent rate is a private rate and that the social discount rate might be lower. The real social discount rate clearly exceeds zero, and the interpretation of our results are not sensitive to choice of alternative rates, say, between two and three percent. We computed present values at a zero rate but do not present the results in this book to conserve space. Our key findings did not vary appreciably for social discount rates within a plausible range (zero to five percent). Higher discount rates tend to deemphasize the costs of smoking incurred in later life. Some studies have reported very high private financial discount rates (e.g., Harrison, Lau, and Williams 2002), but these rates seem inconsistent with other observed behavior (but not necessarily smoking). If the true financial discount rate were 30 percent or so, we would all be debtors since we could borrow from banks and other sources at a much lower rate of interest than this.

Step 7: Compute Smoking-Attributable Cost

Effects of smoking were calculated as the difference between expected values for actual 24-year-old smokers and for nonsmoking smokers of the same age.

Summary

In this chapter, we first distinguished between cross-sectional and life cycle approaches for evaluating losses due to a bad health habit such as smoking. We gave reasons for preferring the life cycle approach, the one we use in this book. The vast majority of studies have used the cross-sectional approach, in large part because it is easier to use, requires fewer underlying assumptions, is less demanding in terms of required data, and yields estimates that some users of the information find compelling and supportive of their positions. We review these studies in the next chapter. A second objective of this chapter was to describe our data. Because this study is about the burden of smoking, we focus on the results linking smoking to various outcomes. Other factors were included in our analysis, and many of these factors also have important influences on the outcomes we study. However, to discuss each of these findings in depth would detract from the topic of our study.

Recent availability of panel data for persons aged 50 and over has allowed a much more complete analysis of life cycle effects of smoking than was possible heretofore. As demonstrated in later chapters, much of the adverse effect of smoking is realized after age 50. The third goal of this chapter was to describe our study's basic methodology. We use this method throughout this book.

3   What We Know and Don't Know about the Cost of Smoking

By 2002, at least one hundred and sixty-five previous studies on the cost of smoking had been completed with the earliest dating from the 1960s, but nearly half of these have been conducted since 1995. Nearly two-thirds of the studies have been conducted in the United States, with only a handful on developing nations such as China and South Africa. In light of all this previous work, it is worth asking, why do another?

The simple answer is that most previous studies have addressed only a single piece of the puzzle—either focusing on one component of costs (e.g., medical) or focusing on a limited perspective (e.g., examining only external costs to nonsmokers, excluding the appreciably larger effects of smoking on smokers and their spouses and children). Some of the few studies that attempted to compute the global cost of smoking to society have been plagued by methodological limitations. In other cases, the methods are strong, but better data are available now than when those studies were conducted.

Although we obtained better data for studying some important impacts of smoking, such as on public and private pensions and on life insurance, as well as impacts of smoking on mortality and morbidity of nonsmoking spouses of smokers, we could not analyze every possible impact of smoking. Thus, examining the other studies is worthwhile, not only for the big picture they reveal about smoking-attributable cost, but also for some of the components of such cost as well, especially those we did not measure.

The earliest cost-of-smoking study we have been able to identify dates to 1966. Most early work focused on developing national estimates of the cost of smoking from a social perspective, and studies typically used a cross-sectional human-capital framework (see chapter 2 for an explanation of this approach) in which losses are quantified on the basis of change in earnings to estimate both expenditures and productivity losses.

State-level estimates of smoking costs did not begin appearing until the early 1980s. In this same period, studies broadened in scope to include costs related to environmental tobacco smoke (ETS), and indeed, a cluster of studies focused exclusively on measuring these costs for infants, children, and adults. Nearly all studies included measures of medical expenditures attributable to smoking, and at least sixty studies focused exclusively on this aspect of cost; nearly one-third of these represent (often litigation-inspired) efforts by states to document their Medicaid losses attributable to smoking.

Outside the United States, the cross-sectional framework has been by far the most commonly used, with most studies making an effort to quantify expenditures, morbidity losses, and mortality losses. As in the United States, a handful of studies have focused exclusively on measuring ETS losses. Both in the United States and abroad, life-cycle-based lifetime cost estimates are far less common, even though these studies have played an important role in public debates about smoking taxes during the 1993–1994 discussions of health care reform in the United States (see Gravelle and Zimmerman 1994) as well as subsequent debate about the tobacco settlement (e.g., Viscusi 2002).

Summary of Cross-Sectional Estimates

Previous estimates of the costs of smoking vary widely even if we try to "standardize" these in terms of costs (e.g., deflate or inflate all estimates into a common year's dollars) per smoker, per pack, or per resident, or express the overall burden as a fraction of gross domestic product (GDP) (table 3.1). For comparability, we have restricted this review to comprehensive estimates of the cost of smoking, that is, those that took into account at least medical costs, morbidity losses, and mortality losses. The vast majority of studies did not estimate the costs of ETS and thus understate the total costs of smoking.

The literature indicates a clear preference for using a human-capital approach rather than willingness-to-pay (WTP) to estimate morbidity and mortality losses. The popularity of the human-capital approach reflects its ease of implementation. Within the academic economics community, the human-capital approach as a summary indicator of benefit from disease reduction has been fully discredited since about the time of the publication of important papers on the subject by

Schelling (1968) and Mishan (1971). A more detailed discussion of our position was provided in chapter 2.

With these caveats in mind, annual costs per U.S. smoker ranged from $1,451 to $7,336, averaging $3,055; median costs were somewhat below the mean. All values in money terms in this study have been converted to 2000 dollars, using changes in national health expenditures to adjust medical costs and changes in gross domestic product to adjust for productivity losses and other costs (e.g., smoking-related fires). This variation is artificially high because the $7,336 estimate resulted from using (more comprehensive) willingness-to-pay values; yet even excluding the WTP estimates, the high-end estimate amounted to $4,988 per smoker—representing more than a threefold difference from the lower bound estimate.

On a per-pack basis, estimates ranged from $2.96 to $18.40, averaging $6.82 (median costs were somewhat lower than the mean), compared to a mean price per pack in the United States of $3.12 in the year 2000 (Orzechowski and Walker 2002).[1] Thus, the total private and social costs of smoking generally appear to have been several multiples of the price currently paid by smokers. However, as discussed in chapter 1, the appropriate level of taxation need not reflect *all* costs of smoking, but rather, according to economists' traditional view, only the external costs.

On a per capita basis, overall losses from smoking ranged from $399 to $1,545, averaging $773 per year; on a per-smoker basis, costs were roughly four times as high as these figures. Finally, based on current estimates, losses due to smoking amounted to at least 0.7 percent of GDP, perhaps as much as 4.3 percent, but averaging 1.7 percent. This is the backdrop against which our estimates presented in the following chapters should be compared.

Summary of Life-Cycle-Based Estimates

After more than a decade of studies based on the cross-sectional methodology, the life cycle approach became more popular in the late 1980s, starting with Oster and colleagues (Oster, Colditz, and Kelly 1984a; Oster 1997b). Unlike the aggregate cross-sectional estimates that preceded them, these life-cycle- or "incidence-based" estimates provided the first picture of the individual-level lifetime costs of smoking, including expenditures and illness-related earnings losses due to early death and disability.[2]

Table 3.1
Previous Comprehensive Estimates of Smoking-Related Costs, United States (2000 Dollars)

	Year Pub-lished	Year of Data	Includes ETS?	Year 2000 Estimate (billions)					Year 2000 Total Costs			
				Total Costs	Expenditures		Productivity Losses		Per Smoker	Per Pack	Per Resi-dent	Percent of GDP
					Medical	Other	Mor-bidity	Mor-tality				
Hedrick	1971	1966	No	138.0	124.2	—	13.8	—	2,263	5.35	683	0.7%
Kristein	1977	1975	Fires	172.1	52.7	9.1	37.2	73.1	2,868	6.03	782	1.5%
Luce and Schweitzer	1977	1975	Fires	188.0	76.0	1.0	35.9	75.1	3,133	6.59	854	1.6%
Wolfe	1977	1976	No	107.5	53.1	—	19.0	35.4	1,772	3.47	484	0.9%
Luce and Schweitzer	1978	1976	Fires	178.1	72.8	1.0	33.9	70.5	2,936	5.75	802	1.5%
Califano—low estimate	1979	1976 (est.)	No	91.0	44.4	—	M/M*	46.6	1,451	2.96	399	0.7%
Califano—high estimate	1979	1976 (est.)	No	140.9	71.1	—	M/M*	69.9	2,248	4.58	618	1.0%
Kristein	1983	1980	No	189.1	58.8	—	M/M*	130.3	2,981	6.24	822	1.7%
Rice and Hodgson	1983	1980	No	178.8	85.8	—	24.6	68.4	2,820	5.90	778	1.5%
Rice et al.	1986	1980	No	162.9	76.7	—	26.3	59.9	2,568	5.38	708	1.4%
Rice et al.	1986	1984	No	155.9	79.0	—	23.5	53.4	2,413	5.23	650	1.4%
Lewit	1985	1964–1983	No	144.0	52.7	—	M/M*	91.3	2,194	4.80	608	1.3%
OTA (Office of Technology Assessment)	1985	1985	No	237.1	66.4	68.1	M/M*	102.6	3,729	7.96	980	2.2%
OTA—low estimate	1985	1985	No	167.1	35.3	68.1	M/M*	63.6	2,627	5.61	690	1.6%

							M/M*					
OTA—high estimate	1985	1985	No	317.2	106.0	68.1		143.1	4,988	10.65	1,311	2.9%
U.S. DHHS	1990	1985	Newborns, fires	141.5	72.7	1.0	24.2	43.6	2,225	4.75	585	1.3%
OTA (Office of Technology Assessment)	1993	1990	No	120.1	39.0	—	11.8	69.2	2,001	4.72	473	1.2%
Rice	1999	1995	No	183.8	105.7	—	11.3	66.7	3,187	7.72	686	1.9%
U.S. Department of Treasury	1998	1998	Fires	147.2	55.9	—	0.6	90.7	2,541	6.37	535	1.5%
U.S. Treasury Dept.—low WTP estimate	1998	1998	Fires	339.8	55.9	—	57.2	226.7	5,868	14.72	1,236	3.4%
U.S. Treasury Dept.—high WTP estimate	1998	1998	Fires	424.9	55.9	—	142.2	226.7	7,336	18.40	1,545	4.3%
Minimum				91.0					1,451	2.96	399	0.7%
Maximum				424.9					7,336	18.40	1,545	4.3%
Median				167.1					2,627	5.75	690	1.5%
Average				186.9					3,055	6.82	773	1.7%

Note: All dollars expressed in 2000 dollars. All medical care spending estimates were updated based on the change in personal health spending in the U.S. between the year of data and 2000. All other direct and indirect costs were updated based on the change in GDP during the same period.
*M/M = morbidity costs are included with mortality figures and listed in mortality column.

Using data from the Netherlands, Barendregt, Bonneux, and Van der Maas (1997) used data on age- and gender-specific incidence and prevalence of five major diseases: heart disease, stroke, lung cancer, a heterogeneous group of other cancers, and chronic obstructive pulmonary disease (COPD). They obtained data on the per capita cost of each of these diseases. The residual category was all other diseases, which accounted for the difference between total costs of health care and the cost of the five diseases, expressed per capita population. Unlike the five diseases, frequency of the residual disease category varied by age and gender but not by smoking status. The authors used three life tables, one for a mixed population of smokers and nonsmokers, one for a population of smokers, and one for a population of nonsmokers. Expected cost was discounted at alternative rates, ranging from zero to ten percent.

Per capita costs rose sharply with age, increasing tenfold between the base age of 40–44 years to 80–85 years of age. At age 65–74, per capita cost was 40 percent higher for male smokers and 25 percent higher for female smokers. However, considering the number of smokers alive by that age, the total cost of care for various age cohorts of male smokers peaked at about age 65–69. For male nonsmokers, the total cost of care peaked at about age 75–79. Far more (over three times) was spent per capita on behalf of male nonsmokers aged 85–89 than on male smokers of the same age. The authors simulated changes in total health costs for the male population after smoking cessation. Irrespective of the discount rate used, smoking cessation caused an initial drop in spending. However, as the population aged, spending increased. Thus, for example, using a discount rate of 3 percent, 31 years after cessation, encouraging people to stop smoking actually increased spending. Using a lower discount rate decreased the breakeven year; with a higher rate, the breakeven year was greater than 31 years.

Other longitudinal studies have yielded different results. Several studies have found smoking to result in higher medical cost, but the amount of the increase depended on the discount rate used and other underlying assumptions (Oster, Colditz, and Kelly 1984a; Leu and Schaub 1985; Manning et al. 1991; Hodgson 1992). Leu and Schaub (1985), in a study of Swiss males, found higher expenditures for nonsmokers than smokers, a result consistent with the above study from the Netherlands. However, according to Miller et al. (1997), "There is some evidence that Leu and Schaub underestimated the level of excess medical care associated with smokers" (p. 5).

Why Do the Cost Estimates Vary So Widely?

Given the substantial variation in the estimates of the aggregate cost of smoking in the United States and in other countries, what explains the differences? We attribute the differences in large part to differences in: (1) analytic approach—life cycle versus cross-sectional, (2) methods for valuing health loss, (3) the time periods used in the analysis, (4) data sources, (5) breadth of impacts considered, and (6) other underlying assumptions.

Choice of Analytic Approach

The life cycle and the cross-sectional approaches must yield different results, given fundamental differences in the underlying methodology (see chapter 2). Inflammatory language such as "death credit" aside (see the quotation from box 1.1 in chapter 1), it remains a reality that from a financial standpoint, deaths occurring before the observational period in question affect cash flows during the period.[3]

Other methodological differences also contribute to the variation in estimates. By discounting in the life cycle approach, expenditures incurred far in the future receive less weight in the calculation. One possible rationale for the cross-sectional approach is that much financing of personal health services and of income support is on a pay-as-you-go (PAYGO) basis. Private and public health insurance and some private and public pensions are financed on PAYGO. Thus, a deceased person neither contributes to nor draws from the plan. Social Security and Medicare are PAYGO systems; the nature of the social contract is that the young finance current payments on behalf of elderly beneficiaries. To the extent that smokers die prematurely, they may contribute more than they receive.

Valuing Health Losses

A few studies valued morbidity and mortality in WTP terms (e.g., U.S. Department of Treasury 1998) and obtained a much higher estimate of loss than studies using lost earnings (the human-capital approach). But even within studies based on a human-capital framework, there was variation in the level of detail used to project future earnings, whether to include fringe benefits as part of earnings, assumed rates of future productivity growth, and whether and how to value household production (e.g., household chores).

Time Period

Studies varied in terms of the time period on which estimates were based. For various reasons, including a change in the content of cigarettes (see e.g., Sloan, Smith, and Taylor 2003), technology, and real cost of treating smoking-related diseases, the real cost of smoking plausibly has varied over time.

Data Sources

Likewise, even if studies have the same base year, differences in the data sources used to estimate the levels and nature of smoking behavior would explain some of the differences in the estimates. All longitudinal studies must use data from a combination of years (chapter 11).

Breadth of Impacts

All studies have accounted for the health of smokers in some way, but they have varied widely in the scope of diseases covered. The earliest studies focused only on the major diseases for which reasonably solid scientific evidence demonstrated a relationship between smoking and disease incidence: heart disease, lung cancer, and selected respiratory diseases. More recent studies have compared health services utilization rates and mortality and morbidity patterns between smokers compared to statistically equivalent nonsmokers (chapter 2), that is, effectively taking into account all diseases and conditions potentially affected by smoking (e.g., Manning et al. 1989, 1991; Viscusi 1999). At least 125 studies we reviewed did not include any costs associated with nonsmoking victims of ETS or fires, whereas more recent studies tend to include at least some ETS and fire effects. But even so, the studies differed in scope, with some taking into account only newborn ETS victims, whereas others focused on children more generally, and still others included both child and adult ETS costs.

Some studies focused exclusively on measuring medical expenditures related to smoking, whereas others include nonmedical expenditures (e.g., property damage due to smoking-caused fires) and productivity losses (e.g., morbidity and mortality losses to smokers).[4] Only a few studies examined productivity losses related to ETS.

Consensus Estimates of Components of Smoking-Related Loss

Because of these variations and limitations, the only way to derive a plausible composite estimate of the annual cost of smoking from the literature is to examine a piece at a time, relying on the best available methods that have been conducted to date for each piece. We discuss our consensus estimates for components of cost.

Medical Expenditures

As of 2002, the literature contained twenty-six different U.S. estimates of smoking-related medical expenditures. They showed more than a fourfold difference in estimated annual expenditures in 2000, ranging from $35.3 billion to $143.7 billion, with a median value of $72.8 billion. These amounts constituted 3.1 to 12.6 percent of all expenditures on personal health services, with a mean value of 6.4 percent. But these estimates are almost certainly too conservative insofar as many of these studies restricted the number of diseases examined, excluded certain types of services such as mental health and mental retardation, or excluded costs of those living in institutions.[5] On a per-smoker basis, the annual medical expenditure estimates ranged from $651 to $2,738, with a mean value of $1,365. For comparison, total per capita health spending in 2000 was roughly $4,070 (inclusive of both smokers and nonsmokers). On a per-resident basis, smoking costs the United States at least $154 per capita in added medical spending each year, but this figure might be as high as $719, with a mean value of $344.

To illustrate sources of variation in estimates, Miller et al. (1999) used a two-part model to compute the smoking-attributable fraction (SAF, explained in chapter 2), with data from the 1987 National Medical Expenditure Survey (NMES). They categorized smokers based on smoking intensity—smoking status (current, former, never) and amount smoked daily. In their regression analysis of probability of use of ambulatory care (mainly physicians' services), and separately, hospital care, coefficients on the smoking variables were highly variable in sign and statistical significance. The overall weighted SAF was 6.4 percent.

Warner, Hodgson, and Carroll (1999) conducted a detailed review of published U.S. cross-sectional studies. With one exception, the studies they reviewed found that annual medical costs constituted about 6 to 8 percent of expenditures on personal health services in the United States. The exception, Miller et al. (1998b), found that smoking-attributable expenditures on personal health care services constituted 12 percent of personal health expenditures. Warner and colleagues attributed the difference between the lower and the higher estimates to reflect a difference in focus on smoking-related diseases (lower) versus an all-inclusive approach (higher). They gave several plausible reasons for their expectation that the all-inclusive approach would yield higher estimates. Smoking causes many diseases not typically included among the most highly prevalent smoking-related diseases.[6] Smoking might also lead to delays in recovery, including longer hospitalizations. Smoking might also increase the severity of certain diseases, even those not initially caused by smoking per se. As seen below, however, all-inclusive estimates have not been consistently higher.

Early cost-of-smoking studies both overestimated spending, by attributing all differences to smoking without accounting for the riskier behavior of smokers in general, and underestimated it, by focusing only on selected diseases known to be related to smoking rather than tracking actual spending differences across all diseases. More recent studies have made the adjustment for nonsmoking smokers (see chapter 2), but the two most sophisticated studies, using the same data, reached widely divergent results.

Using a multistage approach that combined synthetic and analytic methods, Miller et al. (1998b,c) only analyzed heart disease, emphysema, arteriosclerosis, stroke, cancer and other health status effects, concluding that smoking accounts for 12 percent of personal health expenditures. In contrast, using much simpler reduced-form equations, Miller et al. (1999) measured spending differences for all diseases, but concluded that smoking accounts for only 6.5 percent of personal health expenditures. Both studies excluded dental care, psychiatric hospitals, and mental retardation nursing homes and focused only on a civilian noninstitutionalized population.[7]

Hodgson's (1992) study of lifetime medical expenditures provided estimates of total health spending over the course of five years, comparing the existing mix of smokers and nonsmokers to the totals that would occur if all smokers had the same cost profile as nonsmokers. When these figures were adjusted to correspond to the nonsmoking smoker approach of Manning et al. (1989),[8] they implied a SAF for personal health expenditures of 14 percent; hospital, physician, and nursing home services were included in the analysis (Warner, Hodgson, and Carroll 1999). In the Miller et al. (1998b,c) study, these three services together had a SAF of 12.1 percent compared to 11.8 percent for all services together (including prescription drugs and home health). Thus, the 14 percent was roughly equivalent to 13.7 percent were all services included—roughly midway between Miller et al.'s most likely and upper-bound estimates. Averaging the three results (6.5, 11.8, and 13.7), all of which are biased downward due to the exclusion of any costs associated with those living in institutions, produces an intermediate estimate of 10.7 percent for the SAF.

Nonmedical Expenditures

Marks et al. (1990) estimated the long-term special education costs required of infants whose low birth weight (LBW) is attributable to smoking, amounting to $1.6 billion in 2000 dollars. Leistikow, Martin, and Milano (2000a,b) compiled the estimated cost of cigarette-caused fires based on an extensive literature review. From separate estimates of property-related losses from such fires for residential and non-residential fires (Mudarri 1994), we calculate roughly $1 billion in such damages in the form of residential fires.

Productivity Losses

The vast majority of estimates of productivity losses of smoking rely on the human-capital approach for valuing mortality and morbidity losses (table 3.2). The best of these studies (e.g., Rice 1999) accounted for earnings loss due to disease and disability, including an imputed value for household services, based on relative risks of work loss and bed-disability days as well as premature death. All studies have valued losses in household productivity as accruing to the smoker and have not accounted for losses to nonsmokers who provide care for disabled smokers.

On average, morbidity losses amounted to $36 billion and mortality losses to $95 billion a year (in year 2000 dollars). The combined total averaged more than $1,900 per smoker, or $473 per capita, and over

Table 3.2
Estimates of Productivity Losses Due to Smoking, United States (2000 Dollars)

Study	Year of data	Estimated smoking-related productivity losses ($ billions)			Percent of total smoking-related losses	Diseases included[a]	Whose losses included[b]	How losses calculated[c]	Discount rate	Year 2000 Total Costs**		
		Morbidity	Mortality	Total						Per pack	Per smoker	Per resident
Luce and Schweitzer	1975	35.9	75.1	110.9	59.0%	C, M, R, F	S, F	HC	4%	3.89	1,849	504
Luce and Schweitzer	1976	33.9	70.5	104.3	58.6%	C, M, R, F	S, F	HC	4%	3.37	1,720	470
Kristein	1977	37.2	73.1	110.3	64.1%	All	S	HC	10%	3.87	1,838	501
Wolfe	1977	19.0	35.4	54.4	50.6%	C, M, R	S	HC	4%	1.76	897	245
Califano—low	1976	M/M*	46.6	46.6	51.2%	NR	S	HC	NR	1.51	743	204
Califano—high	1976	M/M*	69.9	69.9	49.6%	NR	S	HC	NR	2.27	1,114	306
Kristein	1983	M/M*	130.3	130.3	68.9%	C, M, R, F	S, F	HC	4%	4.30	2,055	567
Lewit	1964–1983	M/M*	91.3	91.3	63.4%	NR	S	HC	NR	3.02	1,440	397
Rice and Hodgson	1980	24.6	68.4	93.0	52.0%	NR	S	HC	NR	3.07	1,467	404
Rice et al.	1984	23.5	53.4	76.9	49.4%	C, M, R	S	HC	4%	2.58	1,191	321
Office of Technology Assesment	1985	M/M*	102.6	102.6	43.3%	C, M, R	S	HC	4%	3.45	1,614	424
OTA—low estimate	1985	M/M*	63.6	63.6	38.1%	C, M, R	S	HC	4%	2.14	1,000	263

		M/M*				C, M, R	S	HC	4%			
OTA—high estimate	1985		143.1	143.1	45.1%	C, M, R	S	HC	4%	4.81	2,250	591
Office of Technology Assesment	1990	11.8	69.2	81.0	67.5%	C, M, R	S	HC	4%	3.19	1,351	319
Rice	1995	11.3	66.7	78.0	42.5%	C, M, R, D, I	S, I	HC	4%	3.28	1,353	291
U.S. Treasury	1998	0.6	90.7	91.2	62.0%	C, M, R, D, I	S, I	HC	4%	3.95	1,575	332
Expenditures	1998	57.2	226.7	283.9	83.5%	C, M, R, D, I	S, I	WTP***	NA	12.30	4,903	1,032
Medical	1998	142.2	226.7	368.9	86.8%	C, M, R, D, I	S, I	WTP***	NA	15.98	6,370	1,341
Minimum		0.6	35.4	46.6	38.1%					1.51	743	204
Maximum		142.2	226.7	368.9	86.8%					15.98	6,370	1,341
Median		24.6	71.8	92.2	55.3%					3.32	1,521	401
Average		36.1	94.6	116.7	57.5%					4.37	1,929	473

Source: Adapted from table 4.5 in Lightwood et al. (2000), with both additions and updates by authors.

*M/M = morbidity costs are included with mortality figures and listed in mortality column.

**Total medical and other direct costs in year 2000 dollars divided by base year units in denominator.

***WTP used for mortality losses only. Morbidity losses shown represent lost earnings due to lower productivity among working smokers while working, exclusive of lost workdays due to illness.

a. C = cardiovascular and circulatory disease (includes Is); Is = ischemic heart disease; G = gastrointestinal disease; D = digestive diseases; M = malignant neoplasms; R = nonmalignant respiratory disease; F = injuries due to fires; I = infants (LBW, SIDS, etc.);

b. S = smokers; A = nonsmoking adults; C = children; I = infants; F = victims of fires (includes smokers, nonsmoking adults, and children);

c. HC = human capital method; WTP = willingness-to-pay.

$4.00 per pack. Productivity losses reported in the literature generally amounted to about three-fifths of the total costs of smoking. Estimates of cost attributable to absenteeism and reduced productivity vary widely, due in part to differences in methodologies and assumptions.

The foregoing studies measured morbidity losses only in terms of work-loss days related to smoking-related illnesses. We found only a handful of specialized studies that examined the effect of smoking on on-the-job productivity. One reason employers claim that smokers are less productive on average is that they take smoking breaks. Alternatively, not smoking for periods of time during the workday may reduce productivity. Parrott, Godfrey, and Raw (2000) studied the cost of employee smoking in the workplace and reviewed previous research on the topic. They based their calculation on assumed productivity losses due to smoking breaks in workplaces at 30 minutes per day, but others have estimated such time losses at as little as 5 minutes daily. These estimates do not seem to have accounted for the fact that nonsmokers also may take breaks. Yet even if this loss is only 15 minutes daily, total annual productivity losses would exceed $5 billion annually.

Effects of Smoking on Health of Others

As discussed more fully in chapter 10, others adversely affected by smoking include nonsmoking spouses of smokers, infants of smoking mothers, children of smoking parents, nonsmoking coworkers and other adults who experience smoking secondhand. Their costs are external to the smoker even though rational smokers generally are presumed to take into account some of these costs, such as those related to spouses or other family members.

ETS has been far less studied than the costs resulting from the adverse health effects on smokers. In addition, several of the best studies have relied on willingness-to-pay methods to estimate ETS costs, resulting in figures that are not strictly comparable to the conventional cross-sectional studies' estimates based on earnings losses. Moreover, no study has included such ETS costs as expenditures on personal health services and productivity losses. Thus, one has to piece together estimates from several sources that use disparate methodologies to get an overall picture.

Most research on the effect of ETS on expenditures on personal health services has focused on infants affected by passive smoking (table 3.3). Aligne and Stoddard (1997) examined both low birth weight and sudden infant death syndrome, whereas Marks et al. (1990) and Lightwood, Phibbs, and Glantz (1999) only assessed LBW infants. Together, expenditures for infants (unavoidably inclusive of pregnancy-related costs for smoking women) and children amount to roughly $3 billion annually.

Nonmedical Expenditures

A specialized literature explores smoking-related fires. From this we could estimate nonresidential fire damage losses as well as legal and administrative costs associated with legal claims arising from all smoking-related fires and fire fighting costs. Together, these amount to roughly $700 million a year. In addition, the U.S. Environmental Protection Agency (EPA) has estimated the extra cleaning and maintenance costs associated with smoking, including replacement of office equipment such as computers, repairs due to smoking-related damage, and similar costs (Mudarri 1994), amounting to roughly $9.2 billion annually. Turnover has been estimated to be 80 percent higher for smokers than for nonsmokers in the military (Klesges et al. 2001), thereby resulting in higher training costs for replacement workers.

Expenditures on tobacco prevention and control, including research and enforcement costs, all relate to interventions undertaken in response to the social costs of smoking. For this reason, there is a strong argument against their inclusion in a social cost analysis of smoking's burden on the United States. Relative to the sizable costs of smoking documented thus far, expenditures on prevention and control are very modest. Total spending on tobacco prevention and control from federal, state, and private sources totaled $950.3 million in 2001, including $58.1 million in federal funding through the U.S. Centers for Disease Control's National Tobacco Control Program, $654.9 million in state expenditures covered through the tobacco settlement, another $218.4 million covered through state excise taxes on tobacco, $9.9 million from state general funds, and $9 million through the American Legacy Foundation (Centers for Disease Control and Prevention 2001a).

These estimates include only funds appropriated specifically for tobacco prevention and control, thereby excluding appropriations for multiple purposes, some of which may have been directed to this activity. Also, actual outlays may differ from appropriations in a given year. Some potential sources of funding such as the Public Health

Table 3.3
Estimated Costs of Environmental Tobacco Smoke, United States (Billions of 2000 Dollars)

	Adams et al. 1997		Aligne and Stoddard 1997	Marks et al. 1990	Stoddard and Gray 1997	EPA 1994		Lightwood, Phibbs, Glantz 1999	Viscusi 1995		Summary		
	Lowest	Highest	1997	1990	1997	Lowest	Highest	1999	Lowest	Highest	Lowest	Average	Highest
Grand Total	**$1.7**	**$2.4**	**$12.4**	**$3.3**	**$1.3**	**$62.3**	**$116.3**	**$0.3**	**$2.2**	**$50.2**	**$14.7**	**$75.4**	**$167.0**
Medical Expenditures											**1.1**	**3.0**	**4.6**
Family—infants	1.7	2.4	1.7	3.3	—	—	—	0.3	—	—	0.3	1.9	3.3
Family—children	—	—	0.8	—	1.3	—	—	—	—	—	0.8	1.1	1.3
Family—adults	—	—	—	—	—	—	—	—	—	—	—	—	—
Nonfamily	—	—	—	—	—	—	—	—	—	—	—	—	—
Nonmedical Expenditures	—	—	—	—	—	7.3	14.4	—	—	—	**7.3**	**10.8**	**14.4**
Morbidity Losses											**2.0**	**4.7**	**8.6**
Family—children	—	—	—	—	—	3.5	8.6[2]	—	—	—	2.0	4.7	8.6
Family—adults	—	—	—	—	—	—	—	—	—	—	—	—	—
Nonfamily	—	—	—	—	—	—	—	—	—	—	—	—	—
Mortality Losses											**4.2**	**56.9**	**139.4**
Family—infants	—	—	7.6[1]	—	—	—	—	—	—	—	1.0	4.3	7.6
Family—children	—	—	2.2[1]	—	—	—	—	—	—	—	1.0	1.6	2.2
Family—adults	—	—	—	—	—	51.5	93.3[2]	—	1.6	13.9[2]	1.6	32.5	93.3
Nonfamily	—	—	—	—	—	—	—	—	0.7	36.3[2]	0.7	18.5	36.3
Base Year of Estimate	1995		1993	1986	1987	1997		1995	1993				

Note: All dollars expressed in 2000 dollars. The overall consumer price index for all urban consumers (CPI-U) was used to update lost earnings, willingness-to-pay and other nonmedical cost components, while the CPI for medical care was used to update medical costs.
1. Monetary value based on lost earnings.
2. Monetary value based on willingness-to-pay.

and Preventive Services block grants, Substance Abuse and Mental Health Services Administration block grants, and Robert Wood Johnson Foundation grants were not included in the analysis.

No studies to date have quantified the effects of smoking on morbidity losses attributable to ETS. Kristein (1983) roughly estimated these at one-fifth of total costs for smokers, based on epidemiological data showing that involuntary smokers suffer a breathing impairment equal to that of light smokers (1–10 cigarettes daily); such smokers have a cancer risk that is one-fifth that of smokers who smoke at least one pack per day.

The U.S. Environmental Protection Agency (EPA) (Mudarri 1994) estimated the number of lung cancer and heart disease deaths that might be attributable to ETS. Others have estimated annual deaths due to nonresidential smoking-related fires. Assuming an average human-capital cost per death of $155,000,[9] total family and nonfamily adult deaths due to ETS amount to $3.5 billion a year.

How Much Does Smoking Cost in Terms of Forgone Flows of Annual Production?

The studies reviewed thus far assessed losses attributable to smoking in terms of the national product that presumably could have been devoted to other uses if people did not smoke. Using the cross-sectional approach, our review of the literature led us to the overall conclusion that smoking costs the U.S. economy $323 billion annually (year 2000 dollars)—far higher than the $187 billion composite estimate based on the major cost of smoking studies that have quantified expenditures and productivity losses (table 3.1).

Interestingly, although we have filled some of the gaps in these studies related to ETS costs, external costs overall—$26 billion—accounted for a very small fraction of the total $323 billion estimate. Thus, the very large majority of costs arose from adverse effects on the health of smokers. In contrast, if willingness-to-pay to avoid death and disability were substituted for the human-capital approach used in the above studies, our estimate of annual cost rises from $323 billion to $3.5 trillion. Although WTP is the preferred method, this estimate of the burden of smoking is implausibly high. After all, in 1999, the manufacturing component of the U.S. GDP was only $1.5 trillion. The health services component was under $600 billion (U.S. Department of Commerce 2001, table 641).

Limitations of Current Estimates

We take the $323 billion estimate as a starting value. The studies on which the estimate is based are subject to several important short-comings. The most important is the limitation of the cross-sectional approach itself. Costs and benefits of smoking accrue over several periods; a single snapshot will not do. If other factors correlated with smoking, such as other behaviors, also affect losses attributable to smoking, the SAF will be overstated. Information still is lacking about transportation costs for: smoking-related medical visits; modifications to homes and vehicles due to smoking-related disability; paid house-hold help due to smoking-related disability; medical costs and other losses attributable to increased morbidity for spouses, workers, and others adversely affected by ETS; morbidity losses for spouses, workers, and other adult victims of ETS; and informal caregiving by family and friends for smoking-related illnesses.[10]

Finally, an important distinction must be made between the cost that smoking imposes on society as a whole and the incidence of such burdens. Although smokers possibly impose a burden in terms of lost output, at the same time, they might more than pay their way. It is to this distinction that we now turn.

Who Bears the Cost of Smoking? Relative Importance of Internal versus External Costs

No one previously has provided a systematic accounting of how the costs of smoking are distributed among smokers and nonsmokers. The estimates provided here are only a first cut, based on existing empirical evidence. In subsequent chapters, we will present more refined esti-mates of the distribution of burden.

For simplicity, we provide such calculations with a cross-sectional framework here, which typically has used the human-capital rather than the willingness-to-pay or WTP approach for valuing losses due to mortality and morbidity, which we will use later (chapters 4 and 9). We neglect financial externalities arising from various forms of insur-ance, which are discussed in later chapters. These estimates indicate only where costs arise, not who actually pays. That is, costs that are at-tributable to smokers in many cases are actually borne by both non-smokers and smokers—for example, medical costs paid through public insurance such as Medicaid or Medicare or through private third-party coverage. Despite these limitations, several important insights emerge from this analysis (table 3.4).

As calculated in the studies through 2002, over 90 percent of the total costs of smoking were incurred on behalf of smokers themselves. Second, two-thirds of this was in the form of actual expenditures, principally on medical care and cigarettes, and only slightly more than one-third reflected productivity (morbidity and mortality) losses. This means that even if smokers completely discounted any adverse health effects of smoking, up to two-thirds of the impact on their own lives would be knowingly borne if smokers were not insulated from the medical cost consequences of their decision to smoke. But if smokers pay only one-fifth of their medical costs out of pocket and pay no higher premiums for their coverage, they shifted an amount onto society (roughly $100 billion) exceeding the amount they now paid for cigarettes. Third, mortality losses were nearly twice morbidity losses, making it imperative to accurately estimate the amount of excess mortality that legitimately can be attributed to smoking—the research task of chapter 4.

Costs imposed on infants and children were about four times as large as those imposed on spouses. As adults, spouses are less susceptible to being viewed as "innocent victims" in the sense that any health consequences they bear might well have already been "compensated" by the smoker within the context of the myriad of adjustments made in any marital relationship (chapter 1); even if uncompensated, most spouses might be viewed as already having made a rational calculation that the benefits of living with a particular smoker outweigh the health consequences. Given the relatively early age at which most smokers begin their habits, relatively few spouses enter into their marital relationships unaware of their partners' smoking habits.

Children, on the other hand, have far less autonomy to exit or adjust to the adverse health consequences they face and, for the most part, presumptively are innocent of any knowledge about such consequences. An important issue is the extent to which smokers take the welfare of their children into account when electing to smoke. The standard economic view is that they do. In terms of medical and nonmedical costs, these presumably are borne by the family (or third parties) rather than the children. In that context, an interesting note is that almost half of smoking's cost on children stems from such losses. The nearly $10 billion in mortality losses might be viewed differently, since it mostly represents future earnings losses imposed on society

Table 3.4
Summary of Estimated Costs of Smoking, by Type of Victim (Billions of 2000 Dollars)

	Grand Total	Family Members			Outside Family
		Smokers	Spouses	Children	
Grand Total	**322.9**	**295.9**	**4.2**	**18.2**	**4.7**
Expenditures	**208.1**	**194.3**	**2.7**	**8.4**	**2.7**
Medical	125.0	122.0	NR	3.0	NR
Nonmedical	83.1	72.3	2.7	5.4	2.7
Productivity Losses	**114.8**	**101.5**	**1.5**	**9.8**	**2.0**
Morbidity	29.7	29.7	NR	NR	NR
Mortality	85.1	71.8	1.5	9.8	2.0
			Percent		
Grand Total	**100.0**	**91.6**	**1.3**	**5.6**	**1.5**
Expenditures	**100.0**	**93.4**	**1.3**	**4.0**	**1.3**
Medical	100.0	97.6	NR	2.4	NR
Nonmedical	100.0	87.0	3.3	6.5	3.3
Productivity Losses	**100.0**	**88.4**	**1.3**	**8.6**	**1.7**
Morbidity	100.0	100.0	NR	NR	NR
Mortality	100.0	84.4	1.7	11.6	2.3
			Percent		
Grand Total	**100.0**	**100.0**	**100.0**	**100.0**	**100.0**
Expenditures	**64.4**	**65.7**	**64.6**	**46.0**	**57.6**
Medical	38.7	41.2	NR	16.2	NR
Nonmedical	25.7	24.4	64.6	29.8	57.6
Productivity Losses	**35.6**	**34.3**	**35.4**	**54.0**	**42.4**
Morbidity	9.2	10.1	NR	NR	NR
Mortality	26.3	24.3	35.4	54.0	42.4

Note: All dollars expressed in 2000 dollars. The overall consumer price index for all urban consumers (CPI-U) was used to update lost earnings, willingness-to-pay and other nonmedical cost components, while the CPI for medical care was used to update medical costs.

rather than borne directly by the smoker. Yet in WTP terms, this estimate would be much larger.

Finally, smokers appear to impose costs outside their own families of less than $5 billion a year. In the context of nearly $70 billion spent on cigarette purchases, this appears to be an extraordinarily modest amount. Since current cigarette taxes now amount to about 30 percent of the retail price, if we accept the standard economic approach for defining externalities, this implies that federal and state governments now collect several multiples of this outside family loss. Of course, the health effects on others do not include the unpleasantness of breathing in someone else's smoke, but it seems doubtful that these excluded external costs are sufficient to alter the conclusion that current excise taxes far exceed the externalities imposed on the health of persons outside the family.

Do Smokers Pay Their Own Way from a Social Perspective?

Composite Estimates for U.S. Smokers

Two longitudinal studies of smoking cost, published during the 1990s, are particularly pertinent to our study. Unlike most of the other studies, these investigations took a broader perspective of cost than just a focus on medical expenditures.

Manning et al. (1989, 1991) assessed the cost of poor health habits, that included smoking, excess alcohol consumption, and lack of exercise. They limited their analysis to external cost. For smoking, such cost consisted of collectively financed costs: medical care, sick leave, group life insurance, nursing home care, retirement pension, fires, and taxes on earnings. To estimate the effect of smoking on medical care cost, the authors estimated utilization equations to control for the effect of other determinants of utilization not causally related to smoking.

There are several differences between Manning et al. and our study. Their primary source of data on use of personal health services came from the Rand National Health Insurance Experiment. The Rand data were limited to persons under age 62 at enrollment in the study. Data came from six sites located throughout the United States. Respondents remained in the study from three to five years. Because the panel was short, the authors did not take advantage of the panel feature of their data. The exclusion of persons over age 62 at enrollment was unfortunate for a study of smoking-attributable utilization because most of the adverse health effects of smoking first become manifest after age 50 (see chapters 4 and 9). Also, since the Rand study randomly assigned respondents to health insurance plans, Manning et al. could not study impacts of smoking on an individual's choice of particular forms of health care coverage. Smokers are overrepresented in some insurance categories, such as Medicaid (chapter 5). For elderly persons, Manning et al. used data from a 1983 supplement to the National Health Interview Survey (NHIS). By contrast, we used 1998 NHIS data, mainly for information on persons under age 50 (see chapter 5). Also, smoker-specific life tables are now available (see chapter 4).

Using these parameters, Manning et al. altered the smoking status of current and former smokers to that of never smokers counterfactually (the nonsmoking smoker approach, chapter 2). Because they only measured external cost, they excluded out-of-pocket payments for personal health services. The result was that the estimated medical cost attributable to smoking was only that part borne by insurance. They considered the medical costs of secondary smoke to be so small that they excluded such costs from the calculations. They implicitly assumed that health insurance coverage did not differ systematically for smokers and nonsmokers.[11] Furthermore, they assumed that people bear the full cost of health insurance. The cost of group insurance was assumed to be borne by employees in terms of reduced wages, an assumption we made also (chapter 5).[12]

For nursing home expense, they assumed that habits do not affect use, but rather depend only on age.[13] They considered such cost for persons only over age 65. Smoking only had an effect on nursing home cost to the extent that it affects longevity. Insurance coverage for dental, eye care, and pharmaceutical expense were not considered. In fact, before the 1990s, such coverage was relatively rare.

The computation for sick leave was only for employed persons. Persons who are not employed do not have collectively financed sick leave. Their estimates of sick leave were obtained from a combination of (1) the probability of being employed, (2) the difference in predicted number of work loss days for smokers versus nonsmokers, (3) the hourly wage rate, and (4) 0.38, the proportion of sick leave costs borne by the employer.[14]

For life insurance, the authors considered only group life insurance, because "most individual life insurance policies adjust premiums for habits (especially smoking status). Group life insurance provided by employers does not" (Manning et al. 1991, p. 38). Surcharging practices of individual insurers is an empirical issue, which we explore in chapter 8. They further assumed that group life insurance ends with retirement. Thus, every person with life insurance was assumed to have a term life insurance policy. In our analysis, we include both term and cash value life insurance.

The Manning et al. study considered both public and private pensions. For Social Security, death of a male pensioner entitled to Social Security benefits results in an increase in payments to the wife if the wife is not eligible for Social Security benefits on her own. In such cases, the payment rises from that for a "wife" to that for a "widow," which is an increase of from 50 to 100 percent of the man's benefit. They included this cost only for men dying between 60 and 79 years of age. At an earlier age, the wife will probably work or remarry. At older ages, the wife might not survive the husband. Unlike our study, they did not assess the impact of smoking on contributions to Social Security plans. Information on mean pension benefits and other social welfare program amounts received was taken from the 1985 Current Population Survey (CPS). In our study, we had individualized measures of benefits and could distinguish between Old Age and Survivors Insurance (OASI) and Social Security Disability Insurance (SSDI).

For pensions, they found that the probability of retiring because of disability was higher for current and former smokers than for never smokers. Patterns of retirement for other reasons did not differ by smoking status. Other Social Security payments varied by smoking status only to the extent that smoking reduced survival. Their method for computing effects of smoking on private pensions and public assistance was not described.

They assumed that medical, sick leave, disability, group life insurance, and retirement benefits were largely financed from premiums paid by the employee, taxes on wages and salaries, and other taxes. For simplicity, they assumed that these costs are financed solely by a constant percentage tax on earnings. The tax rate was set at a proportional 10 percent rate.[15] In contrast to our study (see chapter 6), they did not have data on earnings by smoking status; they based their comparisons on differences in education by smoking status. Earnings data came from a single cross section, the 1985 Current Population Survey (CPS). They did, however, consider that differences in survival and early retirement of smokers reduce the amount smokers pay in taxes below that of nonsmoking smokers.

Viscusi (1999) extended the Manning et al. (1991) methodology in two ways. First, he adjusted for the change in tar content of cigarettes.[16] On a tar-adjusted basis, cigarette consumption has declined much more than on an unadjusted basis. As he acknowledged, adjusting for tar content remains a highly controversial issue; data to indicate that low-tar products are safer are lacking (Stratton et al. 2001). Second, he included a computation for the social cost of ETS. However, as he noted, "The net financial externality from ETS is not significant" (Viscusi 1999, p. 588). His results on the social cost of smoking, based on external costs, and a comparison of his results to Manning et al. (1991), are presented in table 3.5. Additional discussion on ETS cost is provided in box 3.1.

Several features of table 3.5 are particularly noteworthy. First, the bottom line is that the net social cost of smoking is *negative*, even taking into account ETS losses. That is, considering the extra costs imposed on others by smoking (net of smokers' contributions to various programs such as Social Security), smoking has a negative net social cost. As we shall see in subsequent chapters and as others have argued as well, the value of health losses from reduced longevity attributable to smoking far and away exceeds costs of smoking on such programs as Medicaid. Further, this per-pack social cost does not consider smokers' contributions to excise taxes on cigarettes, which nationally in 1995 amounted to 56 cents per pack (see Viscusi 1999, p. 602). Thus, if such payments were added to the negative net social cost estimates summarized in table 3.5, the estimates would be at least triple the negative value shown in the table.

Second, the estimates are insensitive to the precise method used. This of course is within the range of methods they did use.

Third, the largest external cost is for medical care. By contrast, savings from early death account for the negative total net cost. Computations for sick leave and fires might be interesting, but their impact is not consequential. Fourth, the cost estimates were quite sensitive to the discount rate used. For example, the −$0.25 total net cost per pack (the updated Manning et al. estimate reported by Viscusi) is based on a real discount rate of three percent; total net cost using alternative rates of zero and five percent is −$1.26 and $0.22 per pack, respectively. Total net cost rises with higher discount rates because the savings from reduced retirement expense receives a lower weight. Because returns on risk-free securities have been about three percent since early 1900s, a three percent discount rate is the most reasonable one and most widely applied (Viscusi 1995; Gold et al. 1996).

Do Smokers Pay Their Own Way from a Federal or State Government Perspective?

Several efforts have analyzed the distribution of smoking-related medical expenditures by payer (including Medicare and Medicaid), including aggregate estimates reported by the Office of Technology Assessment (1985), at that time, an agency reporting to Congress, and Bartlett, Rice, and Max (1994), as well as lifetime estimates reported by Hodgson (1992). However, the most interesting perspective can be gleaned from data reported by Viscusi (1999), because these estimates allowed us to account for all external costs of smoking, by source (federal, state, and private), and they are the only existing figures that answer the explicit question of whether smokers pay their own way from a government perspective. Viscusi concluded that from the perspective of the federal government, smokers do more than pay their own way, as they generate net savings of 46 cents (tar adjusted) to 53 cents (no tar adjustment) per pack. Likewise, from the perspective of the average state, smokers generate net savings of 8 cents (tar adjusted) to 9 cents (no tar adjustment) per pack.

Medicaid

The cross-sectional approach has been used widely in studies by experts for plaintiffs in tobacco litigation (see e.g., Harris 1997a,b; Max 1997a,b,c). The general methodology has been to derive SAFs for particular health services, such as hospital care, and apply these fractions to data on expenditures (see chapter 2 for a description of this methodology). The SAFs consistently imply excess spending on behalf of smokers (see e.g., Miller et al. 1997; Miller, Ernst, and Collin 1999), and therefore the findings are favorable to plaintiffs in such litigation. Thus, smoking-related cost is always positive.

We illustrate this approach, using a recent study that determined smoking-attributable cost for Medicaid in Massachusetts (Cutler et al. 2000). The authors based their analysis on data from Medicaid and other sources. Excluding some categories of service from consideration because they are not related to smoking (e.g., mental retardation), they

Table 3.5
Lifetime Costs of Smoking (2000 Dollars, per Pack)*

| Elements of Cost | Manning et al. (1991) | | | Viscusi (1999) | | | |
| | Base Case[a] | Lower Bound[b] | Upper Bound[c] | Manning et al. Update[d] | Viscusi Estimates | | |
					No Tar Adjustment[e]	Tar Adjustment[f]	Average[g]
Internal Costs	**$1.846**	**$1.846**	**$7.152**	**$—**	**$—**	**$—**	**$3.615**
Medical costs borne by family	0.214	0.214	0.214	NR	NR	NR	0.214
NICU costs for LBW infants	0.043	0.043	0.043	NR	NR	NR	0.043
Sick time losses borne by family	0.028	0.028	0.028	NR	NR	NR	0.028
Smoker deaths	1.321	1.321	6.627	NR	NR	NR	3.089
Fetal deaths	0.199	0.199	0.199	NR	NR	NR	0.199
Fire-related smoking deaths	0.128	0.128	0.128	NR	NR	NR	0.128
ETS—lung cancer deaths	0.199	0.199	0.199	NR	NR	NR	0.199
ETS—heart disease deaths	NR	NR	NR	NR	NR	NR	NR
External Costs	**(0.264)**	**(0.169)**	**0.485**	**(0.710)**	**(0.577)**	**(0.463)**	**(0.516)**
Total medical care	0.556	0.321	0.641	0.452	0.686	0.568	0.569
Sick leave	0.014	0.014	0.057	0.015	0.015	0.013	0.014
Group life insurance	0.071	0.071	0.085	0.105	0.157	0.131	0.131
Nursing home care	(0.064)	(0.064)	(0.043)	(0.152)	(0.283)	(0.245)	(0.227)
Retirement provision	(0.341)	(0.540)	(0.284)	(1.152)	(1.372)	(1.150)	(1.225)
Fires (property damage)	0.028	0.028	0.028	0.021	0.018	0.018	0.019

Expenditures			------ Included above ------			
Medical	NR	NR	NR	0.001	0.001	0.001
Nonmedical	NR	NR	NR	0.017	0.017	0.017
Productivity Losses	NR	NR	NR	0.171	0.171	0.171
	NR	NR	NR	0.013	0.013	0.013
Morbidity	**0.128**	**0.071**	**0.128**	**0.466**	**0.463**	**0.375**	**0.434**
Total						
Excluding internal costs	0.392	(0.098)	0.613	(0.245)	(0.114)	(0.088)	(0.082)
Including internal costs	2.238	1.748	7.765	(0.245)	(0.114)	(0.088)	3.533
Discount Rate	**5%**	**5%**	**5%**	**3%**	**3%**	**3%**	**3%**

Note: NR = Not Reported.

*Updated from original results using the ratio of the medical CPI in 2000 to the corresponding annual average in the base year. All other components were adjusted using the GDP implicit price deflator (year 2000 value estimated using the average of quarters 2 and 3) and consumer price index 1998 to the corresponding value for 1995. Viscusi presented estimates based on alternative discount rates, 0, 3, and 5 percent. The estimates used a 3% discount rate.

a. Effect of changing current and former smokers to never smokers, with other characteristics held constant.

b. Based on narrow definition of medical costs, with no effects of smoking on early retirement.

c. Comparison with actual never smokers rather than statistical never smokers. Figure for taxes on earnings is based on nonsmoking smoker differential; never smokers actually pay $0.51 more earnings tax than smokers per pack because of higher earnings rates, but it is implausible that their higher earnings rates are causally related to smoking alone.

d. 1995 $ estimates reported in table 1 of Viscusi (1999).

e. Figures based on 30-year point estimates and include tar adjustment.

f. 1999 estimates.

g. For external costs, average excludes the original Manning figures since these were calculated using a 5 percent discount rate. Figures based on WTP value of smoker deaths (to be consistent with use of WTP value for ETS and fire deaths). Cost of in-home nonsmoker deaths are imputed from EPA figures reported in Viscusi showing a breakdown of in-home vs. out-of-home ETS deaths. Figure for fire-related smoking deaths in home derived from nonresidential smoking deaths estimate based on a reported 1328 out of 1366 fire-related deaths being residential (Mudarri 1994).

Box 3.1
Prior Research on Costs from Environmental Tobacco Smoke

Much of the analysis of the costs from environmental smoke has been motivated by the substantial controversy about the adequate level of taxation that fully covers the cost of such externalities. Hay (1991), for example, concluded that accounting for long-term costs of smoking-related LBW implied externalities of $6.10 per pack of cigarettes (in 2000 dollars). Chaloupka and Warner (2000) explained that some important studies conducted prior to their review did not fully account for a number of health consequences of ETS that only recently achieved greater attention, such as its effects on heart disease. The authors also assumed that effects within the family, such as effects on a nonsmoking spouse or children, are internalized by the smoker and hence do not add to the externalities; counting part or all of these effects as externalities and using alternate methods to derive the value of a statistical life to account for premature mortality would significantly raise the optimal level of taxation.

Adams et al. (1999) reviewed several other, U.S.-specific and international, studies of the costs of ETS. The authors cited estimates from an EPA study (Mudarri 1994) for the cost of ETS-related lung cancer and heart disease mortality of $52 to $94 billion (in 2000 dollars) due to ETS. Two other studies estimated ETS-related neonatal intensive care unit (NICU) costs at approximately $1 billion (Aligne and Stoddard 1997; Marks et al. 1990). Other studies have attributed about 10 percent of the cost of smoking to ETS (Collins and Lapsley 1991; Chudy, Remington, and Yoast 1992).

grouped the remaining Medicaid expenses into one of three aggregate categories: adult acute care, long-term care, and care for low-birth-weight (LBW) babies. Adult cost was for care rendered to Medicaid recipients aged 18 and over. For long-term care cost, the sample was limited to persons over age 45. For LBW infants, they considered medical spending only in the first year of life.

They developed two models: an inclusive model and a disease-specific model. Using the former approach, the authors decomposed the share of total medical cost attributable to smoking by the SAF, defined separately for former and current smokers. With the latter, they limited the analysis to specific smoking-related diseases. They obtained a separate SAF for each of these smoking-related diseases. Because the disease-specific model considered only a few diseases, the authors argued that this approach yields a lower bound on Medicaid costs attributable to smoking. Suppose, for example, that smoking increases the length of stay in the hospital from gall bladder surgery; the first approach would reflect such additional cost. The latter would exclude them because gall bladder disease has not been linked to smoking.

The Centers for Medicare and Medicaid Services (CMS, formerly the Health Care Financing Administration or HCFA), the federal agency responsible for administering Medicaid, provides Form 64 data on Medicaid spending by category and state. These data were used for aggregate Medicaid expenditure in Massachusetts. They used Medicaid claims data to split the expenditure aggregates into age/gender groups, and data on smoking status from the respondents to the Massachusetts Tobacco Survey and the Massachusetts component of the Behavioral Risk Factor Surveillance Survey (BRFSS) who were enrolled in Medicaid at the time of the surveys. To ascertain whether the smoking rates obtained from these sources were likely to be representative, they compared smoking prevalence rates from these two sources with national data on Medicaid recipients from the NHIS.

The SAFs for the inclusive model were based on an analysis of the determinants of utilization, including smoking status, using data from the NHIS. Expenditures were assumed to vary with relative utilization of current, former, and never smokers. Thus, the authors specified and estimated a two-part model. In the first part, the dependent variable was the probability that a type of service (e.g., hospital care) was used during the year. The second part was the amount used, conditional on having used at least one unit during the year. With measures of predicted use from these regressions, SAFs were calculated. As noted above, controlling for other potential determinants of expenditures is desirable, but adding covariates generally had little effect on the estimated effects of smoking on use of services. In fact, in some cases, adding these variables increased the size of the smoking effect rather than decreasing it, as one would generally assume adding additional covariates to a utilization equation would do. Overall, using the inclusive model, Cutler et al. estimated that smoking accounts for three to seven percent of physician visits and from 15 to 23 percent of hospital days covered by Medicaid.

For the disease-specific approach, the authors first summed all the Medicaid claims for persons diagnosed with each smoking-related condition. Thus, for example, claims for X-rays and for open-heart surgery were counted, the former even if the X-ray bore no relationship to smoking. It only mattered that the claim be filed on behalf of someone with a smoking-related diagnosis.

The SAF was the share of persons who got a particular disease due to smoking. It was this share that represented smoking's contribution to cost rather than particular services, such as x-rays, that were attributed to smoking versus other underlying reasons for use. These SAFs were obtained from data on the relative risks of dying from that disease.[17] For example, if smoking increases the probability of dying of lung cancer by 24, then the SAF for lung cancer is 0.96. Of course, people in the cross-sectional sample were alive, and the authors implicitly assumed that relative risks of dying also apply to the living.

The SAF for a disease such as lung cancer was multiplied by a disease-specific spending differential, which was the difference in spending for Medicaid recipients with the smoking-related disease and such spending by persons of the same age and gender who did not have *any* of the smoking-related diseases. The product was then multiplied by the number of Medicaid recipients in the age/gender category. The results for each smoking disease type/age/gender category were summed to arrive at disease-specific Medicaid spending attributable to smoking. Details of computation for the long-term care and one-year LBW components of Medicaid spending differed somewhat from adult acute care, which we have described in detail.

The two approaches led to the conclusion that smoking-attributable expenditures were about seven percent of Medicaid expenditures in Massachusetts for inpatient, outpatient, and long-term care and approximately 5.6 percent of total Medicaid spending. Current costs to Massachusetts Medicaid were about the same as payments to Massachusetts under the Master Settlement Agreement of November 1998, implying that the compensation was just about right.

Medicare

Gori and Richter (1978) were the first to observe that disease prevention efforts—including smoking cessation—might have adverse effects on government transfer programs such as Social Security and Medicare. Their study, described in more detail earlier, is too aggregated to permit conclusions to be drawn about the specific effects on Medicare. At the other extreme, Daviglus et al. (1998) compared differences in Medicare costs for middle-age patients, showing that those with favorable cardiovascular risk profiles (including not smoking) in middle age had lower average annual Medicare expenditures in older age. But again, there is no way to disentangle the specific contribution of smoking to their reported cost differentials.

Wright (1986) was the first to specifically address the potential impact of smoking cessation on Medicare, taking into account both the contribution and expenditure sides of the equation. In the first step, Wright used American Cancer Society data on mortality rates for male light smokers and never smokers to determine the proportion of the mortality gap between these two groups that is removed at successive years after light-smoking men quit. From this, the author calculated the additional quitters alive (AQA) in each year through age 99 for a cohort of 100,000 quitters. She then calculated the additional contributions to and expenses from the Medicare Part A hospital insurance fund, including interest earnings on the added fund balance to obtain a net financial effect by year. She then calculated the present value per quitter, using alternative discount rates and assumptions. Under the pay-as-you-go financing approach used by Medicare, any additional contributions are used to pay for current beneficiaries and therefore do not remain in the fund long enough to earn interest. Under the opposite extreme, "self-insured" financing, all contributions remain in the fund until they are needed to pay for added expenses of AQAs. An intermediate approach, "half-and-half," splits the difference between these approaches.

The Wright (1986) study showed that using the generally recommended discount rate of 3 percent, the net present cost per quitter ranges from $934 with the self-insured approach, to $952 using the intermediate approach, and to $2,745 using pay-as-you-go financing. Bartlett, Rice, and Max (1994) found that Medicare covered 20.4 percent of total smoking-attributable medical spending among the civilian noninstitutionalized population in 1987. Among the elderly, Medicare covered 41.2 percent of all smoking-attributable expenditures.

Bartlett, Rice, and Max (1994) used 1987 data from the National Medical Care Expenditures Survey (NMES), a single cross-sectional survey, and the Smoking-Attributable Mortality, Morbidity, and Economic Costs (SAMMEC) attributable-risk approach to determine SAFs for hospital care, physician services (including hospital outpatient care and emergency room), prescription drugs, and home health; this yielded a weighted average for the noninstutionalized U.S. population.

The data used by Bartlett, Rice, and Max (1994) excluded persons living in institutions such as nursing homes. This might not be a serious omission insofar as Medicare only covers a limited amount of nursing home care; however, such individuals are heavy users of other Medicare-covered services such as hospital and physician services, so the exclusion means these estimates are biased downward.

Social Security

Shoven, Sundberg, and Bunker (1989) focused entirely on the Social Security cost of smoking. They examined the consequences for Social Security of smoking for 100,000 men born in 1920 and 100,000 women born in 1923 (the three-year age difference reflected the common age differential between husbands and wives in this cohort). The authors did not have access to data on earnings histories of smokers compared to nonsmokers. However, they used life tables that accounted for smoking.

The overall conclusion of the Shoven, Sundberg, and Bunker analysis (1989) was that the median male smoker paid Social Security nearly $36,000 (2000 dollars) more than he could expect to receive. The corresponding value for the median female smoker was half as large. The authors concluded that "the aggregate implications of our results are that smokers 'save' the Social Security system hundreds of billions of dollars.... Looked at this way, it is not surprising that the large potential for increasing life span that reduced smoking offers has sizeable consequences for Social Security" (p. 244).

One weakness of the Shoven et al. study was the failure to consider the impact of smoking on wage rates. To the extent that smokers earn less than nonsmokers because, for example, they miss more work due to sickness, smokers' payments into the Social Security system would be reduced relative to nonsmokers. This would have led to an overestimate of the savings to Social Security from smoking. Our analysis in chapter 6 fills this gap by taking into account this earnings differential.

More recently, Leistikow (2000) estimated the total amount of Social Security Survivors Insurance benefits paid based on the average number of youths per adult in different age, sex, and education categories. Leistikow examined only the expenditure side of Social Security Survivors Insurance and did not consider the effects of premature parental mortality on contributions to this fund as we do in chapter 6.

Summary and Link of Previous Literature to Our Research

This chapter has covered a lot of territory. These are the main take-away messages: first, on balance, the life cycle approach is superior to the cross-sectional approach, which has been used in the majority of smoking cost studies and more recently, by plaintiffs in tobacco litigation. Second, there is substantial variation in findings, especially among the cross-sectional studies. We have explained some reasons for these differences in results. Third, less variation is found in results from the life cycle studies. In contrast to the cross-sectional research, the bottom line of the life cycle studies is that the cost of smoking is not great and may even be cost saving. This picture changes dramatically, however, if one considers the cost of bad health attributable to smoking, especially lost life years. Lost life years, not lost lives, should be part of the calculation of smoking-attributable cost. Using the willingness-to-pay value of lost lives, some estimates of smoking-attributable cost have exceeded the gross domestic product of the U.S. manufacturing and health sectors, which is implausible, and is based on the flawed assumption that nonsmoking smokers, our counter-factual smokers, would not have died anyway. Fourth, most past research has neglected to identify winners and losers from smoking and public policies related to smoking. Public policy is often guided more by the issue of who gains and who loses than by whether all parties, given compensation of the losers, could, as a theoretical possibility, be made better off ("Pareto optimality"). We used estimates of external cost from the literature when we did not quantify such cost ourselves.

We will now turn to the results of our own research, based on the methodology described in chapter 2.

4   Effects of Smoking on Mortality

Smoking is the world's leading cause of preventable premature deaths. Each year, more than four million people die from the consequences of smoking (World Health Organization 2002). In the United States alone, a consensus estimate for the number of smoking-attributable deaths is 400,000, or about 35–40 percent of all deaths annually (McGinnis and Foege 1993), and the World Health Organization (WHO) estimates the number of deaths caused by smoking in developed countries between 1950 and 2000 to amount to fifty-two million among males and more than ten million among females (World Health Organization 1997). A difficulty in deriving a precise estimate of the number of smoking-attributable deaths arises from the substantial time lag between the behavior and its consequences. The full mortality effects of smoking can generally be observed thirty to forty years after the onset of habitual smoking, although many adverse health effects began earlier and risks remain elevated for those who survive longer.

Longitudinal studies highlight not only the deleterious effects of smoking on health, but also the chronology of the harm's manifestation. A recent 25-year follow-up of the Seven Countries Study found the probability of death was elevated from 30 percent for smokers of fewer than 10 cigarettes per day relative to never smokers to 180 percent for smokers of 10 or more cigarettes per day (Jacobs et al. 1999). In this study, after 25 years of follow-up for males aged 40 to 59 at enrollment between 1957 to 1964, 57.7 percent of very heavy smokers had died, compared with 36.3 percent of never smokers. The study revealed clear dose-response relationships.

In a 40-year follow-up study of more than 30,000 British physicians (the British Doctors Study), Doll, Peto, and Wheatley (1994) found mortality rates to be significantly higher among smokers compared with never smokers. Smoking raised the probability of death approximately threefold at ages 45–64 and the risk doubled at ages 65–84. The authors found that physicians who stopped smoking before middle age avoided virtually all of the smoking-related excess mortality and that even quitting smoking in middle age translated into substantially reduced mortality risks. The clinical pathways through which smoking causes premature death are well known. Cardiovascular disease and cancers account for the cause of death for approximately 80 percent of persons who die from smoking. The vast majority of these deaths occur among persons who smoke, but a small number of deaths (in the context of the total smoking-related deaths) occur among children who are exposed to cigarette smoke and among persons killed in accidental fires.

The harmful affects of smoking have been widely publicized. Certainly, nearly everyone has heard some of the public messages and/or has been advised not to smoke by a personal physician (Sloan, Smith, and Taylor 2003).

Gains in Life Expectancy from Smoking Cessation

Not only has smoking been found to be detrimental to one's health, but smoking cessation has been linked to improvements in health. The U.S. Surgeon General completed an exhaustive study of the health benefits of smoking cessation in 1990 and documented the following positive attributes of cessation (U.S. Department of Health and Human Services 1990). First, smoking cessation results in almost immediate improvements in general health, and the benefits accrue both to persons with smoking-related illnesses as well as those with other ailments. Second, persons who stop smoking increase their longevity. For example, a 50-year-old former smoker reduces his or her risk of death by age 65 by half (Ibid). Third, smoking cessation has been linked to reductions in the risk of developing lung and other types of cancer as well as heart disease. It reduces both morbidity as well as mortality from these causes. Fourth, pregnant women who stop smoking have lower risks of smoking-related complications including low birth weight. Fifth, health benefits of smoking cessation more than offset any adverse health consequences from the average five-pound weight gain that sometimes occurs after smoking cessation.

In a recently published study (Taylor et al. 2002), some of us simulated the impact on life expectancy of the entire U.S. population if all persons were to stop smoking. We used data from the Cancer Prevention Study II (CPS-II), a cohort of 1.2 million U.S. adults, surveyed at baseline and intermittently thereafter to identify the life years that could be saved by stopping smoking at various ages. Current smokers had higher all-cause mortality rates compared to never smokers, regardless of their age or gender, and the relative risk of death rose with increasing age, peaking at age 50–59 in men and age 60–69 in women, and then fell among older smokers. Death rates among former smokers older than 50 in 1982 were nearly always higher than never smokers, regardless of how long prior to 1982 they had quit smoking. For former smokers younger than 50, the risk of death was not usually different from that of never smokers. Among former smokers, the relative risk of death by years since cessation in 1982 rises with increasing age until age 70–79 and then declines. Alternatively, given a particular age group in 1982, the relative risk of death fell as the years since cessation increased, showing that cessation at earlier ages reduced mortality. The pattern for women was similar.

Males who smoked at age 35 and continued to do so had a life expectancy of 69.3 years compared to 75.9 for those who stopped smoking by age 35, a difference of 6.6 years; clearly showing that mortality is lower for persons who stop smoking. After adjustment for the subsequent quit rate among current smokers at baseline, the life extension from cessation at age 35 rose to 8.5 years. Female smokers who were age 35 and continued to smoke had an expected 6.3 fewer years than those who quit at age 35, 7.7 years when adjusting for smoking cessation. Quitting earlier had clear advantages in terms of average life years saved relative to continuing to smoke. However, even among 65-year-old smokers, those who quit at age 65 had an expected increase in life span of 2.0 years for males and 3.7 for females relative to 65-year-olds who continued to smoke, showing that cessation as late as age 65 yields substantial increases in life expectancy.

The analysis of CPS-II data demonstrates that people live substantially longer when they stop smoking, regardless of the age at which they quit. Virtually all the excess mortality from smoking could be avoided by quitting smoking at age 35, and most of it by stopping smoking in middle age. Even smokers who quit around age 65 stand to gain 2.0 years of life expectancy among men and 3.7 years among women relative to those who continue to smoke. These findings reinforce the urgency of emphasizing smoking cessation to all smokers, irrespective of age, and never assuming that a smoker is "too far gone." The estimates of life extension that would accrue from smoking cessation are conservative, principally because some persons who were current smokers in 1982 stopped smoking during the follow-up period used to estimate the relative risk of death from smoking. Thus, we underestimate the negative effect of continued smoking as well as the benefits of cessation. Our calculation of the benefits of smoking cessation in terms of life extension agrees with the recent findings using data on British doctors (Doll, Peto, and Wheatley 1994)—stopping smoking at any age reduces the risk of mortality, and doing so by age 35 avoids essentially all the excess risk of smoking. The estimate of life extension gained from stopping smoking by age 35 identified by Taylor et al. (2002) is much larger than that found by Tsevat (1992). Using information from the Framingham Study, a longitudinal (1950s-to-1980s) database from Framingham, Massachusetts, he found that smoking cessation by age 35 would yield an average life extension of 0.8 years for males and 0.7 years for females, relative to the life expectancy of 35-year-olds who continued to exhibit population-based smoking behavior, including some smokers who subsequently stopped smoking. The similar comparison from the Taylor et al. study was 3.6 to 4.6 years for men and 3.9 to 5.1 years for women.

The estimate of the effect of never smoking is more similar to that found in the second half (1971–1991) of the British Doctors Study. Doll, Peto, and Wheatley (1994) determined that 35-year-old never smokers had a life expectancy that was 8 years longer than 35-year-olds who smoked until death, compared to around 8.5 years for men and 6.7 years for women in our study. Between 1951–1971 and 1971–1991, life expectancy increased by over 3 years in the British Doctors Study. If the survival benefit of smoking cessation continues to increase over time as it did during the British Doctors Study, Taylor et al. (2002) have likely underestimated the benefit of cessation for life extension since our study period (1982–1996) is later and our follow-up period was shorter.

Life Table Used in This Study: Rationale and Methods

Although other life tables exist, including the one developed for Taylor et al. (2002), we desired to have a life table using the same methodology as in the analyses presented in the next six chapters. Other life tables did not include survival probabilities for nonsmoking smokers (see chapter 2 for discussion of the concept of nonsmoking smokers). Also, the well-publicized estimate of deaths in the United States attributable to smoking of over 400,000 per year seemed high to us. It seemed unlikely that the estimate sufficiently considered the effects of health habits on mortality other than smoking that are likely to be correlated with smoking (e.g., excessive alcohol use, lack of exercise). We wanted to derive an independent estimate, particularly as our estimates of burdens over the life cycle would depend on the life table estimates we used.

For our analysis of smoking effects on mortality, we combined information from a published life table from Strauss and Shavelle (2002), data from the 1998 National Health Interview Survey (NHIS), 1999 population data from the U.S. Census Bureau, and the first four waves of the Health and Retirement Study (HRS) to assess the effects of smoking on mortality. At the time we conducted our study, data on deaths between waves four and five were not yet available.

We used the NHIS to obtain estimates of the number of current, former, and never smokers by age. Since recent quitters are likely to relapse or may have quit because of a recent health shock (Taylor et al. 2002; Sloan, Smith, and Taylor 2003), we considered former smokers who had quit within the last five years to be "current" smokers. Separately for males and females, we used *multinomial logit* analysis, to estimate the probability of being a current, former (as we defined it), or never smoker. Multinomial logit is a statistical technique appropriate when there are more than two mutually exclusive categories. With the parameter estimates from the regression, we predicted the probability of being a current, former, or never smoker as a function of age, starting with age 18 and ending with age 100. We then multiplied the predicted probabilities by population by year of age and gender, for the United States in 1999. In this way, we derived the total number of smokers, former smokers, and never smokers by age and gender in 1999.

The usual procedure would be to apply life tables of smokers and former smokers to these numbers to estimate the total number of deaths per year due to smoking. However, as emphasized in chapter 2 in our discussion of the concept of the "nonsmoking smoker," simply comparing the mortality experience of smokers and nonsmokers may overstate the impact of smoking on mortality. What one needs is the counterfactual of the mortality experience of the types of persons who took up smoking, that is, what the mortality experience of these persons would have been had they not begun smoking. For example, smokers tend to be less educated than never smokers. If we had not developed counterfactual estimates, the effect of educational attainment and other factors would remain embedded in the estimated effect of smoking on mortality.

The Health and Retirement Study is particularly rich in potential determinants of mortality that are correlated with smoking and may have independent effects on mortality. Among these variables are the HRS measures of risk and time preference (see chapter 2), variables not available in the NHIS and in other data sets containing information on smoking behavior. By relying on the HRS to generate counterfactual life tables as well as in analyses in subsequent chapters, we made the restrictive assumption that these variables exert similar proportional impacts on mortality for persons at other ages. This is a restrictive assumption; we would like to have had more data.

We used the mortality experience of respondents to the first four waves of HRS to derive an estimate of the fraction of excess mortality attributable to smoking that more accurately accounts for factors other than the person's smoking behavior. With logit analysis, an appropriate technique to use when there are only two mutually exclusive categories (here, alive or dead), we estimated equations by gender for the probability that a person died between two adjacent HRS waves, a two-year period. We included covariates for: current smoking; former smoking, as well as years since quitting; light/moderate, heavy, and problem drinking; body mass index (BMI); risk preferences; financial-planning horizon; marital status; race; and education; as well as separate binary variables for each wave. Smoking and drinking variables were interacted with age to allow for time-varying effects of these characteristics on mortality. Time-varying explanatory variables were defined for the beginning of the two-year period. Deaths were measured until the end of the period.

Using parameter estimates from the model, which relate the effects of each independent variable to the probability of death, we calculated predicted probabilities for (1) current smokers and former smokers, and (2) nonsmoking current and nonsmoking former smokers. The latter were calculated by setting the binary variables for current and for former smoking equal to zero. Using these probabilities, we calculated the excess mortality risk attributable to smoking, and the excess (or reduced) mortality risk attributable to differences in other covariates, separately for current and former smokers (see box 4.1).

Using life tables of current, former, and never smokers, and non-smoking smokers, we calculated age-specific smoking-attributable excess probabilities of death among smokers and former smokers relative to never smokers, and multiplied these by the number of smokers and

Box 4.1
Detailed Description of Method for Calculating Effect of Smoking on Mortality

We calculated predicted probabilities of death for current, former, and never smokers, as well as with smoking variables set to zero, using parameter estimates from logistic regression models. To derive estimates of mortality risk of "nonsmoking smokers," we predicted mortality rates setting the parameter estimates on binary variables for current smokers and for former smokers to zero and then predicting mortality based on the parameter estimates on the other explanatory variables and sample mean values for both current and former smokers.

Using age-, gender-, and smoking-status-specific weighted sample means of the predicted probabilities, we converted these probabilities into log odds of two-year mortality for current smokers, former smokers, and nonsmoking smokers. The difference between the estimates for smokers and nonsmoking current smokers represents the "best" estimate of the effect of *smoking*. Similarly, the difference between the measures for former smokers and nonsmoking former smokers represents the "best" estimate of the effect of *former smoking*.

The difference in the estimates between counterfactual nonsmokers and actual nonsmokers represented the excess risk of death among smokers *not* attributable to smoking, but instead attributable to other factors. The share of smokers' excess risk attributable to smoking was not related to age; we therefore calculated a single, sample-size weighted mean of the share of risks for each combination of gender and smoking status. We implicitly assumed that the ratio of the excess risks due to characteristics other than smoking and the total excess risk of death among current smokers and former smokers remains constant over a person's life.

former smokers to calculate the number of excess deaths in 1999. We calculated each person's life expectancy at age 24 as the sum of the probabilities of survival to each age between 24 and 100, conditional upon survival to age 24.

Empirical Results

Characteristics of Respondents by Smoking Status
Individual characteristics differed by smoking status (table 4.1). Current and former smokers were much more likely to be heavy or problem drinkers than were never smokers. Current smokers also had a higher risk tolerance, that is, were less risk averse (although the difference between current and never smokers was not statistically significant at conventional levels for females), and were more likely to

Table 4.1
Differences between Current Smokers, Former Smokers, and Never Smokers at Wave 1 of the Health and Retirement Study

| | Smoking Status | | | | | | | | |
| | Females | | | Males | | | Total | | |
Variables[1]	Current[2]	Former	Never	Current	Former	Never	Current	Former	Never
Number of respondents (N)	2,209	1,417	3,106	2,156	2,172	1,483	4,365	3,589	4,589
Age	53.3**	54.3**	53.7	56.2**	57.7***	56.7	54.7	56.3***	54.7
Light/moderate drinker	55.6***	61.2***	45.8	55.3	62.0*	57.9	55.5***	61.7***	49.7
Heavy drinker	4.4***	1.5**	0.6	15.2***	7.4***	3.8	9.7***	5.1**	1.7
Problem drinker	12.5***	8.7***	3.2	29.7***	20.4***	10.1	21.0	15.8	5.4
BMI 25–29.9	33.0	33.0	34.0	44.6***	52.8	50.3	38.7	45.0	39.2
BMI 30+	21.4***	29.1	27.5	17.5***	23.0	22.9	19.4	25.4	26.0
Risk tolerance	24.0	24.6**	23.3	25.4**	23.8	24.0	24.6	24.1	23.5
Short financial planning horizon	32.8**	26.5	28.8	27.4***	23.5	21.1	30.1	24.7	26.3
Long financial planning horizon	7.7	9.5	7.9	7.3	9.4*	7.6	7.5	9.4	7.8
White	78.0	79.0	77.5	77.5	86.0***	79.4	77.7	83.2	78.1
Less than high school education	34.3***	23.1**	26.7	36.4***	28.7***	22.3	35.3	26.5	25.3
College graduate	9.0***	19.8**	16.1	12.6***	23.0***	29.7	10.7	21.7	20.5
Married	65.6***	73.1**	77.5	78.0***	88.1***	84.2	71.7	82.2	79.6

1. Numbers are percent with specified characteristic, except for age (in years).
2. *, **, and *** refer to statistically significant differences in means relative to never smokers, at the 0.05, 0.01, and 0.001 levels, respectively.

have a shorter financial-planning horizon than never smokers. They were much more likely to have less than a high school education and less likely to be college educated. They were less likely to be married. On the other hand, smokers, especially male smokers, were less likely to be overweight or obese than were never smokers.

Logit Analysis of Mortality between Consecutive HRS Waves

Probabilities of dying during a two-year period were substantially elevated for current smokers (see chapter 4, appendix A). At age 60, the probability of death was 3.07 times as high for current as for never smokers among women and 5.24 times as high for men.

Life Tables

Since our estimated life tables are likely useful to future research, we present them in appendix B to this chapter. Among female smokers, "lifetime smokers," defined as persons who smoked at age 24 who are projected to never quit, had the lowest expected survival (figure 4.1, panel A). However, most smokers will quit at some point during their lifetime. For the average women who smoked at age 24, a "typical 24-year-old smoker," survival was better than for lifetime smokers. Never smokers had the best survival experience. Nonsmoking smokers had slightly less expected longevity than this. We found essentially no difference in survival by smoking status until the women reached about their midfifties. Differences in survival were most pronounced in the seventies and eighties.

Qualitatively, the pattern for males was the same as for females, but the differences by smoking status were more pronounced (fig. 4.1, panel B). Differences in survival probabilities emerged at about age 40, but as with females, the differences by smoking status were largest for persons in their seventies and eighties.

Remaining Life Expectancy at Age 24

In table 4.2, we show estimates of life expectancy of persons at age 24 based on our life tables. Female lifetime smokers had an average remaining life expectancy of 53.3 years, compared with 59.3 years for female never smokers, a difference of six years. For typical 24-year-old smokers, many of whom would quit subsequently, a more realistic

Panel A. Females

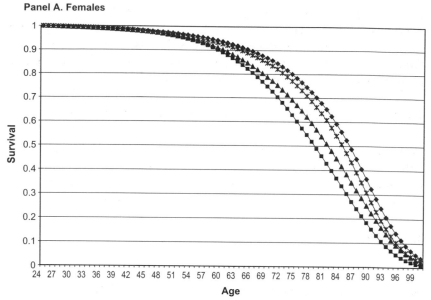

Panel B. Males

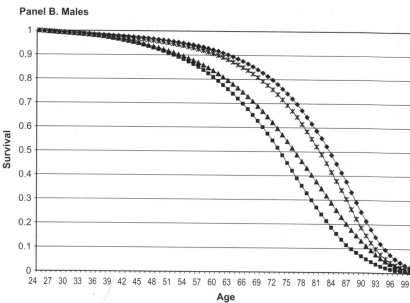

Figure 4.1
Survival probabilities for female and male smokers, never smokers, and nonsmoking smokers. ▪ Lifetime smoker; ▲ Typical 24-year old smoker; ◆ Never smoker; ✳ Nonsmoking smoker.

Table 4.2
Effect of Smoking on Life Expectancy at Age 24

		Actual	Non-smoking Smoker	Effect of Smoking
Female	Lifetime smoker	53.3	57.8	−4.5
	Typical 24-year-old smoker	55.5	57.8	−2.4
	Never smoker	59.3	59.3	0.0
Male	Lifetime smoker	47.1	54.2	−7.1
	Typical 24-year-old smoker	49.8	54.2	−4.4
	Never smoker	56.2	56.2	0.0

assumption than assuming that such persons never quit, the difference in life expectancy between female smokers and female never smokers was not quite as large. Thus, on average, a woman who smoked at age 24 was expected to live another 55.5 years, reducing the mortality differential relative to never smokers to 3.8 years. Female nonsmoking smokers would have a remaining life expectancy of 57.8 years, 1.5 fewer years than never smokers. For an average 24-year-old female smoker, the net expected smoking-related loss in life expectancy was 2.4 years.

Life expectancy was lower for males. Male lifetime smokers had a remaining life expectancy of 47.1 years, compared to 56.2 remaining years for male lifetime never smokers, a much greater differential of 9.1 years. On average, a 24-year-old male smoker had a 6.4-year lower remaining life expectancy than a 24-year-old who would never smoke over his lifetime. The smoking-attributable reduction in remaining life expectancy was 4.4 years for the average 24-year-old male smoker. These results confirm the mortality gains from quitting from earlier studies.

Annual Smoking-Related Deaths

Based on our calculations, we estimate the number of excess deaths, relative to never smokers, among smokers aged 24 to 100 to be 439,000 in 1998–1999 (table 4.3, panel A). Correcting for the other factors correlated with smoking reduced this estimate to 422,000 deaths (panel C).

More smoking-attributable deaths occurred among men than among women and among current smokers relative to former smokers. About sixty percent of excess deaths occurred among persons 65 and over;

Table 4.3
Estimated Annual Number of Smoking-Related Deaths by Age, 1998–1999

	Females		Males		
	Current	Former	Current	Former	Total
A. Excess deaths relative to the mortality experience of never smokers					
Age 24–50	7,435	1,570	43,818	7,632	60,454
Age 51–64	25,403	6,139	58,217	24,671	114,430
Age 65+	51,355	37,985	70,484	104,137	263,962
Total	84,193	45,694	172,519	136,440	438,845
B. Share of smokers' excess risk of death attributable to smoking					
	85.5%	96.8%	81.7%	110.0%	
C. Excess deaths controlling for differences in characteristics other than smoking					
Age 24–50	4,156	1,298	36,594	8,856	50,904
Age 51–64	21,642	5,476	51,361	28,207	106,687
Age 65+	41,716	33,093	58,816	130,546	264,171
Total	67,515	39,867	146,770	167,609	421,761

Sources: 1998 National Health Interview Survey; 1999 population data by single year of age; 1992-to-1998 Health and Retirement Study.

about a quarter occurred among persons aged 51 to 64. Of the excess risk among female smokers, 85.5 percent was attributable to smoking, compared to 81.7 percent of excess risk among male smokers (panel B). Of the excess risk among female former smokers, 96.8 percent was due to smoking, while 110.0 percent of the observed excess risk among male former smokers was attributable to smoking. The value for male former smokers implies preferential selection on characteristics other than smoking. That is, they were drawn from a pool of men for whom mortality risk would have been lower than average, had they never smoked. Controlling for these differential baseline risks, due to factors such as risk tolerance, time preference, and education, yielded the estimates in panel C. Underlying this adjusted estimate is a greater number of deaths among male former smokers and fewer deaths among male current smokers and female current and former smokers.

Valuing Losses from Mortality

A vast literature has been written on the value of a statistical life and its determinants. In part, this reflects the high demand for such information. Values are widely used by policymakers in the field of the environment. They also are used in litigation, especially in wrongful

Table 4.4
Value of Life Years Lost[1]

		Value of Life Years Lost
Female	Lifetime smoker	93,864
	Typical 24-year-old smoker	52,385
	Never smoker	0
Male	Lifetime smoker	174,584
	Typical 24-year-old smoker	113,923
	Never smoker	0

1. Discounted at 3% per year to age 24, valued at $100,000 per year.

death cases. Despite the numerous studies, the topic is surrounded by much controversy. Although the quality of analysis has substantially improved (see e.g., such recent studies as Krupnick et al. 2002, which addresses many of the criticisms of past work), a consensus on the most appropriate approach of life valuation is lacking. For this reason, and in view of the widely discrepant findings (see Viscusi 1993; Mrozek and Taylor 2002; and Viscusi and Aldy 2003), no single dollar figure for the value of a statistical life is generally accepted. Individual literature reviews have arrived at consensus estimates, but the consensus varies.

A recent meta-analysis of more than forty value-of-a-statistical-life studies concluded that the value of a statistical life is from $1.5 million to $2.5 million (Mrozek and Taylor 2002). This is about the level of recent estimates based on contingent valuation (see in particular, Krupnick et al. 2002), but below other estimates (see, e.g., Krupnick 2002; Viscusi and Aldy 2003). This includes pecuniary, for example, lost earnings, as well as nonpecuniary loss. Earlier studies implied a value of life ranging from $3 million to $7 million (Viscusi 1993). Based on the latter estimates, Cutler and Richardson (1997) used a conservative value of $100,000 per life year lost, which is the value we use. This is conservative in that estimates from many value of life studies imply much higher annual estimates.

Using a value of $100,000 per life year lost, for female smokers at age 24, the value of lost life years estimated above (2.4 years for females) and the three percent real discount rate we have used throughout this study translates into a present value of loss of $52,000 per smoker (table 4.4). For male smokers of this age (who lost 4.4 years), the corresponding present value is $114,000. For female and male smokers at age 24 who never quit, the present values of losses are $94,000 and $175,000 for women and men, respectively. Assuming higher or lower values for the value of a lost life year would change these present values proportionately, but it is important to remember that the value we used is at the low end of what has been used in the literature.

Discussion and Conclusions

More studies of the effects of smoking have focused on mortality than on any other single end point. The result that smoking is a major cause of death comes as no surprise. A woman who smoked at age 24 could expect to lose 2.4 years of life because she smoked. For men of this age, the expected loss was 4.4 years. However, that we were able to replicate the result that more than 400,000 persons die of smoking-related causes annually is particularly noteworthy. Before conducting our own research on the issue, we had suspected that this estimate was too high. But, in our own analysis, after controlling for other factors, estimated smoking-attributable deaths were reduced only slightly. We did control for a number of other factors. Of course, other covariates might have been included, for example, occupational and environmental exposures to risk, that might be correlated with smoking. However, the fact that adjusting for the factors we included in our analysis did not have much of an effect on the estimated influence of smoking suggests that inclusion of these other factors would not have had much of an impact on our findings for smoking either.

Our estimate of excess deaths was well above 400,000 per annum (422,000) after adjustment. A woman who smoked at age 24 could expect a loss attributable to premature mortality of $52,000 in present value terms; for men of this age, such loss was $114,000.

The survival curves demonstrate the importance of the life cycle approach. A simple calculation might have been to multiply the number of deaths due to smoking by a value of a life from the value-of-a-statistical-life studies. The impact of not smoking is to delay, not avert, death. Therefore, when the death occurs is of great importance in determining the "cost" of such an early death to either an individual household or society as a whole.

A word of caution: readers who prefer alternative estimates of the value of a life year can use their preferred values (express their values as a proportion of ours and multiply) to derive alternative estimates of the mortality cost of smoking. Those who argue that policy should be guided by the external effects of behavior implicitly place a zero value on such loss for public policy decision making, arguing that smokers foresaw their earlier demise on account of the smoking habit, but chose to smoke anyway. Such an approach is misleading and if applied in many other realms of policy would ascribe nearly all harm to private households leaving little legitimate role for public policy.

In analyses for the following chapters, we used the life tables presented in this chapter. We also took account of the same propensities to quit smoking as in this chapter.

Appendix A to Chapter 4: Regression Analysis of the Probability of Death Within Two Years of a Health and Retirement Study Interview

Probabilities of dying during the two-year period were substantially elevated for current smokers (table 4.A.1). Although parameter estimates taken individually were not statistically significant at conventional levels, the joint effects with interactions were statistically significant with $p < 0.001$ for both male and female current smokers. For former smokers, the joint tests indicated statistical significance for men ($p = 0.0012$) but not for women ($p = 0.135$). The effect of smoking on mortality increased in age for men and deceased in age for women. The difference plausibly reflects gender-specific differences in age of initiation, or of smoking intensity at various ages.

Holding other factors constant, we found heavy drinking (joint $p < 0.001$ for females and $p = 0.034$ for males), problem drinking for females ($p = 0.0020$ and $p = 0.256$, for women and men, respectively), and short time horizon (for males), race (for females), and education (for females) to be statistically significant determinants of two-year mortality. The effect of body mass index showed that, if anything, excess weight was a protective factor.

Some traits more prevalent among smokers amplified mortality effects of smoking. For example, among females, having less than a high school education was related to increased mortality risk; female smokers were more likely to lack a high school diploma than female never smokers. For men who smoked, there was a positive association between having a short financial time horizon and mortality.

Table 4.A.1
Results from Two-year Mortality Analysis of the Health and Retirement Study Cohort

	Odds Ratios with 95% Confidence Intervals in Brackets[1]			
	Females		Males	
Age[2]	1.02	[0.95; 1.09]	0.88*	[0.79; 0.98]
Current smoker	3.58**	[1.59; 8.06]	1.89	[0.72; 4.98]
Current smoker × Age	0.98	[0.91; 1.07]	1.11	[0.99; 1.24]
Former smoker	2.99	[0.89; 10.10]	1.20	[0.38; 3.73]
Former smoker × Age	0.93	[0.83; 1.05]	1.09	[0.97; 1.24]
Years since quitting −5	0.99	[0.90; 1.08]	0.99	[0.94; 1.04]
Years since quitting × Age	1.00	[0.99; 1.01]	1.00	[0.99; 1.00]
Light/moderate drinker	0.97	[0.48; 1.95]	0.55*	[0.32; 0.94]
Light/moderate drinker × Age	0.95	[0.88; 1.02]	1.02	[0.97; 1.08]
Heavy drinker	4.56	[1.00; 20.80]	0.31**	[0.13; 0.75]
Heavy drinker × Age	0.60***	[0.49; 0.73]	1.10*	[1.01; 1.20]
Problem drinker	2.79*	[1.19; 6.55]	1.35	[0.77; 2.34]
Problem drinker × Age	0.96	[0.88; 1.05]	0.99	[0.94; 1.05]
BMI 25–29.9 (overweight)	0.66*	[0.46; 0.95]	0.63**	[0.48; 0.85]
BMI 30+ (obese)	1.01	[0.69; 1.48]	0.65*	[0.46; 0.92]
Risk tolerance	1.74	[0.64; 4.71]	1.07	[0.43; 2.66]
Short financial planning horizon[3]	1.27	[0.92; 1.75]	1.53**	[1.15; 2.02]
Long financial planning horizon[3]	1.26	[0.71; 2.22]	0.99	[0.60; 1.63]
White	0.65**	[0.48; 0.90]	0.80	[0.59; 1.08]
Less than high school education	1.39*	[1.01; 1.91]	1.10	[0.82; 1.47]
College graduate	0.62	[0.33; 1.17]	0.82	[0.56; 1.21]
Married	0.75	[0.55; 1.03]	0.88	[0.65; 1.19]
Wave 2	3.00***	[2.01; 4.48]	3.84***	[2.75; 5.36]
Wave 3	5.14***	[3.62; 7.28]	3.78***	[2.76; 5.18]
N	24,710		21,159	
N (died)	227		311	
Joint effect of main effect and age interaction at age 60, and test of joint significance				
Current smoker	3.07***		5.24***	
Former smoker	1.51		2.93**	
Years since quitting −5	0.99		0.98	
Light/moderate drinker	0.56*		0.68**	
Heavy drinker	0.03***		0.78*	
Problem drinker	1.87**		1.25	

1. *, **, and *** indicate statistical significance at the 0.05, 0.01, and 0.001 levels, respectively.
2. Age defined as "age minus 50 years"; the same applies to interactions involving age.
3. Reference group is medium financial planning horizon.

Appendix B to Chapter 4: Life Tables by Gender and Smoking Status

Life tables by gender and smoking status, ages 24–100, are shown in table 4.B.1. To our knowledge, these are the first published life tables by smoking status that make the adjustment for "nonsmoking smokers."

Table 4.B.1
Life Tables by Gender and Smoking Status, Ages 24–100

Age	Females				Males			
	Lifetime Smoker	Typical Smoker	Never Smoker	Nonsmoking Smoker	Lifetime Smoker	Typical Smoker	Never Smoker	Nonsmoking Smoker
24	100,000	100,000	100,000	100,000	100,000	100,000	100,000	100,000
25	99,939	99,939	99,953	99,946	99,850	99,850	99,870	99,841
26	99,876	99,876	99,905	99,889	99,702	99,701	99,743	99,685
27	99,812	99,812	99,855	99,831	99,558	99,557	99,618	99,533
28	99,746	99,746	99,805	99,771	99,417	99,415	99,497	99,385
29	99,676	99,676	99,751	99,709	99,276	99,273	99,375	99,236
30	99,603	99,604	99,694	99,642	99,131	99,126	99,250	99,083
31	99,525	99,527	99,634	99,572	98,980	98,974	99,121	98,926
32	99,443	99,445	99,571	99,498	98,824	98,815	98,986	98,761
33	99,353	99,357	99,503	99,418	98,662	98,649	98,846	98,589
34	99,259	99,264	99,430	99,333	98,491	98,474	98,698	98,408
35	99,158	99,164	99,352	99,242	98,313	98,291	98,544	98,222
36	99,047	99,056	99,267	99,143	98,127	98,099	98,383	98,025
37	98,943	98,952	99,172	99,031	97,783	97,776	98,269	97,886
38	98,831	98,840	99,068	98,911	97,422	97,440	98,148	97,739
39	98,709	98,720	98,958	98,782	97,043	97,089	98,021	97,583
40	98,579	98,591	98,840	98,645	96,641	96,720	97,886	97,419
41	98,439	98,452	98,713	98,496	96,212	96,331	97,741	97,243
42	98,297	98,310	98,572	98,331	95,765	95,922	97,601	97,072
43	98,142	98,154	98,420	98,154	95,286	95,488	97,450	96,889

44	97,976	97,987	98,257	97,964	94,775	95,028	97,289	96,692
45	97,797	97,807	98,081	97,758	94,225	94,538	97,114	96,480
46	97,604	97,614	97,890	97,536	93,638	94,017	96,926	96,252
47	97,286	97,318	97,736	97,356	93,014	93,478	96,697	95,973
48	96,942	96,999	97,567	97,160	92,344	92,902	96,448	95,671
49	96,569	96,656	97,385	96,948	91,625	92,290	96,180	95,346
50	96,163	96,284	97,187	96,716	90,858	91,642	95,892	94,997
51	95,722	95,882	96,970	96,464	90,042	90,961	95,585	94,625
52	95,250	95,457	96,720	96,173	89,179	90,237	95,285	94,261
53	94,734	94,997	96,445	95,854	88,256	89,471	94,961	93,870
54	94,173	94,498	96,146	95,506	87,269	88,657	94,613	93,449
55	93,561	93,957	95,817	95,124	86,209	87,790	94,236	92,993
56	92,895	93,373	95,460	94,709	85,067	86,863	93,826	92,499
57	92,081	92,686	95,084	94,273	83,798	85,837	93,350	91,925
58	91,187	91,938	94,669	93,792	82,422	84,732	92,827	91,295
59	90,209	91,126	94,212	93,263	80,930	83,542	92,253	90,606
60	89,145	90,249	93,712	92,684	79,317	82,263	91,627	89,854
61	87,991	89,305	93,166	92,053	77,583	80,896	90,943	89,034
62	86,711	88,254	92,570	91,364	75,836	79,473	90,182	88,125
63	85,324	87,124	91,917	90,612	73,964	77,953	89,353	87,135
64	83,832	85,917	91,208	89,795	71,963	76,334	88,454	86,064
65	82,239	84,637	90,445	88,917	69,837	74,618	87,480	84,908
66	80,550	83,287	89,625	87,975	67,591	72,808	86,432	83,666
67	78,742	81,847	88,745	86,966	65,202	70,842	85,257	82,278
68	76,844	80,344	87,808	85,893	62,724	68,800	84,010	80,809
69	74,838	78,764	86,804	84,747	60,144	66,571	82,679	79,248

Table 4.B.1 (continued)

Chapter 4

Age	Females				Males			
	Lifetime Smoker	Typical Smoker	Never Smoker	Nonsmoking Smoker	Lifetime Smoker	Typical Smoker	Never Smoker	Nonsmoking Smoker
70	72,697	77,083	85,715	83,506	57,446	64,440	81,248	77,577
71	70,398	75,286	84,527	82,154	54,618	62,090	79,704	75,779
72	68,053	73,367	83,154	80,597	51,603	59,568	77,935	73,731
73	65,567	71,336	81,673	78,922	48,498	56,949	76,047	71,556
74	62,950	69,196	80,082	77,129	45,332	54,251	74,044	69,263
75	60,213	66,954	78,379	75,218	42,133	51,493	71,933	66,862
76	57,375	64,622	76,573	73,197	38,932	48,694	69,721	64,363
77	54,661	62,108	74,604	71,004	35,878	45,935	67,097	61,423
78	51,851	59,494	72,517	68,691	32,853	43,156	64,381	58,407
79	48,939	56,771	70,299	66,245	29,868	40,357	61,564	55,309
80	45,913	53,922	67,927	63,645	26,921	37,530	58,634	52,122
81	42,768	50,935	65,384	60,875	24,019	34,671	55,576	48,833
82	39,767	47,935	62,424	57,675	21,296	31,712	52,183	45,233
83	36,674	44,813	59,285	54,310	18,629	28,733	48,652	41,543
84	33,502	41,575	55,965	50,786	16,057	25,763	45,012	37,802
85	30,270	38,232	52,464	47,107	13,631	22,854	41,312	34,067
86	27,008	34,801	48,789	43,292	11,388	20,051	37,601	30,396
87	24,066	31,647	44,708	39,114	9,768	17,614	33,224	26,176
88	21,164	28,474	40,560	34,933	8,261	15,294	29,025	22,238
89	18,344	25,321	36,394	30,808	6,879	13,112	25,043	18,615
90	15,644	22,226	32,261	26,791	5,634	11,085	21,315	15,333

91	13,105	19,230	28,211	22,938	4,528	9,229	17,874	12,409
92	10,765	16,377	24,305	19,307	3,568	7,558	14,748	9,853
93	8,658	13,711	20,606	15,956	2,753	6,083	11,964	7,669
94	6,808	11,274	17,177	12,935	2,078	4,808	9,536	5,847
95	5,228	9,093	14,062	10,272	1,534	3,731	7,465	4,365
96	3,913	7,184	11,290	7,980	1,107	2,840	5,735	3,188
97	2,849	5,551	8,878	6,055	779	2,120	4,322	2,277
98	2,015	4,190	6,829	4,481	535	1,550	3,193	1,589
99	1,383	3,087	5,136	3,234	359	1,110	2,312	1,084
100	921	2,219	3,773	2,274	234	778	1,639	721

5

How Much Does Smoking Increase Outlays for Personal Health Care?

In view of the substantial size of the health care sector as well as its growth, there is considerable interest in why the sector is as large as it is, why it has grown historically, how much growth can be anticipated in future years, as well as in public policies that may succeed in reducing the rate of growth in expenditures on personal health care services. For states, Medicaid is one of the largest single components of state spending and is increasing as a share of total spending. For the federal government, Medicare is one of the largest programs. Medicare expenditures are increasing and will surely increase in the future, irrespective of cost containment policies that are adopted to constrain its growth.

Smoking is a major cause of mortality, and previous studies have demonstrated a link between smoking and health care spending. At least at first glance, it would appear that if we could convince everyone not to smoke, and improve other health behaviors, we would realize a huge dividend in terms of reduced expenditures on personal health services. This dividend would appear to be potentially much greater than the savings achievable by many health cost containment policies that have been implemented in the past or are under active consideration currently.

In litigation against the tobacco manufacturers, the issue for states and for the federal government has been the burden that smoking has allegedly imposed on public programs. Much, if not most, of the burden is said to be in terms of increased health expenditures by public health insurers. Their private counterparts have not been as active in litigation against the tobacco companies, but private insurers and their employer sponsors may be next. For these reasons, knowing the impact of smoking on outlays for personal health services is important, as are the distributional impacts of these outlays.

This chapter evaluates the impact of smoking on health care spending and on the expenditure burden borne by health insurers and ultimately by the public at large in the form of increased taxes, health insurance premiums, and out-of-pocket payments. We assess impacts on spending on behalf of adults in three age groups, 24–50, 51–64, and 65+. Especially for Medicare and Social Security, there is a natural division between age 65 and earlier ages. There is no natural split before age 65, and the division between the first two age groups was made for reasons of data availability.

To analyze the effects of smoking in the 24-to-50 cohort, we used data from the 1998 National Health Interview Survey (NHIS). The Health and Retirement Study's (HRS) first five waves (1992, 1994, 1996, 1998, and 2000) were used for the age 51-to-64 cohort. We used the first four waves of the Asset and Health Dynamics of the Oldest Old (Soldo et al. 1997) study conducted in 1993, 1995, 1998 and 2000 for the 65+ age group.

Our analytical approach represents an improvement over past cost-of-smoking studies in several respects. First, to our knowledge, ours is the first national study to use a life cycle approach to assess the effects of smoking on all major sources of payment rather than on an individual payer, such as Medicaid.[1]

Second, because all three surveys provided data on source of payment for personal health services, we were able to distribute the cost burden of smoking across payers. In the past, no study has explicitly considered effects of smoking on payer status and incorporated this information into an analysis of the cost burden of smoking. Because smoking worsens health, which in turn influences employment, income, and payer status (which in the United States is employment related), this is an important adjustment.

Third, in previous work, incorporating changes in smoking status and their effects has not been possible. In fact, during middle age cessation is quite common, and this change should affect the trajectory of health care cost. As seen in figure 5.1, which gives smoking rates of current and never smokers relative to the total number of persons alive at each age, in 1998 (actual values and polynomials fitted values to actual values), the share of current smokers of the noninstitutionalized population peaked around age 38, declining slowly until about age 50, and declining at a faster rate at later ages. At age 50, about 33 percent of persons smoked.[2] At this age, about 45 percent of persons were never smokers, the remaining 22 percent of persons being former

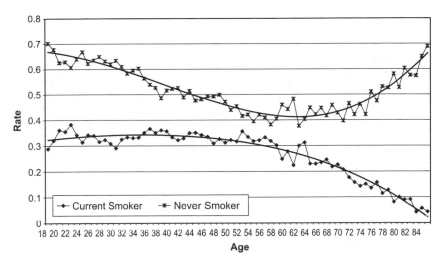

Figure 5.1
Cross-sectional smoking rates by age, 1998 National Health Interview Survey.

smokers (not shown). The share of never smokers was lowest at about age 62. By age 64, about 25 percent smoked, 43 percent were never smokers, and 32 percent were former smokers. The change in composition reflects a combination of higher mortality of current smokers and quitting.

Fourth, unlike most studies, we did not limit our analysis of health services utilization and payer burden to "smoking-related" diseases as some studies have done (chapter 3). Our approach allowed us to capture effects on other diseases as well. Smoking also affects the course of recovery from various diseases, irrespective of whether the diseases are "smoking-related." The effect of smoking on recovery is complex and does not always disadvantage smokers (see, e.g., Hasdai et al. 1999).

Overall, our estimates of the increased cost attributable to smoking are substantial, even for persons aged 24–50. Mortality-related reductions in the older age groups tend to reduce or offset smoking-related utilization increases, with a relatively small net effect for public insurance programs. The burden is unequally distributed among types of health insurance. Private insurance premium payers bear the largest share of the health insurance burden of smoking. If Medicare could be viewed as a business, this program would be said to profit from smoking. The burden on Medicaid, and more particularly on the taxpayers who finance this program, is somewhere in between private insurance

Box 5.1
Utilization Measures

With the NHIS, we measured utilization as the numbers of nights in the hospital during the year before the interview and physician visits during the two weeks prior to the interview. With HRS and AHEAD, we measured utilization as the number of hospital nights and physician visits since the previous wave interview, that is, during the previous two years for most surveys but for three years between waves 2 and 3 of AHEAD. For the oldest age group (65+), we also considered effects on nursing home use between interviews for AHEAD.

All estimates of physician visits and hospitalizations were made for the year; that is, we multiplied two-week estimates by 26 and divided the number of hospital nights and nursing home use by the number of years between adjacent waves. The implied visit rates based on a two-week recall exceeded those based on two- to three-year recall of visits in the HRS and AHEAD. Because visit rates based on a two-week recall are plausibly more accurate, we adjusted for underreporting of visits in the HRS and AHEAD samples based on comparisons in visit rates between HRS/AHEAD and NHIS.

and Medicare. If the policy goal is to compensate for losses incurred as a consequence of smoking, it is critical to account for differences in burdens by payer.

In the next section, we describe the methodology for this chapter's analysis, which is followed by our findings. Finally, we place the findings in a larger policy context.

Assessing the Effects of Smoking on Utilization of Personal Health Services

To assess the effects of smoking on utilization of personal health services, we used data from three surveys, NHIS, HRS, and AHEAD. All three surveys contained data on physician visits, hospitalizations, and the number of nights spent in hospitals during specified time periods. Precise descriptions of the dependent variables are provided in box 5.1.

Our analysis accounted for the propensity to stop smoking over the life course by incorporating age-specific quit rates. We also accounted for differential survival of smokers, former smokers, and never smokers and for smoking-related differences in type of health insurance coverage—Medicare, Medicaid, other government, private, and uninsured. To assess the effect of smoking behavior on the number

Box 5.2
Types of Regression Analysis Used to Study Utilization Patterns

We estimated negative binomial models with NHIS for the 24–50 age group, and random effects negative binomial models for HRS and AHEAD (Hausman, Hall, and Griliches 1984). A negative binomial model has several appealing features. First, it explicitly deals with count data. Second, it allows for inclusion of covariates. Third, it accounts for the large proportion of zeros in our utilization measures and the skewed distribution of positive values. Fourth, it allows for overdispersion (variance greater than the mean), unlike the Poisson model. The random effects model accounts for repeated observations on the same individual, which is possible with panel data, such as HRS and AHEAD (see chapter 2 for descriptions of these surveys).

We estimated random effects logistic regression for whether the person had spent any nights in a nursing home since the last interview, and random effects regression for the number of nights spent in a nursing home since the previous interview conditional on being admitted.

of physician visits, and hospital and nursing home nights, we used various types of regression analysis (box 5.2).

In analysis based on HRS and AHEAD, data on the dependent variables represented the experience since the last interview. Utilization of health care services between the waves was converted to annual utilization and made to depend on levels of variables in the previous wave. Thus, we defined explanatory variables for the preceding wave. For this reason, our panel used dependent variables from HRS waves 2 to 5, and AHEAD waves 2 to 4, with wave 1 used exclusively for information on explanatory variables. We used repeated observations on each respondent, as long as respondents were of ages 51–64 at the beginning of the interval during which utilization was measured. Since NHIS is a single cross section, dependent and independent variables were measured contemporaneously. The explanatory variables were described in chapter 2.[3] AHEAD did not contain information on the quitting age of respondents; we therefore assumed a fixed quitting age of 55 for persons who reported in the survey that they were former smokers.[4]

To calculate the total number of hospital nights and physician visits for persons in each age group, we first predicted the number of hospital nights and physician visits for every person at every age in the respective age range, using parameter estimates from the negative binomial models. We used respondents' actual, self-reported smoking histories to predict utilization between age 24 and the survey year. We incorporated estimated probabilities of quitting to predict utilization for current smokers after the survey year and before the person reached the upper limit of the age range.

Next, using methods described in chapter 2, we adjusted the predictions for differential survival between current smokers, former smokers (again defined as those who had quit for five years or more prior to the interview with those quitting for a shorter time period than this classified as current smokers), and never smokers, and converted each individual's predicted (unconditional) physician visits and hospital nights at each age to expected utilization, conditional only on survival to age 24, the person's actual smoking history between age 24 and the survey date, and predicted smoking status during each year between the survey year and the upper limit of each age range.[5]

Third, age-specific estimates of expected utilization were brought to a present value at age 24, using a 3 percent discount rate.

Fourth, we used multinomial logit analysis to assess effects of smoking on health insurance status, with specifications of insurance categories described in box 5.3.

Fifth, we multiplied probabilities of having particular types of insurance coverage from the multinomial logit analysis with the predicted, discounted, survival-adjusted utilization to estimate the share of the utilization burden borne by each payer at every age. Aggregating the gender- and smoking-status-specific means within each age range yielded estimates of the total discounted utilization for each individual during these time periods. Many persons 65+ had both Medicare and private health insurance. For these individuals, we had to make assumptions to allocate smoking-attributable cost between payers (box 5.4).

Sixth, to translate utilization into cost to each payer, we first used data on Medicare payment per hospital day.[6] We then calculated prices for the other payers, adjusting for price/cost margins paid by each payer[7] and prices per physician encounter,[8] also adjusted for payer payment differentials.[9] We also used average daily charges by payer from the 1999 Nursing Home Survey,[10] and we used the consumer price index to convert all values to year 2000 dollars.

Finally, we predicted unconditional utilization and insurance choice at each age. For nonsmoking smokers, we predicted utilization and insurance choice by switching the smoking variables off (that is, setting the binary variables equal to zero) but holding all other characteristics

Box 5.3
Insurance Categories Used in Analysis of Effects of Smoking on Health Insurance Status

For the younger age group, mutually exclusive categories for the dependent variable were: uninsured, Medicare for the disabled persons receiving Social Security Disability Insurance benefits and persons with end-stage renal disease (ESRD), Medicaid, other public coverage, and private coverage. Some sample persons had more than one type of coverage. To develop mutually exclusive health insurance categories, we developed a hierarchy of types. Specifically, private insurance was considered the first payer, followed in order by other government, Medicare, and Medicaid. For example, if a person had both Medicare and Medicaid, we considered the person to be covered by Medicare. The omitted reference group was private coverage. Unlike HRS and AHEAD, the NHIS did not distinguish between individual and group insurance. A person was considered to be uninsured only if there was no other coverage.

In the oldest age group, where Medicare coverage is virtually universal, the differences in coverage were the types of insurance the person possessed in addition to Medicare. For example, "private insurance" is "private insurance and Medicare." Otherwise, we used the same explanatory variables as in the analyses of utilization. Age-specific probabilities of each individual's using a particular payer were calculated from the predicted probabilities of the multinomial logit analysis.

of that individual constant. We calculated counterfactual mortality risks using methods described in chapter 2. We applied these counterfactual risks to our hypothetical sample of 24-year-old smokers to calculate each person's counterfactual probability of survival to each age between 24 and 50, 51 and 64, and 65 to 100. The difference in payer-specific predicted utilization between smokers and nonsmoking smokers (counterfactual nonsmokers), multiplied by payer-specific unit costs of each type of utilization yielded an estimate of the expenditures attributable to smoking.

Contributions to Health Insurance Plans

Overview

Smokers and nonsmokers contribute to private and public health insurance plans through several channels—in a combination of foregone

Box 5.4
Allocations of Smoking-related Costs Between Medicare and Other Payers

For persons 65+ who (1) had Medicare (over 99%) (2) had private health insurance, and (3) were *not* employed full time (over 95%), Medicare was the primary payer. For such persons, we allocated 90 percent of smoking-attributable hospital cost to Medicare, 5 percent to private insurance, and 5 percent to Medicare. For physicians' services, we allocated 80 percent to Medicare, 10 percent to private insurance, and 10 percent to self-pay. For nursing home care, we allocated 10 percent to Medicare, 30 percent to private insurance, and 60 percent to self-pay.

For persons 65+ employed full-time with private health insurance coverage, we allocated 90 percent of smoking-attributable cost to the private plan for hospital care, 80 percent for physicians' services, and 30 percent for nursing home care. Medicare as a secondary payer was assumed to bear from five to 10 percent of such cost depending on the service. When there was no private supplemental coverage, Medicare was assumed to bear the major part of such cost, with the exception of nursing home care. The Medicare benefit for nursing home care is extremely limited.

The obvious omission from our analysis is pharmaceutical expense. None of the data sets contained information on such expense.

For persons over 65 without private insurance or other coverage, we allocated all of the amounts allocated to private insurance for non-employed Medicare beneficiaries with insurance to self-pay. The final category was persons with other government coverage, such as Medicaid or Veterans Administration coverage, and Medicare. In such cases, we allocated the amounts allocated to private insurance for the non-employed beneficiaries with private insurance to Medicaid or the other government payer.

wages, payroll tax assessments, and taxes that constitute general revenue for federal, state, and local governments. Each type of contribution is distinctive and involves its own set of complexities.

Our approach for assessing the impact of smoking on contributions to health insurance plans involved these steps. First, we started with an estimate of the effects of smoking on expenditures for personal health services by payer. The goal was to determine who ultimately bore the burden of these extra expenditures. Second, for reasons given below, we assumed that all employed individuals, irrespective of their compensation levels, paid equal amounts in terms of lost earnings for the additional cost incurred by employer-based insurance plans. Based on the empirical evidence presented below, we also assumed that

Table 5.1
Allocations of Smoking-Attributable Costs between Medicare and Other Payers

Type of Coverage	Hospital Services	Physician Services	Nursing Home Care
Private insurance, not employed	Medicare: 90% Private insurance: 5% Self-pay: 5%	Medicare: 80% Private insurance: 10% Self-pay: 10%	Medicare: 10% Private insurance: 30% Self-pay: 60%
Private insurance, employed	Medicare: 5% Private insurance: 90% Self-pay: 5%	Medicare: 10% Private insurance: 80% Self-pay: 10%	Medicare: 10% Private insurance: 30% Self-pay: 60%
Medicaid or other government payer	Medicare: 90% Medicaid/other: 10%	Medicare: 80% Medicaid/other: 10% Self-pay: 10%	Medicare: 10% Medicaid/other: 40% Self-pay: 50%
No additional coverage	Medicare: 90% Self-pay: 10%	Medicare: 80% Self-pay: 20%	Medicare: 10% Self-pay: 90%

for individual health insurance plans, all policyholders paid equal amounts in the form of additional premiums. We estimated premium contributions over the life cycle for Medicare Part A. Third, this left a residual smoking-related expenditure burden not covered by payments from these sources. Funds for this residual mainly came from general public revenue (personal income taxes, corporate income taxes, sales taxes, etc.). Taxes paid by families reflect their income. We estimated the effect of smoking on family income. The result was a total estimate of contributions by smokers and nonsmokers.

Contributions to Employer-Based Private Health Insurance Plans

Adults under age 65 with health insurance are covered by employment-based insurance, private individual insurance, or public plans (primarily Medicaid). Determining who pays in the case of private individual coverage and public insurance is straightforward: people pay for their own individual coverage. Taxpayers pay for public coverage from various sources. However, for employment-paid benefits, the question is more complicated. In many employers' view, the answer is simple. The employer bears that part of the cost of the fringe benefit that the employee does not pay, for example, in the form of a payroll deduction.[11]

To economists, the answer is quite different from the notion that employers pay for the health insurance provided to their employees. Although some argue that specific fringe benefits are offered to attract a certain type of workforce,[12] the firm is basically indifferent to how it compensates its employees: in money (inclusive of payroll taxes), in kind, or some combination of each. If employees prefer to be paid in fringe benefits rather than in wage compensation, this will be done.

Employees have two main reasons to prefer receiving part of their compensation in the form of employer-provided health insurance. First, the administrative cost, or load, on employer-provided health insurance tends to be much lower than for individually purchased health insurance, especially for large employer groups.[13] Second, provided that the employer meets government requirements, compensation in the form of health insurance, unlike wages and salaries, is not subject to taxation under federal or state personal income taxes. The benefit of this exclusion varies directly with the employee family's marginal tax rate on personal income. For both reasons, the advantage to the employee of obtaining health insurance through the employer is likely to be quite considerable.

Employees with unhealthy family members may also prefer employer-based health insurance, as their use of personal health services is more highly cross-subsidized by their healthier coworkers. But this factor works both ways, decreasing demand for employer-based insurance among the healthy and increasing it for those with less healthy family members. Because smokers on average are less likely to be healthy or expect to remain healthy, they should demand employer-based coverage for this reason. However, other factors may operate in the opposite direction. For example, to the extent that smokers are less risk averse, which some empirical evidence indicates is so,[14] then less insurance of all types would be demanded.

Because employers do not impose an extra contribution on employees who smoke, a plausible assumption is that any effect of smoking on plan outlays is borne equally by employees enrolled in the plan, which is what we assumed in our analysis of contributions to employer-based health insurance plans. Furthermore, to the extent that smoking increases outlays incurred by private insurance plans, there is some additional tax revenue that does not accrue to the public treasury. This amount is approximately the product of the average marginal federal and state income tax rate multiplied by the extra expense incurred by private health insurance plans that is attributable to smoking.

Individual Health Insurance Premiums

In principle, the actuarial value of the loss attributable to smoking could be charged to smokers who purchase individual health insurance policies. If so, smoking-attributable expense paid by individual health insurance plans would be borne by the smokers themselves. At the other extreme, if insurers do not surcharge for smoking at all, the extra cost of smoking is borne equally by all holders of individual health insurance policies.

We used data from the Health and Retirement Study to assess variations in premiums paid by respondents for individual health insurance (appendix A to chapter 5). Holding other factors constant, current smokers were 13 percent less likely than never smokers to have individual health insurance. We found no statistically significant difference between former and never smokers in the probability of having individual coverage. Among those with such insurance, and holding other factors constant, policyholders who were current smokers paid $341 less in premiums annually than did never smokers. There were no statistically significant differences in premiums between former and never smokers for such coverage.

Rather than really indicating that current smokers faced lower premiums, there could have been important differences in the amount of coverage or in other characteristics of the individual health insurance plans. The HRS did not obtain information on characteristics of insurance policies. The fact that current smokers were less likely to purchase individual insurance, holding such factors as risk tolerance constant, suggests that the comparisons may not be apples-to-apples. Given no basis for assuming that individual health insurers routinely impose surcharges on premiums paid by smokers, we adopted the assumption that premiums for such insurance did not differ by smoking status.

Contributions to the Medicare Trust Fund

Medicare Part A, which is mainly for hospital coverage, is funded by a payroll tax, the revenue from which is placed in the Medicare trust fund. Medicare Part B is mainly for coverage of physicians' services. It is funded from Part B premiums paid by Medicare beneficiaries and from general federal revenue. We consider contributions to Part B below.

Until 1990, for Part A, the Medicare contribution was computed as a fixed percentage of the person's earnings up to the limit on taxable earnings set by Social Security. The rate increased over time from 0.70 percent in 1966 to 2.9 percent in 2002. In 1991, the Medicare contribution limit was increased to $125,000 and was completely eliminated in 1994, making all earnings subject to taxation. Historically, the program has been underfunded; realistically, this is largely a pay-as-you-go program.[15]

Smokers might contribute less than nonsmokers if they are less productive in the workplace on average. They might miss more work due to illness or might be sick on the job (see chapter 9). Lower productivity may translate into a lower market wage. Assuming that the reservation wage for market work (the minimum hourly pay a person requires to supply a given number of work hours) is not meaningfully affected by smoking, smokers may work less during their "working years." For these reasons, their contributions to Medicare may be lower.

The question is what to hold constant other than smoking per se. One approach is to simply compare actual contributions of smokers versus others and assess any cross-subsidy that may result. An alternative is to hold constant other factors that may be correlated with smoking, such as other health behaviors, education, time and risk preferences, and other factors, and, as in the previous chapter, compare contributions by a hypothetical nonsmoking smoker to those of never smokers. We selected the latter approach. Because we included many other factors, some of which are correlated with smoking, our analysis provides a conservative estimate of the effects of smoking on contributions to the Medicare trust fund.

To study contributions to Medicare, we used a file provided by the Social Security Administration to HRS on respondents to wave 1. To our knowledge, no other data set links contributions to so many variables on the individual and his or her household as does HRS. We had information on contributions to Social Security back to 1951. For Medicare, the data extended back to 1966, Medicare's first year.

The objective of our analysis was to compare lifetime contributions with lifetime benefits. Medicare benefits accrue after age 65, but almost all contributions are made before the person's sixty-fifth birthday. To match the contributions estimates based on HRS with the benefits from AHEAD, we estimated contribution regressions to predict representative individuals' lifetime contributions to Medicare.

In total, data on Social Security taxable earnings were available on 7,306 persons from HRS. In 1966, such persons were mostly aged 25–

35. Thus, the data covered most of the period during which Medicare has been in existence. Using annual contribution rates, we calculated Medicare contributions as a percentage of Social Security taxable earnings. For ages 62 and older, we modeled contributions to Medicare as a nonlinear function of age based on estimates between the ages of 45 and 61. The raised earnings limits after 1991 (eliminated in 1994) did not apply to Social Security, therefore our data on Social-Security-taxable earnings captured most, but not all contributions to Medicare.

The dependent variable was the person's age-specific Medicare contribution inflated to year 2000 dollars. In addition to the smoking variables, we included explanatory variables in our basic specification (see chapter 2). The only time-varying explanatory variable was age. All other variables were time invariant, that is, defined as of the HRS baseline survey in 1992.[16] Interactions between explanatory variables and age allowed for the effects of covariates on contributions to vary with age. On smoking status, we distinguished between former smokers who quit before age 40 and those who quit later. Based on the regression results, predicted contributions were calculated for every person at every age between 24 and 64, including contributions by nonsmoking smokers.

We converted our unconditional age-specific predictions to expected contributions at each age. We calculated each person's lifetime contributions as the sum of the age-specific annual expected contributions, discounted to age 24 at three percent per year.

Contributions to General Revenue-Funded Plans

Several health programs are funded from general revenue: Medicare Part B, Medicaid, and small government programs such as Veterans Administration and Tricare (formerly Champus). General revenue comes from many difference sources, including personal income, sales, and excise taxes, in this context, excise taxes on cigarettes in particular. Also a portion of revenue to Part B comes from premiums paid by Medicare beneficiaries.[17]

To make the computations manageable, we did not distinguish among sources of public revenue. Rather, we determined the effect of smoking on family income. Then we made different assumptions about the progressivity of taxation. In the baseline case, we assumed that federal and state taxes rise in direct proportion to family income. There is some evidence to support this assumption for the United States, although the share of taxes borne by very high income individuals rose during the 1990s (Feenberg and Poterba 1993; Kasten, Sammartino, and Toder 1994; Petska and Strudler 2002).[18] Alternatively, we assumed that taxes are more progressive than this to test the sensitivity of our results to alternative assumptions.

To assess the impact of smoking on family income, we used family income data from the 1998 National Health Interview Survey. Family income was provided in categories, with nine ordered categories below $75,000 and one above $75,000, plus two additional categories for nonresponses—less than $20,000 and $20,000 or more. Based on parameter estimates from ordered logit analysis, we predicted each person's probability of falling into each income category.[19] We calculated each person's federal/state tax burden using two extreme scenarios—a proportional income tax set at a 25 percent rate ("flat tax") and a highly progressive tax, ranging from a zero marginal tax rate for the lowest income category to a 45 percent rate for persons in the highest income category. For families with two spouses, the person's tax burden was obtained by dividing by two. Using the total number of smokers and never smokers at age 24, we allocated the cost of smoking to each group. Dividing by the number of persons in each group yielded the share of the cost of smoking borne by each individual.

Results: Effects of Smoking on Personal Health Services Expenditures

Based on our results discussed below, smoking increased expenditures on personal health services over the life cycle by surprisingly little, much less than the value of life years lost due to smoking reported in chapter 4.

Health Insurance and Smoking Status

Overall, current smokers were less likely to have private health insurance than were former and never smokers (table 5.2). For the overwhelming majority of persons 65+, private health insurance was supplemental to Medicare. In this age group, 95 percent or more reported being covered by Medicare with virtually no one being uninsured. Among those under age 65, Medicare covers disabled persons and persons with end stage renal disease.

Table 5.2
Health Insurance Coverage by Age and Smoking Status

| | Percent Reporting Coverage | | | | | |
| | Females | | | Males | | |
	Current	Former	Never	Current	Former	Never
A. Ages 24–50						
Private	67.2	88.2	79.1	68.2	87.8	80.4
Medicaid	9.8	1.8	5.1	3.9	1.3	1.7
Medicare (disabled/ESRD)	1.7	1.1	0.9	2.5	1.6	1.0
Other gov. insurance	3.7	3.2	2.2	4.0	1.9	2.4
Uninsured	19.5	6.8	13.8	24.1	8.9	16.0
B. Ages 51–64						
Private	71.3	81.7	79.8	72.3	84.8	83.3
Medicaid	5.5	3.9	3.2	3.2	1.5	2.4
Medicare (disabled/ESRD)	4.0	3.9	2.1	5.7	4.2	3.7
Other gov. insurance	3.7	4.5	3.2	8.8	7.5	5.0
Uninsured	20.2	12.3	15.4	17.5	10.0	11.9
C. Ages 65+						
Private	70.7	76.5	74.3	68.9	81.4	77.6
Medicaid	13.3	11.8	10.4	8.7	5.6	5.7
Medicare	95.1	97.2	97.3	94.6	97.5	96.7
Other gov. insurance	3.9	1.8	2.3	5.9	4.7	5.1
Uninsured	0.5	0.4	0.7	0.9	0.3	1.0

Note: Percentages add to more than 100 because multiple types of coverage could be reported.

Private insurance coverage was almost equally prevalent in all three age groups, with 67.2 to 88.2 percent of persons reporting such coverage. Among persons over age 65, however, as already noted, such insurance covered only a minor part of the insured's medical expense. In all age and gender groups, former smokers had the highest rates of private insurance coverage, followed by never smokers.

Among current smoker younger than 65, the probability of being uninsured was substantial. For men, the likelihood of being uninsured declined with age; 24.1 percent of male current smokers in the 24-to-50 cohort (panel A) reported being uninsured. Even at 51 to 64, the share of uninsured was considerable, 17.5 percent. Among women, rates of uninsured were highest in the HRS cohort (panel B), 20.2 percent among smokers. Fractions of uninsured were high even among never smokers, but they were consistently lower than for current smokers. Rates were lowest among former smokers.

Current smokers were also relatively more likely to be Medicaid recipients, especially relative to never smokers. Nearly 10 percent of current female smokers below age 50 were enrolled in Medicaid versus 5.1 percent of never smokers. The highest fraction of Medicaid recipients was for women 65+, but, at this age, Medicaid is a secondary payer to Medicare for hospital and physicians services, even though Medicaid covers far more nursing home expense.

Medicare coverage for disability or end-stage renal disease was higher for the 51-to-64 than for the 24-to-50 age group. Again, current smokers were relatively more likely to have such coverage. Likewise, other government coverage, such as Veterans Administration and Tri-care tended to be higher for smokers than others and, at least for men, higher for the 51-to-64 than for the 24-to-50 age group.

In regression analysis, we assigned each respondent to a primary payer (appendix B to chapter 5). The payers were defined to be mutually exclusive. Holding other factors constant, current smokers were more likely to be uninsured or to have Medicare, Medicaid, or other government insurance coverage, and less likely to have private health insurance coverage than were never smokers, the omitted reference group. For both women and men aged 24–50, current smokers 24–50 were about twice as likely to be covered by Medicaid and by Medicare relative to the omitted reference group, privately-insured persons, than were never smokers.

Although not all results were statistically significant for current smokers 51–64, there were substantial differences in coverage, nevertheless, especially for Medicaid and Medicare for female current smokers and in the probability of having other government insurance coverage for male current smokers. By contrast, there were only minor differences in coverage between former and never smokers. Male former smokers were less likely to be uninsured than were never smokers aged 24–50 as were both genders among former smokers aged 51–64. Male former smokers 51–64 were much less likely to have been enrolled in Medicaid than were never smokers.

Among persons over age 65, female current smokers were 44 percent more likely to be covered by Medicare only than were never female smokers. Differences between current and never female smokers were even greater for Medicaid and other government insurance coverage. For men, there was only one statistically significant difference between current or former and never smokers aged 65+. Former smokers were less likely than never smokers to have had Medicare as the primary payer.

Utilization of Hospital, Physician, and Nursing Home Care by Smoking Status

Utilization of physicians and hospitals was low irrespective of smoking states among persons aged 50 and under (table 5.3). Rates of utilization were higher for females than males. Never smokers had the lowest rates. By ages 51–64, utilization rates were considerably higher than for the youngest age group, especially for males. Rates of use were appreciably higher for person over age 65, but among persons 65+, nursing home utilization was lower among current smokers than among never smokers, but lowest among former smokers.

Results based on regression analysis are more definitive since they allow the researcher to hold factors other than smoking constant. The regression results on utilization are presented in appendix C to chapter 5. Here we discuss key findings from the regression analysis.

In the youngest cohort, smokers had higher rates of utilization of both physician and hospital services. The differences were larger for males than for females. Among middle-aged individuals, if anything, smokers had lower rates of physician visits. These results are based on regression analysis, which accounted for other determinants of such use, such as risk and time preference and educational attainment. Female smokers had 44 percent higher rates of hospitalizations and 39 percent more nights in the hospital. Male smokers had 30 percent more hospitalizations and spent 26 percent more nights in the hospital. Rates of hospital utilization were also elevated for former female smokers.

In the oldest age group, smokers had lower rates of physician visits among both men and women. Current and former smoking raised rates of hospital utilization and the probability of any nursing home use for females, but not for males. Smoking had no statistically significant effects on the number of nights spent in a nursing home conditional on being admitted to such facilities. If anything, use rates for smokers were lower than those for nonsmokers.

Aggregating expected utilization across all ages in the three age ranges, we obtained estimates for the total expected utilization of 24-year-old smokers and nonsmokers during each of the three stages of their adult lives (table 5.4). The estimates are expected values of

Table 5.3
Smoking and Health Care Utilization: Mean Utilization

	Mean Utilization					
	Females			Males		
	Current	Former	Never	Current	Former	Never
A. Ages 24–50						
Physician visits in past 2 weeks	0.28	0.29	0.24	0.19	0.22	0.13
Number of hospital stays in past year	0.15	0.09	0.12	0.09	0.06	0.04
Number of hospital nights in past year	0.48	0.22	0.32	0.31	0.22	0.12
B. Ages 51–64						
Physician visits in past 2 years	7.39	6.48	6.06	5.83	5.07	4.80
Number of hospital stays in past 2 years	0.29	0.21	0.19	0.37	0.25	0.18
Number of hospital nights in past 2 years	1.12	0.85	0.66	1.39	0.98	0.69
C. Ages 65+						
Physician visits in past 2 years	8.03	8.40	7.77	7.02	7.79	7.30
Number of hospital stays in past 2 years	0.60	0.52	0.44	0.52	0.50	0.48
Number of hospital nights in past 2 years	3.02	2.79	2.43	2.78	2.70	2.43
Number of nights in nursing home in past 2 years	12.97	11.97	17.71	6.77	6.14	11.22

Note: Reference period for self-reported physician visits and hospital utilization differed across the NHIS, HRS, and AHEAD.

Table 5.4
Predicted Lifetime Utilization for a Representative Person by Smoking Status at Age 24 (Not Discounted)

| | Predicted Utilization | | | | Effects of Smoking[1] | |
| | Females | | Males | | Females | Males |
	Smoker	Nonsmoker	Smoker	Nonsmoker		
A. Ages 24–50						
Physician visits	191.2	161.8	124.8	88.8	25.5	33.1
Number of hospital stays	3.8	3.2	2.0	1.1	0.5	0.7
Number of hospital nights	12.1	8.9	8.2	3.5	2.0	3.8
B. Ages 51–64						
Physician visits	115.2	117.5	85.4	99.3	0.9	–6.9
Number of hospital stays	2.3	1.7	1.6	1.5	0.6	0.1
Number of hospital nights	8.1	6.4	6.0	5.7	1.8	0.3
C. Ages 65+						
Physician visits	197.1	213.7	160.5	210.1	–33.9	–62.2
Number of hospital stays	5.3	4.9	4.5	5.4	0.2	–1.3
Number of hospital nights	21.2	19.9	19.1	22.8	0.4	–5.4
Number of nursing home nights	299.4	275.8	91.4	185.1	1.4	–99.5

Note: Utilization is nominal, i.e., not discounted.
1. Difference between actual and counterfactual predicted utilization. The absolute levels of the counterfactual (nonsmoking smoker) is not shown.

persons who smoked or did not smoke at age 24, based on utilization rates by age, quitting propensities over the life cycle, differential survival probabilities by smoking status, and the other factors that went into the calculation of the nonsmoking smoker. The panels show use during a particular phase of the life cycle. These estimates (but not estimates in later tables) assume a zero discount rate.

We estimate that women who smoked at age 24, will have 191 physician visits between the ages 24–50, 115 between 51–64, and 197 visits after the 65th birthday. By contrast, women who did not smoke at age 24 have 162, 118, and 214 visits in the three age ranges, respectively.

For physician visits, the results indicate that smoking caused increases in use before age 51, but smoking decreased use subsequently, in part because of excess mortality attributable to smoking. The net effect of smoking was to decrease physician visits, albeit slightly. For women, the net effect of smoking on physician visits was to decrease such visits by 7.5, which is not much over a lifetime. For men, the effect of smoking was to decrease physician visits by 36 on average, mostly due to early mortality.

For hospital stays, the effect of smoking over the life cycle was minuscule. For nursing home nights, the effect was to decrease use for men because of the effects of smoking on survival. For women, there was a trivial increase.

In table 5.5, we show utilization burdens of smoking by payer. The burden of additional physician visits among females in the youngest age group was nearly evenly split between the uninsured, Medicaid, and private health insurance plans. The greatest beneficiary of the reduced expected utilization of physician visits in the oldest age group is private insurance (in conjunction with Medicare). Among men, private insurance bore the largest share of the excess burden of smoking-related physician visits in the youngest age group, but also benefited from the reduced expected value of physician visits in the oldest age group. The uninsured bore a large part of the burden in the youngest group. Medicare was the main beneficiary of a lower number of expected hospital nights in the oldest age group, particularly among men. Medicare and private insurance benefited from the lower expected number of nursing home nights.

Discounting by three percent and converting utilization into expenditures, we obtained estimates of the burden imposed by smoking by payer category (table 5.6). The bottom line is that each woman who smoked at age 24 generated an extra $3,757 increase in real expendi-

Table 5.5
Effects of Smoking on Lifetime Utilization of Physician, Hospital, and Nursing Home Care by Gender, Smoking Status, Age, and Payer (Not Discounted)

Unit of Utilization	Gender	Age Group	Effects of Smoking by Payer[1]					
			Uninsured	Medicaid[2]	Medicare	Other Government	Private	Total
Physician visits	Females	24-50	7.7	6.9	1.3	2.7	6.8	25.5
		51-64	-0.5	1.0	0.9	0.2	-0.7	0.9
		65+	-0.1	-0.2	-2.5	-0.9	-30.2	-33.9
	Males	24-50	8.0	1.6	1.6	1.4	20.5	33.1
		51-64	-2.5	-0.4	0.2	1.4	-5.6	-6.9
		65+	-0.8	-0.2	-18.5	-1.9	-40.8	-62.2
Hospital nights	Females	24-50	0.7	0.7	0.1	0.2	0.3	2.0
		51-64	0.3	0.2	0.1	0.0	1.1	1.8
		65+	0.0	0.0	0.6	-0.1	-0.2	0.4
	Males	24-50	1.1	0.3	0.3	0.2	2.0	3.8
		51-64	0.0	0.0	0.0	0.1	0.2	0.3
		65+	-0.1	0.0	-2.0	-0.2	-3.1	-5.4
Nursing home nights	Females	65+	0.1	-0.1	8.1	-1.7	-5.0	1.4
	Males	65+	-0.5	-0.5	-38.6	-2.4	-57.4	-99.5

1. Difference between smokers and nonsmoking smokers. Insurance assignment for multiple types of coverage is described in the text.
2. Medicaid implies Medicaid only. In the oldest age group, most persons covered by private insurance are also covered by Medicare.

Table 5.6
Cost of Personal Health Services Attributable to Smoking by Payer (2000 Dollars)

Gender	Age Group	Estimated Cost[1]		Medicare			Other Govern-ment	Private	Self-Pay	Total
		Uninsured	Medicaid	Part A	Part B	Total				
Females	24–50	976	1,188	69	82	151	386	993	219	3,913
	51–64	79	121	53	34	87	21	563	68	939
	65+	0	0	83	–933	–851	–3	–128	–114	–1,096
	Total	1,056	1,308	205	–818	–613	405	1,428	173	3,757
Males	24–50	1,168	325	150	92	242	212	3,823	728	6,499
	51–64	–95	–17	18	8	26	110	–198	–61	–235
	65+	–30	–1	–1,431	–1,601	–3,031	–9	–243	–333	–3,647
	Total	1,044	306	–1,262	–1,501	–2,763	313	3,383	334	2,617

1. 2000 U.S. Dollars. Difference between the cost of actual and counterfactual predicted utilization, discounted at 3% per year. Cost allocation accounts for cost sharing for all ages. Cost sharing for the 65+ age group is described in table 5.1.

tures on health care services over the life cycle. For male smokers of this age, $2,617 of extra spending resulted from a 24-year-old's decision to smoke.

For women, Medicaid and private health insurance plans incurred the largest burdens. By contrast, there was a $613 saving to Medicare per female 24-year-old smoker. Most of the extra burden reflected higher expenditures before age 50. For men, there were savings in outlays for Medicare ($2,763 per 24-year-old male smoker), which largely offset an extra burden imposed on private health insurance plans (and their sources of financing). The extra burden on such plans occurred in financing services for men aged 24–50. There was an uneven distribution imposed by smoking by payer, which was mitigated by rather small absolute levels of smoking-attributable expenditures. The effect of smoking on Medicaid expenditures per 24-year-old smoking was to raise such spending by $1,308 for female smokers, and $306 for male smokers.

Results: The Other Side of the Coin—Effects of Smoking on Contributions to Health Insurance Plans

We now turn to the revenue side. Again, we first review results of some of the steps taken to reach our finding, that, excluding cigarette excise taxes (to be considered in chapter 11), smokers contributed slightly less to health insurance plans over the life cycle as a consequence of their smoking. By slightly, we mean less than $1,000 per smoker.

Lifetime Medicare Part A contributions varied mainly by gender, with females contributing less over the life cycle, $5,059 by smokers at age 24 and $5,040 for never smokers, than by male smokers at $11,699 and $13,099, respectively (table 5.7). Nonsmoking smokers would have contributed slightly more than we estimate smokers at age 24 contributed. Differences in contributions between actual and nonsmoking smokers were quite small. We estimate that lifetime contributions of female smokers were $115 lower than those of nonsmoking smokers, and that male smokers contributed $933 less than otherwise identical nonsmoking smokers.

Part of the cost of smoking to general tax-revenue-funded insurance programs was borne by smokers and part was borne by nonsmokers (table 5.8). We allocated $895 in smoking-attributable expenditures over the life course to general revenue for women and a savings attributable to smoking of $882 for men.

Table 5.7
Present Value of Expected Lifetime Medicare Contributions (2000 Dollars)

	Females	Males
(A) Actual Smoking Status		
Smoker	5,059	11,699
Never Smoker	5,040	13,099
(B) Counterfactual Nonsmokers		
Smoker	5,173	12,632
Never Smoker	5,040	13,099
(C) Difference (A) − (B)		
Smoker	−115	−933
Never Smoker	0	0

Note: Ages 24–64, 2000 dollars, 3% discount rate.

Table 5.8
Tax Burden by Smoking Status Due to Smoking's Cost to General Revenue-Funded Programs (2000 Dollars)

	Tax Burden per Smoker		Who Is Bearing the Burden?[2]			
	Cost per Smoker		Smokers		Nonsmokers	
	Female	Male	Female	Male	Female	Male
Medicaid	1,308	306	362	368	368	407
Medicare Part B	−818	−1,501	−569	−580	−578	−640
Other Government	405	313	169	172	172	190
Uninsured[1]	528	522	250	255	254	282
Total	1,423	−360	212	216	215	239

1. Assumed to be 50% of the smoking-related cost among the uninsured.
2. Assuming a flat tax scenario. A progressive tax scenario would have increased the tax burden for male nonsmokers by $9, and decreased the burden for female nonsmokers by $2.

In the table, we show results of the estimated tax burden by smoking status, comparing two alternative tax scenarios, on the share of the tax burden borne by smokers and nonsmokers. The estimates reflect (1) the total burden due to all male and female smokers, and (2) the total tax base composed of all male and female smokers as well as non-smokers. The scenarios are very similar; therefore, for simplicity, we discuss only the first scenario, a flat tax using actual probabilities of smokers' family income falling into each of the ten income categories described above. The effect of using smokers' actual versus counter-factual earnings was similarly small (not shown).

Overall, the burden was distributed relatively evenly among in-dividuals, regardless of smoking status. A typical 24-year-old male smoker would have expected to pay $215 more in general tax revenue (excluding excise taxes on cigarettes), a combination of (1) a $368 bill to fund the Medicaid burden of smoking, with (2) tax savings due to $578 lower Medicare Part B expenses, $172 to cover extra expense of other government health insurance programs (including Veterans Adminis-tration), and $254 to defray smoking-attributable expenditures on per-sonal health services for the uninsured. Under the progressive tax regime, the total burden increased by one dollar (not shown). For male 24-year-old nonsmokers, the increase was to $239 versus $248 under a proportional tax.

Combining the tax burden borne by smokers with the smoking-related overall burden and the contributions differential for Medicare, with the excess burden on Medicare Part A, yields the net cost for per-sonal health care services that smoking imposes on nonsmokers (table 5.9). A female smoker imposed net externalities of $947 due to excess utilization of Medicaid-covered services, $319 for Medicare Part A, a savings of $249 for Medicare Part B, and $236 for other govern-ment programs. A male smoker imposed net externalities of −$61 for Medicaid-covered services, −$329 for Medicare Part A, −$923 for Medicare Part B, and $141 for other government programs.

Discussion and Conclusions

This analysis has covered a lot of territory. Over the life cycle, smoking caused an increase in health expenditures of $3,800 per 24-year-old female smoker. For men, the corresponding increase was $2,600. The increase in expenditures was in the 24-to-50 age range, the time of life before serious adverse health effects of smoking occur. Increased

Table 5.9
Distribution of the Added Health Insurance Cost of Smoking by Smoking Status (2000 Dollars)

| | | | Cost of Smoking Borne by Smokers versus Nonsmokers | | | |
| | | | Medicare | | | |
	Uninsured	Medicaid	Part A	Part B	Other Govern- ment	Private	Self-Pay
Total cost per female smoker	1,056	1,308	205	–818	405	1,428	173
Total cost per male smoker	1,044	306	–1,262	–1,501	313	3,383	334
Cost borne by female smoker	778	362	–115	–569	169	1,233	173
Cost borne by male smoker	776	368	–933	–578	172	1,233	334
Net cost per female smoker	278	947	319	–249	236	195	0
Net cost per male smoker	268	–61	–329	–923	141	2,149	0

Note: Net costs are "per smoker." Self-pay represents the part of expenditures that persons with insurance pay out-of-pocket.

expenditures after age 50 were more than offset by lower survival of smokers after midlife. Thus, smoking actually saved the Medicare program money, $2,800 per male smoker aged 24 and $600 per female. The largest losers were private health insurance plans, largely because expenditures on behalf of insured males below age 51 were appreciably elevated. Medicaid was also a loser, experiencing a loss of about $1,300 per smoking female and $300 per smoking male. As discussed more fully in chapter 11, such loss does not justify the $206 billion in payments (undiscounted) from tobacco manufacturers that the Master Settlement Agreement provides.

Since smoking-attributable personal health care expenditures were not that large, the impacts on contributions to cover such expenditures were also quite small and not sensitive to alternative assumptions about the progressivity of general taxes used to pay for the extra expenditures.

Several limitations of our analysis should be noted. First, the National Health Interview Surveys exclude the institutionalized population. HRS and AHEAD excluded such persons at baseline, but collected information on respondents who became institutionalized subsequently. We did not include nursing home use among persons under 65 since nursing home utilization rates among such persons are low. We may have underestimated utilization of nursing homes among persons over age 65. Our estimates of use of hospital and physicians' services may not accurately reflect the use patterns of persons who live in institutions. Second, some types of health expenditures were not considered at all. We did not measure expenditures on pharmaceuticals, durable medical equipment, dental care, home health, and hospice care. In total, such expenditures constituted less than 25 percent of spending on personal health care services in the United States in 1999 (U.S. Department of Commerce 2001, table 122).

Third, we did not account for smoking/payer interactions. It is possible, for example, that smoking among persons enrolled in the Medicare disabled or ESRD programs had smaller or larger impacts on utilization than the average. We did not have sufficient statistical power to obtain precise estimates of such interactions.

Appendix A to Chapter 5: Variation in Individual Insurance Premiums by Smoking Status

Table 5.A.1 shows the odds ratio and associated confidence intervals for the smoking variables from logit analysis of whether or not the

Table 5.A.1
Effect of Smoking on the Probability of Having Private Individual Health Insurance Coverage and on Premiums for Such Coverage

	Parameter Estimates[1]	
	Current Smoker	Former Smoker
Has individual health insurance	0.87*	0.95
	[0.76; 0.99]	[0.83; 1.07]
Annual premium for individual	−340.52**	−142.25
health insurance	(129.92)	(144.13)
Log annual premium for individual	−0.18**	−0.10
health insurance	(0.06)	(0.06)

Note: Individual health insurance refers to coverage other than Medigap or other supplemental health insurance that was purchased directly or through a membership association such as the American Association of Retired Persons.
1. Odds ratios with 95% confidence intervals, and parameter estimates with standard errors in parentheses. The logit (for the probability of coverage) and ordinary least squares analyses (for premiums) controlled for smoking, drinking, body mass index, age, working status, education, race, sex, risk aversion, marital status, proxy response and wave indicator variables.
*, **, and *** indicate statistical significance at the 0.05, 0.01, and 0.001 levels, respectively.

Health and Retirement Study respondent had health insurance, and conditional on having such insurance, parameter and associated standard errors from analysis of premiums paid. We estimated the premium equations with, alternatively, annual premium and log of annual premium as the dependent variables.

Appendix B to Chapter 5: Effects of Smoking on Health Insurance Coverage

This appendix presents results from a multivariate analysis of effects of smoking status on the HRS or AHEAD respondent's primary source of health insurance coverage. Not having coverage was one of the mutually exclusive categories.

In table 5.B.1, which shows main findings from our multinomial analysis of primary source of coverage for both men and women aged 24–50 (panel A), all differences between current and never smokers were statistically significant at conventional levels. The relative risk ratio imply substantial differences in coverage patterns by smoking status. Results for the other two age groups are described in the text.

To gauge the economic significance of the effect of smoking, its effect on insurance coverage is most relevant (table 5.B.2). In the youngest

Table 5.B.1
Smoking and Health Insurance Coverage: Results from Multivariate Analysis

| | Relative Risk Ratios from Multinomial Logit[1] | | | |
| | Females | | Males | |
	Current	Former	Current	Former
A. Ages 24–50				
Uninsured	1.49***	0.75	1.29**	0.67*
	[1.27; 1.74]	[0.53; 1.05]	[1.10; 1.52]	[0.49; 0.92]
Medicaid	2.34***	0.72	1.92**	0.63
	[1.84; 2.98]	[0.42; 1.24]	[1.29; 2.88]	[0.28; 1.44]
Medicare (disabled/	2.37***	1.17	2.21**	1.54
ESRD)	[1.47; 3.82]	[0.54; 2.55]	[1.36; 3.60]	[0.62; 3.85]
Other government	1.90***	1.66	1.65**	0.73
insurance	[1.36; 2.66]	[0.96; 2.85]	[1.15; 2.35]	[0.37; 1.42]
B. Ages 51–64				
Uninsured	1.24*	0.77**	1.12	0.69**
	[1.05; 1.47]	[0.64; 0.93]	[0.90; 1.41]	[0.54; 0.86]
Medicaid	1.92***	0.99	1.26	0.50*
	[1.41; 2.61]	[0.70; 1.40]	[0.77; 2.08]	[0.28; 0.89]
Medicare (disabled/	1.92***	1.37*	1.61*	0.96
ESRD)	[1.44; 2.55]	[1.01; 1.86]	[1.08; 2.39]	[0.63; 1.45]
Other government	1.30	1.08	2.42***	1.60*
insurance	[0.83; 2.03]	[0.66; 1.77]	[1.59; 3.68]	[1.04; 2.44]
C. Ages 65+				
Uninsured	1.38	1.10	1.70	0.38
	[0.55; 3.47]	[0.57; 2.13]	[0.58; 5.00]	[0.14; 1.03]
Medicaid	2.25*	0.93	0.16	0.85
	[1.04; 4.90]	[0.45; 1.90]	[0.02; 1.46]	[0.29; 2.47]
Medicare	1.44**	1.13	1.22	0.74**
	[1.16; 1.80]	[0.98; 1.29]	[0.92; 1.61]	[0.61; 0.89]
Other government	2.35*	0.70	1.42	0.79
insurance	[1.21; 4.57]	[0.39; 1.24]	[0.76; 2.66]	[0.50; 1.27]

1. Relative risk ratios relative to private insurance. 95% confidence intervals in brackets. Insurance assignments were based on primary payer. Omitted category in panel C was Private and Medicare. 9.2% of wave 1 respondents with private insurance reported to be working for pay; of those 33.9% (3.1% of privately insured) were working full-time (1,500+ hours per year).
*, **, and *** indicate statistical significance at the 0.05, 0.01, and 0.001 levels, respectively.

Table 5.B.2
Effects of Smoking on Health Insurance Coverage

| | Marginal Effects of Smoking on the Probability of Coverage[1] | | | | | |
| | Females | | | Males | | |
	Current	Former	Never	Current	Former	Never
A. Ages 24–50						
Private	−8.4	1.1	0.0	−5.6	3.4	0.0
Medicaid	3.6	−0.4	0.0	1.1	−0.3	0.0
Medicare (disabled/ESRD)	0.6	0.1	0.0	0.9	0.5	0.0
Other government insurance	1.1	1.1	0.0	0.9	−0.4	0.0
Uninsured	3.1	−1.9	0.0	2.7	−3.2	0.0
B. Ages 51–64						
Private	−4.7	2.1	0.0	−4.0	2.9	0.0
Medicaid	1.8	0.1	0.0	0.3	−0.7	0.0
Medicare (disabled/ESRD)	1.0	0.6	0.0	1.1	0.1	0.0
Other government insurance	0.2	0.1	0.0	2.1	1.0	0.0
Uninsured	1.7	−2.9	0.0	0.5	−3.4	0.0
C. Ages 65+						
Private	−6.9	−1.5	0.0	−4.2	4.6	0.0
Medicaid	0.5	−0.1	0.0	−0.3	0.0	0.0
Medicare	5.1	1.9	0.0	2.8	−3.8	0.0
Other government insurance	1.2	−0.4	0.0	1.1	−0.4	0.0
Uninsured	0.1	0.0	0.0	0.5	−0.4	0.0

1. Percentage point difference in the probability of coverage by specified type of insurance between smokers and nonsmoking smokers.

age group (panel A), relative to never smokers, female current smokers had a 0.036 higher probability of being on Medicaid, 0.006 of receiving Medicare disability or end-stage renal disease (ESRD), a 0.011 higher probability of having other government coverage, and a 0.031 higher probability of being uninsured. They had a 0.084 lower probability of having private insurance coverage. For men, the respective effects were increased probabilities of 0.011, 0.009, 0.009, and 0.027, for Medicaid, Medicare, other government coverage, and being uninsured, respectively, and a 0.056 reduced probability of private coverage.

Compared with the effects of current smoking, those of former smoking were relatively small. Male former smokers had a 0.034 increased probability of private insurance and a 0.032 reduced probability of being uninsured. Female former smokers had a 0.011 increased probability of private insurance and a 0.019 reduced probability of being uninsured. The direction and magnitude of the marginal effects of smoking and former smoking are similar in the HRS cohort (panel B).

In the 65+ cohort, being a current smoker had the effect of increasing the probability of primary Medicare coverage by 0.051 for females and 0.028 for males. It reduced the probability of primary private coverage by 0.069 and 0.042, respectively.

Appendix C to Chapter 5: Effects of Smoking on Health Care Utilization

Results for the smoking variables from multivariate analysis are shown in table 5.C.1. When physician visits and hospital utilization measures were dependent variables, equations were estimated with a negative binomial model. For nursing home use, we used logit analysis for whether or not the respondent was in a nursing home at all, and conditional on same use, we used ordinary least squares in analysis of the number of nights in a nursing home.

Holding other characteristics constant, smoking increased all types of utilization in the youngest cohort relative to never smokers (table 5.C.2, panel A). Women who smoked had 18 percent greater rates of physician visits, 21 percent higher rates of hospitalizations, and 29 percent more hospital nights. Among men, the differences between current and never smokers were even greater: 41, 75, and 112 percent, respectively. With one exception, the parameter estimates for former smokers were not statistically significant at conventional levels. The one significant result indicated that male former smokers had 43 percent higher rates of physician visits.

Effects on utilization based on our regression analysis are shown in table 5.C.2. Since the effects are relative to nonsmokers, the effects in the never smoker column are always zero. For physician utilization, there were no noteworthy differences, except for those over 65. For this group, current smoker visit rates, holding other factors constant, were lower for current smokers than for never smokers (about 2.6 visits per year for men and about 1.5 visits for women). Current female smokers were higher utilizers of hospitals. Differences in numbers of nights in a nursing home were small, especially considering that the estimates apply to a year.

Table 5.C.1

Smoking and Health Care Utilization: Parameter Estimates

| | Parameter Estimates[1] | | | |
| | Females | | Males | |
	Current	Former	Current	Former
A. Ages 24–50				
Physician visits in past 2 weeks	1.18* [1.02; 1.36]	1.08 [0.87; 1.34]	1.41*** [1.16; 1.71]	1.43* [1.05; 1.94]
Number of hospital stays	1.21* [1.03; 1.43]	0.92 [0.66; 1.27]	1.75*** [1.34; 2.28]	1.13 [0.76; 1.68]
Number of hospital nights	1.29* [1.04; 1.61]	0.72 [0.49; 1.05]	2.12*** [1.52; 2.95]	1.19 [0.70; 2.03]
B. Ages 51–64				
Physician visits per 2 years	0.99 [0.95; 1.03]	1.06** [1.02; 1.11]	0.91*** [0.87; 0.96]	1.04 [0.99; 1.09]
Number of hospital stays	1.44*** [1.31; 1.60]	1.23*** [1.11; 1.37]	1.30*** [1.17; 1.46]	1.02 [0.92; 1.14]
Number of hospital nights	1.39*** [1.28; 1.51]	1.21*** [1.11; 1.31]	1.26*** [1.15; 1.38]	1.03 [0.94; 1.12]
C. Ages 65+				
Physician visits per year	0.87*** [0.81; 0.93]	0.97 [0.93; 1.01]	0.76*** [0.70; 0.84]	0.97 [0.92; 1.03]
Number of hospital stays	1.35*** [1.19; 1.53]	1.14** [1.06; 1.24]	0.94 [0.80; 1.10]	1.05 [0.95; 1.17]
Number of hospital nights	1.32*** [1.18; 1.48]	1.13** [1.05; 1.21]	0.93 [0.80; 1.09]	1.05 [0.95; 1.16]
Any nursing home nights	2.49*** [1.76; 3.53]	1.35* [1.07; 1.69]	0.40** [0.22; 0.73]	0.72 [0.52; 1.00]
Conditional number of nights	−13.33 (30.17)	−26.91 (20.00)	−92.03 (54.52)	−30.73 (26.59)

1. Incidence rate ratios, odds ratios, and parameter estimates, respectively. Incidence rate ratios from negative binomial models of physician visits and hospital utilization, odds ratios from logistic regression for "any nursing home nights," parameter estimates from ordinary least squares regression model for "conditional number of nights." 95% confidence intervals in brackets, standard errors in parentheses.

*, **, and *** indicate statistical significance at the 0.05, 0.01, and 0.001 levels, respectively.

Table 5.C.2
Effects of Smoking on Health Care Utilization

| | Marginal Effects[1] | | | | | |
| | Females | | | Males | | |
	Current	Former	Never	Current	Former	Never
A. Ages 24–50						
Physician visits per year	0.04	0.02	0.00	0.06	0.07	0.00
Number of hospital stays	0.03	−0.01	0.00	0.04	0.01	0.00
Number of hospital nights	0.11	−0.08	0.00	0.22	0.03	0.00
B. Ages 51–64						
Physician visits per year	0.00	0.02	0.00	−0.02	0.01	0.00
Number of hospital stays	0.05	0.03	0.00	0.03	0.00	0.00
Number of hospital nights	0.18	0.09	0.00	0.11	0.01	0.00
C. Ages 65+						
Physician visits per year	−1.45	−0.32	0.00	−2.61	−0.31	0.00
Number of hospital stays	0.07	0.03	0.00	−0.02	0.01	0.00
Number of hospital nights	0.26	0.11	0.00	−0.08	0.05	0.00
Number of nights in nursing home	2.18	0.35	0.00	−2.06	−1.07	0.00

1. Mean difference in predicted utilization.

6 Effects of Smoking on Social Security

Increased longevity and changing employment and earnings patterns portend financial implications for Social Security that have gained great importance in recent years, given the baby boomers' approaching retirement. Expectations are that Social Security trust fund reserves will be depleted in the foreseeable future. Trust fund outlays are due to exceed revenues in 2016, and the fund is expected to be depleted by 2038 (Concord Coalition 2001; U.S. Social Security Administration 2001). Between these years, the fund is expected to incur a total revenue shortfall of up to four trillion dollars (Concord Coalition 2001).

Public health policy aims to improve health and longevity by achieving reductions in such bad health habits as smoking, excess alcohol use, and lack of physical activity (U.S. Department of Health and Human Services 2000b). The eradication of smoking in particular has become a public health orthodoxy, owing to the reams of evidence showing that smoking shortens life span and causes enormous morbidity. To the extent that such public health interventions succeed, however, the financial health of such public programs as the Social Security program, especially the component providing pension and survivor benefits (Old Age and Survivors Insurance, or OASI), may be threatened further.

Both political parties have avoided the realities of the future fate of OASI's finances (Rosenbaum 2002). The reason for the threat to OASI's solvency is the aging of the U.S. population. The program works on the principle that each generation of workers pays taxes that cover its parents' retirement benefits. In 2002, there were 3.4 persons employed for each retiree. By 2010, when baby boomers begin to retire, the ratio will be 3.1. By 2030, the ratio will only be 2.1. If smoking were to be further reduced beyond present projections, the dependency ratio would be even less favorable for OASI.

The other Social Security program is Social Security Disability Insurance (SSDI). The SSDI program provides income support for persons under the age of 65 who are totally work disabled. SSDI enrollments have been growing as have disability income support programs in other countries (U.S. Social Security Administration 1999). Unlike OASI, improvements in health resulting from such behavioral changes as reduction in smoking rates would tend to improve the financial viability of SSDI.

Quantifying the effect of smoking on OASI contributions and benefits is important for two reasons: first, as we demonstrate below, smoking reduces earnings over the life course as well as longevity, both of which directly influence payments into and out of Social Security. It is therefore important to quantify smoking's contributions to the fund's long-term fiscal viability. Second, Social Security is inherently a redistributive program in which benefit receipts increase with, but are not proportionately related to, contributions. To the extent on balance that healthy behaviors are subsidized by Social Security, this public program provides incentives for healthy behaviors; at the same time, it redistributes income to individuals engaged in such behaviors. Proposals that would convert Social Security from a defined-benefit program (with payments based on a formula, only partly based on the individual's contributions) to a defined-contribution pension program (based entirely on the individual's contributions) would reduce the redistributive aspect of Social Security as well as any adverse incentive the program might provide with respect to taking care of oneself.[1]

Our results shed light on both issues. We provide the most thorough estimates to date of the effects of smoking patterns on Social Security, accounting for smoking-related differences in both contributions and benefits. We used Social Security earnings data for the years 1951 through 1991 for almost 8,000 participants in the Health and Retirement Study (HRS), a national longitudinal survey of persons in late middle age, which began in 1992, to estimate lifetime earnings profiles and Social Security contributions by smoking status. Using respondents' characteristics at wave 1 (in 1992), and, if married, the characteristics of their spouses, we estimated the present value of each individual's lifetime Social Security benefits, accounting for the earnings histories and smoking-dependent life expectancies of both spouses. Our analysis accounted for other potentially important observable characteristics that differ by smoking status, including demographic characteristics, risk and time preferences, alcohol consumption, and education. With our estimates, we identified the relative extent to which smoking and other observable characteristics of individuals have caused differential OASI contributions and benefits.

We performed identical calculations for SSDI contributions, and estimated lifetime receipt of SSDI benefits using separate methods described below. The issues for SSDI are different since improving health should lead to reductions in SSDI outlays.

In general, researchers have made inferences about effects of various factors on earnings from cross-sectional evidence. The Social Security earnings file that was made available to us is indeed a unique data source on individuals' earnings histories. Although the primary issues reported in this chapter pertain to Social Security, we also report effects of smoking on Social Security taxable earnings over the life course.

Background

Contributions into the Social Security trust fund are related to a person's earnings and duration of market work. Outlays from the fund are related to the benefit level, longevity, and, assuming a positive discount rate, the timing of benefit payments (see table 6.1).

Smoking-related morbidity and mortality have direct effects on Social Security. They affect both the contribution and benefit sides of the program, with a theoretically undetermined net effect on the Social Security trust fund's finances. For contributions, the level of earnings at a given age is a function of productivity, which is influenced by smoking. The direction of this effect is plausibly to decrease earnings and thereby contributions.

The timing of earnings is primarily a function of education, risk preferences, and other characteristics that are correlated with a person's internal discount rate but not necessarily attributable to smoking. The duration of earnings is affected by both the program and smoking. The program may encourage earlier retirement, while smoking may decrease wages, raise the likelihood of disability, and/or decrease life expectancy. Lower earnings potential and increased disability may lead to exiting the workforce.

For benefits, the most important factors are smoking-related differences in life expectancy, reduced benefit levels, and early onset of benefit receipt. Social Security benefits are not dependent on a person's life expectancy at retirement; therefore, longer survival translates directly into greater lifetime benefits. On the other hand, persons with lower

Table 6.1
Determinants of Lifetime Contributions to and Benefits from Social Security for Survivors to Retirement Age

Component	Relationship to Smoking	Effect of smoking
Contributions		
Earnings levels	Smoking may result in	
	—reduced productivity due to higher morbidity	—
	—time cost of smoking	—
	—direct cost to the employer	—
Duration of earnings	Smoking decreases life expectancy	—
	Smoking may result in early retirement	—
	—due to increased morbidity	
	—due to early onset of work disability	
	—due to lower earnings	
Tax level/earnings limit	No relationship to smoking	
Effect of smoking on contributions		—
Benefits		
Benefit level	Contribution levels influence benefit levels	—
	Onset of benfits influences benefit levels	—
Life expectancy	Smoking decreases life expectancy	—
Timing of onset	Smoking encourages early retirement	+
	—due to increased morbidity	
	—due to early onset of work disability	
	—due to lower earnings	
Effect of smoking on benefits		(—)
Net Effect		
Effect on benefits minus effect on contributions		?

earnings (and payroll contributions) also receive lower benefits, as the monthly benefit amount is calculated as a function of a person's average monthly earnings. However, the formula determining a person's benefit amount is progressive, with the result that large differences in contributions translate into comparatively small differences in benefits. One must also consider the complex issue of the timing of benefit onset, that is, the age at which a person starts receiving Social Security benefits. Reduced productivity in the marketplace due to higher morbidity could lead to greater rates of early retirement among smokers, as the opportunity cost of retirement in terms of forgone income would be expected to be lower. Although adjustments for early retirement are intended to be actuarially fair on average (that is, they reduce monthly payments inversely to the period over which benefits are expected to be paid out), they do not account for differential life expectancy based on the person's smoking status. Therefore, persons with information that they have below-average life expectancy, such as smokers, may be able to gain from early retirement with reduced benefits, while those with above-average life expectancy would be better off waiting for full retirement benefits. The effect of early retirement on total lifetime benefits could be positive, negative, or zero.

Finally, some persons are subject to payroll taxation for Social Security over a number of years, but do not survive to retirement age and hence do not receive any OASI benefits. Smokers' higher mortality rates prior to retirement age may partially or fully offset lower contributions by such persons; compared to nonsmokers, each surviving smoker is "supported" by contributions of a relatively larger number of smokers who do not survive to retirement age. However, OASI benefits are not terminated upon a person's death; widowed spouses may receive benefits on their dead spouses' earnings records.

Therefore, smoking has the effect of reducing an individual's contributions to the Social Security trust fund, but it also may reduce benefits. These effects work in opposite directions, and the question answered in this chapter is, given differential contribution levels and differential life expectancy, what is the net financial effect of smoking on Social Security?

Public health interventions aimed at discouraging initiation of smoking and/or promoting smoking cessation could have important consequences for the future viability of the Social Security trust fund if such programs lead to dramatic improvements in longevity, and hence, to a greater duration of Social Security benefit receipt, particularly if contributions to the fund do not increase commensurately. Especially because smoking has been such a prevalent cause of death (chapter 4), it is important to assess the net effect of smoking on Social Security contributions and benefits, the task of this chapter.

The answer to the question above can be framed in two different ways: (1) as the net amount of Social Security benefits a smoker loses or gains due to early mortality and differential contributions to the program; or (2) the amount the Social Security program would lose or gain if every smoker had the earnings history and life expectancy of an otherwise identical nonsmoker. Numerically, the answers to these questions are identical. Quantifying the effect of smoking and changes in smoking behavior on Social Security contributions and benefits is essential to evaluating the fund's long-term viability, as health status and longevity of the population undoubtedly will increase.[2]

Previous Literature

Our review of literature on the cost of smoking to Social Security yielded only a small number of studies specifically addressing this issue; however, other relevant studies have focused on the effects of smoking on earnings and on the effects of increased longevity on pension plans. A review of the main findings is provided below.

Smoking and Earnings

As contributions to OASI depend on earnings, we searched for studies relating smoking to earnings. Levine, Gustafson, and Velenchik (1997) and Lye and Hirschberg (2000) assessed the impact of smoking on earnings. Most of the published evidence is indirect, and much of it relates to the topics of other chapters as well—employer-based health insurance (chapter 5), absenteeism (chapter 9), and life insurance (chapter 8).

One type of study has examined the effects of smoking on employer-provided fringe benefits. As explained in chapter 5, such fringe benefits are largely financed by employees in the form of reduced earnings. In a review of the effects of smoking on the insurance industry, Bell (1996) cited smoking-related increases in health insurance premiums of between 38 and 122 percent relative to nonsmokers, as well as increases in life insurance premiums of 112 percent. However, as explained in the previous chapter, we were unable to document that individual health insurance premiums paid by smokers are subject to surcharges of this magnitude. Furthermore, a surcharge of 122 percent implies that smoking results in a more than doubling of expenditures on health services.

Smokers' higher rates of absenteeism have been used to explain their relatively lower earnings, as employers pass on the additional costs in the form of reduced wages. In addition to absenteeism, increased employment-related costs may reflect decreased productivity due to higher morbidity or time-outs for cigarette breaks,[3] increased life insurance premiums, and costs of designated smoking areas.

Although absences are often covered by sick leave, repeated absences plausibly result in lower earnings and hence reduced payroll contributions to Social Security, as may nonproductive time while ostensibly at work. Ryan, Zwerling, and Orav (1992) and Bush and Wooden (1995), using Australian data, and Leigh (1995), using U.S. data, found higher rates of absenteeism for smokers relative to nonsmokers. Bertera (1991) estimated the illness cost of smoking at $1,214, while Hocking, Grain, and Gordon (1994) estimated the cost of absenteeism at $329 per year (year 2000 dollars). Stickels (1994) reported a substantial cost of smoking in terms of lost productive time. Bell (1996) put the average annual cost of employing a smoker at $4,900.

A somewhat smaller number of studies have analyzed effects of smoking and smoking cessation on pension benefits. Most have come to the conclusion that the additional costs to pension programs due to cessation-related increased longevity outweigh cost savings to health insurance programs due to decreased morbidity. This finding is not really surprising given the enormous effects of smoking on longevity. In 1993, U.S. male (female) smokers' life expectancy at age 65 was only 14.5 (17.4) years, while never smokers could expect to live an additional 19.8 (21.4) years (Richards and Abele 1999). Compared to smokers, nonsmoking Social Security recipients could therefore expect to receive benefits for an additional 5.3 (4.0) years. However, the general notion that smoking may "save" money is contentious, given its many negative consequences for morbidity and life expectancy.

Smoking and Financial Status of Public Programs

An analysis of the effects of smoking in the Czech Republic on public programs, funded by Philip Morris's Czech subsidiary, has been particularly controversial, but the study has also served to bring the topic to the public's attention (Arthur D. Little International 2001). Philip Morris subsequently apologized for release of the study. The text of the apology is interesting for what it reveals about the changed environment (box 6.1).

The study found a net savings to the public budget in the Czech Republic of about $160 million in 1999. Interestingly, in that study, "pension and social expense savings due to early mortality" amounted to only $5.5 million, or 0.9 percent of the "direct and indirect positive effects" of smoking, equivalent to about $0.50 per person. By far the largest source of net savings (89.3 percent) resulted from revenue from

Box 6.1
Text of Philip Morris Press Release Regarding the Czech Study

> "Last month a study commission by the Czech affiliate of Philip Morris International was released. The funding and public release of this study which, among other things, detailed purported cost savings to the Czech Republic due to premature deaths of smokers, exhibited terrible judgment as well as complete and unacceptable disregard of basic human values.
>
> For one of our tobacco companies to commission this study was not just a terrible mistake, it was wrong. All of us at Philip Morris, no matter where we work, are extremely sorry for this. No one benefits from the very real, serious and significant diseases caused by smoking.
>
> We understand the outrage that has been expressed and we sincerely regret this extraordinary unfortunate incident.
>
> We will continue our efforts to do the right thing in all our businesses, acknowledging mistakes when we make them and learning from them as we go forward."
>
> Philip Morris Companies Inc./New York/26 July 2001.
> ⟨www.philipmorrisinternational.com/pages/eng/press/pr_20010726.asp⟩

excise and value-added taxes on cigarettes, an issue we discuss in chapter 11. This result may not generalize to the United States, given the lower tax rates on cigarettes in the United States relative to the Czech Republic in particular, and to other countries in general (Smoking and Health Action Foundation 2002).

Smoking and Social Security

Few studies have specifically studied effects of smoking on Social Security finances. The consensus view is that smoking reduces Social Security expenditures more than it reduces its revenues; smokers incur a net loss, and hence, a net transfer occurs from smokers to nonsmokers (Shoven, Sundberg, and Bunker 1989; Viscusi 1999). In the most comprehensive analysis of the cost of smoking to Social Security, Shoven, Sundberg, and Bunker (1989) analyzed Social Security benefit receipt by smoking status for the 1920 birth cohort. Using 1966 relative mortality rates by smoking status, Social Security Administration (SSA) life tables for the 1920 birth cohort, and gender-specific median earnings, the authors calculated smoking-status-specific benefit receipts separately for single men, single women, and one- and two-earner couples.

They estimated households' smoking-related reductions in the present value of Social Security benefits, ranging from $15,575 for one-earner couples in which only the wife smokes to $48,918 in two-earner couples in which both spouses smoke (in year 2000 dollars), with other household configurations falling in between these estimates.

However, unlike our study, Shoven and colleagues used no individual-level data on the earnings history of benefit recipients and their spouses, and earnings by smoking status were measured only at the cohort level. Therefore, for example, variations in spouses' age- and benefit-level differences, and the resulting nonlinearities in annual household benefit amounts, could not be directly assessed in their analysis. The effect of smoking on earnings, and hence on contributions, were not accounted for other than through differential mortality prior to retirement. Relative mortality risks were estimated 35 years ago and have likely changed with today's earlier diagnoses of smoking-related illnesses and improved treatment options. Finally, they did not conduct a separate evaluation of the effects of being a former smoker.

Other studies of the effects of smoking on pension programs came to similar conclusions. Atkinson and Townsend (1977) analyzed pensions and health care costs to the National Health Service (NHS) in Britain, and found that health care cost savings from a 40 percent reduction in smoking would be more than offset by increased costs of pensions. Similarly, Gori, Richter, and Wu (1984) found that Ford Motor Company's savings from improved health of their employees would be outweighed by increased costs to pension plans due to increased longevity. A study of the cost of smoking to the French pension system (Kopp and Fenoglio 2000) analyzed reductions in contributions to the social insurance system due to early mortality but not reduced benefit receipt.

Viscusi (1995) estimated smoking-related *savings* to state retirement plans at between $0.076 and $0.091 per pack of cigarettes, and the federal cost of smoking due to reduced payroll taxes, including Social Security taxes but excluding income taxes, at between $0.21 and $0.26 per pack of cigarettes (year 2000 dollars). The federal savings, by comparison, amounted to between $0.82 and $0.99 per pack. In an updated study that included adjustments for changes in tar levels in cigarettes, Viscusi (1999) estimated the early mortality-related savings to pensions and Social Security at $1.23 per pack, while the cost due to uncollected health and Social Security taxes amount to $0.41 per pack (year 2000 dollars). These estimates, however, included not only Social Security, but also Supplemental Security Income (SSI), public assistance, veterans' compensation, and pension income.

New Features of Our Analysis of Effects of Smoking on Social Security

Our empirical analysis improved on prior research in three important respects. First, like our analysis of Medicare contributions (chapter 5), our research was based on a unique data source in which contributions by Health and Retirement Study respondents to Social Security from 1951 to 1991 provided by the U.S. Social Security Administration were merged with HRS data. In 1951, most (future) HRS respondents were 10 to 20 years old. From the HRS interviews, we had information on the smoking status of each respondent. For those who had stopped smoking prior to the HRS baseline interview that was conducted in 1992, the HRS asked how many years previously the individual had quit. The HRS also provided data on important covariates relating to other health behaviors and to other factors potentially affecting contributions and benefits from Social Security (chapter 2). Second, our analysis was for a much more recent period than those in past studies. Third, we assessed effects of smoking on both OASI and SSDI.

New Evidence on Effects of Smoking on Social Security Data

We used data from wave one of the Health and Retirement Study (HRS),[4] merged with individual-level earnings data from the SSA.[5] SSA data spanned ages from before entry into the work force through age 62, that is, they provide a nearly complete earnings history for the working life of the cohort.

Contributions to OASI

We calculated annual contributions to OASI from 1951 to 1991 based on reported earnings, annual contribution rates, and annual earnings limits for all persons who had attained the age of 18 during the year,[6] inflated to 2000 dollars.

To assess the relationship between smoking and contributions to OASI, we estimated contributions regressions, as in the analysis of contributions to Medicare Part A in chapter 5, separately for males and females (box 6.2).[7]

Based on the regressions, we predicted contributions for every person at every age between 24 and 64. This step was needed to allow us to isolate the influence of smoking, and to predict respondents' age-

Box 6.2
Data and Methods of Analysis of Contributions to OASI

> The data set was constructed as a panel with the observational unit being the person at each year of age over age 18. The dependent variable was the contribution to OASI at each year of age, expressed in year 2000 dollars. Explanatory variables were: smoking (current, quit before age 40, quit at 40 or older, never smoker), alcohol consumption, a history of problem drinking, body mass index (BMI), age, race, education, residence in a metropolitan statistical area (MSA), risk tolerance, financial planning horizon, and whether the person had any children at wave one (including stepchildren).
>
> We estimated random effects equations separately by gender. Observations were weighted to ensure that estimates, too, were representative of population totals in the 1931 to 1941 birth cohort. With the parameter estimates, we predicted OASI contributions by year of age for every person in the HRS cohort, including those not represented in the Social Security earnings data.

specific earnings after 1991, enabling us to update estimated benefit levels, which increased with additional OASI taxable earnings through age 64.

Using life tables and respondents' smoking histories, we converted predicted age-specific OASI contributions to expected contributions that accounted for deaths occurring between the ages of 24 and 64 (chapters 2 and 4). Our estimates of contributions to OASI accounted for respondents' smoking statuses at age 24, their smoking histories observed in the survey, their predicted future smoking patterns, and the associated mortality effects. Our estimates accounted for survival-related selection of respondents into the sample according to their smoking status at age 24 and differential expected survival of current and former smokers relative to never smokers through age 100. We calculated each person's lifetime Social Security contributions as the sum of the age-specific annual expected contributions, given survival to age 24 and discounted to age 24 at three percent per year.

Contributions to SSDI

We calculated lifetime SSDI contributions using exactly the same methods as for OASI contributions. We used annual SSDI tax rates,

Box 6.3
Method for Calculating an Individual's Expected Benefits from OASI

The *primary insurance amount (PIA)* describes the estimated monthly benefit amount the respondent would have received based on his or her work history. PIAs depend on past earnings subject to Social Security payroll taxes. Using the PIA formula (for 1998), we calculated PIAs for each individual and age combination between ages 24 and 64 using respondents' actual earnings through 1991, and projected earnings from 1992 until the person was to reach the age of 65 (in 2000 dollars). We projected individuals' earnings based on earnings regressions, using the same specification as for OASI contributions. We used these earnings estimates to project values of the earnings measure used by Social Security for computing benefits (average indexed monthly earnings, or AIME) at each age.

We regressed respondents' 1991 AIME, reported to the HRS, against past earnings to estimate mean marginal contributions of age-specific earnings to a person's AIME. Marginal contributions were extrapolated to age 64 by regressing age-specific coefficients against age and age squared, weighted by the number of respondents at each age whose earnings we observed in SSA earnings data. Using the 1991 AIME, actual earnings until 1991, and predicted earnings for the remaining years between ages 24 and 64, we predicted each person's AIME at each age between 24 and 64.

Third, we computed monthly benefit amounts based on the AIME and the 1998 PIA formula. The PIA was calculated as 90 percent of a respondent's AIME up to $477, plus 32 percent of the additional AIME up to $2,875, plus 15 percent of the AIME above $2,875. The amount was later multiplied by twelve to obtain an annual benefit amount.

For each person, we calculated the present value of Social Security benefits at 65, the normal retirement age. We assumed the maximum age of death to be 100.

We used the same life tables for the individual and his or her spouse, if applicable (chapter 4's appendix). For single respondents, the expected value of their benefits at any age was calculated as the product of the person's PIA and probability of being alive at that age (multiplied by 12 to convert monthly to annual benefits).

For married respondents, the expected benefit depended on both spouses' survival probabilities and both spouses' PIAs. We assumed that they maintained the same marriage from the earlier of (1) the onset of benefit receipt, or (2) the date of the wave one HRS interview, until death of the other spouse. The spouse's survival probability depended on his or her age and smoking status; the spouse's PIA in a given year depended on whether he or she was under age 65 during the year. If the spouse had not yet retired, additional earnings could have increased the AIME and, hence, the spouse's PIA.

Box 6.3 (*continued*)

For each married respondent and at each age, we distinguished among three scenarios: (1) spouse alive and not retired (spouse < 65); (2) spouse alive and retired (spouse ≥ 65); and (3) spouse deceased.* Respondents' benefits terminated when the respondent died; however, the spouse might have continued to receive benefits as a widow or widower. For all persons, the age-specific expected benefit was calculated as the sum of the expected benefits from each scenario multiplied by the probability of the scenario's occurrence. We computed the present value of expected OASI benefits at age 65 as the sum of the discounted (at three percent) annual benefit estimates for ages 65 to 100. We also estimated benefits for retirement at age 62. Monthly own benefits were "actuarially reduced" by 20 percent, spouses' benefits by 25 percent, and widowers' benefits by 17.1 percent due to the choice of early retirement 36 months prior to the assumed normal retirement age of 65 for all respondents.

*In scenario 1, prior to the spouse's retirement, the respondent receives a benefit based only on his own PIA, i.e., the expected benefit is the product of the respondent's PIA and the probability is that both spouses are alive. In scenario 2, after the spouse's retirement, the respondent's benefit is equal to the greater of his own PIA and 50 percent of the spouse's PIA, multiplied with the probability that both spouses are alive. In scenario 3, the respondent's benefit is equal to the greater of his own PIA and the spouse's PIA, multiplied with the probability that the respondent is alive and the spouse is dead, accounting for the spouse's PIA's dependency upon the age of death if death occurred prior to retirement. For married spouses aged 65 and over in 1992, annual benefits of 12 times their own PIA were assumed between their retirement at age 65 and 1991. We did not have information on former spouses of respondents or their earnings, which may also influence benefit receipt.

starting in 1957, to calculate age-specific SSDI contributions, the dependent variable in our random effects models. We predicted contributions for every age between 24 and 64 and calculated expected lifetime contributions given each person's smoking status at age 24.

Benefits from OASI

Expected benefits for an individual were calculated as a function of: (1) the person's own benefit amount and, if married, the benefit amounts a person may receive on the spouse's earnings record; and (2) the probabilities that either or both spouses survive to specific ages (box 6.3).

Box 6.4
Method for Calculating an Individual's Expected Benefits from SSDI

First, we estimated a logistic regression model to predict the probability of benefit receipt at every age between age 24 and 64. As above, we included binary variables for current smokers, former smokers who quit by age 40, and those who quit after age 40.

We used nine age splines to allow for nonlinear effects of age on benefit receipt, as well as a quadratic term for the last age spline, age 45 and over. This allowed for predictions through age 64 even though the oldest person in our sample was only aged 61 in 1991. We also controlled for race, education, alcohol consumption, body mass index, residence in an MSA, risk tolerance, and time preferences, as well as a continuous year variable to control for possible changes in eligibility determination over time.

Next, we multiplied each respondent's age-specific predicted probability of benefit receipt with his or her estimated PIA at that age, multiplied by 12 to convert monthly benefit amounts to annual benefit estimates. Using the methods described above, we converted these predictions to expected age-specific benefits conditional on their observed past and predicted future lifetime smoking patterns. After discounting these survival-adjusted expected benefits to age 24, and aggregating across the entire age range, we obtained the expected value of lifetime Social Security disability benefits accruing to the worker.

Using published data from 1991 (U.S. House of Representatives Committee on Ways and Means 1992), we calculated the ratio of benefits for spouses and dependent children of disabled workers relative to their own benefits. We multiplied the expected benefit amounts with these ratios to obtain estimates of the benefits paid out on each person's earnings record to dependents of disabled workers. Adding the two amounts yielded the total expected lifetime benefits from SSDI.

Benefits from SSDI

The data on respondents' Social Security earnings history also contained monthly data on the amount of benefits received during every month between January 1962 and December 1991. We aggregated benefits by year of age, and estimated age-specific probabilities of benefit receipt for every person between age 24 and 64 (box 6.4).

Computing the Effect of Converting Smokers to Nonsmokers

We next estimated the change in contributions and benefits if everyone became a nonsmoker. We computed OASI and SSDI contributions,

Table 6.2
Present Value of Expected Lifetime Social Security Contributions (2000 Dollars)

	Females	Males
(A) Actual Smoking Status (at Age 24)		
Smoker	23,642	58,875
Never smoker	23,214	64,447
(B) Nonsmoking Smokers		
Smoker	23,879	62,702
Never smoker	23,214	64,447
(C) Difference (A) − (B)		
Smoker	−238	−3,827
Never smoker	0	0

Note: Ages 24–64, 2000 dollars, 3% discount rate.

as well as earnings and PIA estimates for nonsmoking smokers. The nonsmoking smoker estimates therefore reflected both differential earnings and mortality experiences attributable to smoking behavior, including those of spouses (if the person was married). The mean differences between expected contributions and benefits of smokers and "nonsmoking smokers," accounting for both differential earnings and mortality rates of both spouses, described the net effect of smoking on OASI and SSDI contributions and benefits. The net effect on OASI and SSDI outlays was the difference in the differences of contributions and benefits.

Results

Contributions to OASI

Females who smoked at age 24 contributed $23,642 to Social Security OASI over their lifetime; $428 more than female never smokers, who contributed $23,214 on average (table 6.2). Male smokers, on average, contributed $58,875; $5,572 less than male never smokers, who contributed $64,447. Nonsmoking smokers would have contributed more than smokers; $23,879 for females, and $62,702 for males. The differences that are attributable to smoking, −$238 for females and −$3,827 for males, reflect differential survival as well as differential earnings between smokers and otherwise identical nonsmokers.

Benefits Accruing from OASI

Even with a shorter life expectancy, lifetime Social Security benefits were higher for males than for females in the same smoking category (table 6.3). Among women, nonsmokers married to smokers received the highest benefits, in part due to survival, but also because, for many females, survivor benefits based on their spouses' earnings records were greater than Social Security pension benefits based on their own earnings records. Among unmarried women, nonsmokers' expected benefits were nearly $6,000 greater than those of smokers.

Among men, never smokers married to female smokers had the greatest expected lifetime Social Security benefits ($55,227), almost 20 percent higher than those of female never smokers married to male smokers ($46,423), and much more than male smokers married to female smokers ($38,733). Single female smokers had the lowest expected benefits ($29,006). Due to generally greater life expectancy among females relative to males, expected lifetime benefits of males were less sensitive to their spouses' smoking status than were those of females. For female smokers, on average, benefits were $7,000 to $10,000 higher if they were married. Relative to nonsmoking smokers, reduced earnings and survival among smokers caused benefit reductions of $11,324 for each male smoker, and $2,729 for each female smoker.

Combining results for both spouses, we obtained benefits per couple. Smokers married to smokers experienced a loss in OASI benefits of $14,066 (table 6.4). When the husband smoked but the wife did not, the loss in such benefits was $8,326. When the wife smoked but the husband did not, the loss in such benefits to the couple was $4,709. Since men have a lower life expectancy than women, the survivor benefit was lower when the wife smoked.

Most of the benefit differences across smoking categories were attributable to smoking rather than differences in other covariates (not shown). Differences in life expectancy by smoking status (benefit duration) accounted for most of the differences in estimated lifetime benefit amounts. A small positive selection effect was found for female former smokers and single male former smokers, whose benefits—assuming life expectancy and earnings of never smokers—increased to levels greater than those of never smokers. This means that these smokers would have earned more than never smokers if they had not become smokers.

Table 6.3
Present Value of Expected Lifetime Social Security Benefits by Smoking Status of Recipients and Their Spouses (2000 Dollars)[1]

| | Females | | | Males | | |
| | Married to | | | Married to | | |
	Smoker	Nonsmoker	Singles	Smoker	Nonsmoker	Singles
(A) Actual Smoking Status (at Age 24)						
Smoker	39,624	36,304	29,006	38,733	39,900	32,355
Never smoker	46,423	42,306	34,969	55,227	54,232	47,771
(B) Nonsmoking Smokers						
Smoker	40,649	41,103	33,410	51,774	52,753	43,873
Never smoker	41,896	42,306	34,969	55,137	54,232	47,771
(C) Difference (A) − (B)						
Smoker	−1,025	−4,799	−4,404	−13,041	−12,853	−11,518
Never smoker	4,527	0	0	90	0	0
(D) Net Effect of an Average Smoker[2]	−2,729				−11,324	

Note: 2000 dollars, 3% discount rate.
1. Assumes that both persons retained marital status observed at ages 51–62 until death of the spouse.
2. Accounts for relative benefit reductions for spouses of nonsmoking smokers relative to smokers.

Table 6.4
Present Value of Expected Lifetime Social Security Benefits for Married Couples by Smoking Status of Both Spouses (2000 Dollars)[1]

	Smoking Status of Husband (at Age 24)	
	Smoker	Never Smoker
(A) Smoking Status of Wife (at Age 24)		
Smoker	78,357	91,531
Never smoker	86,323	96,538
(B) Nonsmoking Smoker (Both Spouses)		
Smoker	92,423	96,240
Never smoker	94,649	96,538
(C) Difference (A) − (B)		
Smoker	−14,066	−4,709
Never smoker	−8,326	0

Note: 2000 dollars, 3% discount rate.
1. Assumes that both persons retained marital status observed at ages 51–62 until death of the spouse.

Contributions to SSDI

Female smokers contributed $2,767 to Social Security Disability Insurance over their lifetimes, more than female nonsmokers who contributed $2,694 (table 6.5). Smoking had a very minimal negative effect on SSDI contributions for females—$4 for each female smoker. For men, the effect was greater. Male smokers contributed $6,902 to SSDI, about $600 less than male never smokers, who contributed $7,546 on average. For every male smoker, smoking cost SSDI $446 in lost contributions due to lower earnings and early mortality.

Benefits Accruing from SSDI

Male smokers could have expected to receive the most benefits from SSDI—$9,275 over their lifetimes (table 6.6)—roughly equivalent to one year of benefits for each male smoker during his lifetime. Male never smokers could have expected to receive $6,947 in SSDI benefits during their lifetimes, over $2,000 less than smokers. Expected benefits were much lower for women, largely due to lower lifetime earnings and consequently lower benefit amounts. Female smokers could have expected to receive $2,439, while female nonsmokers receive $1,378, on

Table 6.5
Present Value of Expected Lifetime SSDI Contributions (2000 Dollars)

	Females	Males
(A) Actual Smoking Status (at Age 24)		
Smoker	2,767	6,902
Never smoker	2,694	7,546
(B) Nonsmoking Smokers		
Smoker	2,771	7,348
Never smoker	2,694	7,546
(C) Difference (A) − (B)		
Smoker	−4	−446
Never smoker	0	0

Note: Ages 24–64, 2000 Dollars, 3% discount rate.

Table 6.6
Present Value of Expected Lifetime Social Security Disability Benefits (2000 Dollars)

	Expected Value of SSDI Benefits (including benefits for dependents)[1]	
	Females	Males
(A) Actual Smoking Status (at Age 24)		
Smoker	2,439	9,275
Never smoker	1,378	6,947
(B) Nonsmoking Smokers		
Smoker	1,461	7,488
Never smoker	1,378	6,947
(C) Difference (A) − (B)		
Smoker	978	1,787
Never smoker	0	0

Note: 2000 dollars, 3% discount rate.
1. Dependent benefits are assumed to be 11.2% of worker's own benefits, based on cumulative payments in 1991.

average, over their lifetimes. Smoking had the effect of increasing benefit receipt, despite greater mortality, which serves to offset age-related increases in benefit receipt for smokers and nonsmokers at older ages. Female nonsmoking smokers could have anticipated receiving $978 less over their lifetime, while male nonsmoking smokers would have received $1,787 less in lifetime benefits.

Net Effect of Smoking on Social Security

Combining estimated differences in contributions and lifetime benefit amounts by smoking status yields the net effect of smoking on Social Security (table 6.7). The bottom line is that women who smoked incurred a net loss of $1,519, consisting of a loss of $1,761 in benefits, which was offset in part by lower contributions in the amount of $242. For female nonsmokers married to smokers, there was a gain in OASI benefits due to their spouses' early mortality, which accounted for the fact that female nonsmokers on average realized a gain in OASI benefits of $1,999.

Male smokers incurred a much greater loss on average, $6,549. This reflected a loss of $12,609 in OASI benefits, which was offset in part by lower contributions to both OASI and SSDI, especially the former, and a higher SSDI benefit receipt. Marital status does not affect benefits from SSDI per se, although it may do so indirectly through its relationships to the number of dependents. We did not consider this source of variation in benefits in our analysis; we assumed that this difference did not vary by smoking status. Therefore, the estimates in the cells in the SSDI row are same within gender.

Finally, we considered the effect of changing the assumed initial receipt of OASI benefits from age 65 to 62 (table 6.8). The main effect of assuming a lower age at which OASI benefits are initially received was to lower the loss in OASI benefits to smokers. For men, the loss in benefits was reduced by about $1,400. For women, the reduction was about $900.

Effects of Smoking on Social Security–Taxable Earnings

In general, inferences about effects of earnings determinants are made from cross-sectional evidence. By contrast, for this study, we obtained longitudinal data on earnings covering a period of over four decades.

Table 6.7
Net Effect of Smoking on Social Security Contributions and Benefit Receipt (2000 Dollars)

	Females				Males			
	Married to Smoker	Married to Nonsmoker	Singles	Total[3]	Married to Smoker	Married to Nonsmoker	Singles	Total[3]
(A) Effect on OASI Contributions[1]								
Smoker	−116	178	−528	−238	−4,184	−3,315	−3,916	−3,827
Never smoker	0	0	0	0	0	0	0	0
(B) Effect on OASI Benefits								
Smoker	−1,025	−4,799	−4,404	−2,739	−13,041	−12,853	−11,518	−12,609
Never smoker	4,527	0	0	1,999	90	0	0	22
(C) Effect on SSDI Contributions								
Smoker	9	42	−37	−4	−483	−391	−448	−446
Never smoker	0	0	0	0	0	0	0	0
(D) Effect on SSDI Benefits[2]								
Smoker	978	978	978	978	1,787	1,787	1,787	1,787
Never smoker	0	0	0	0	0	0	0	0
(E) Net Effect (B + D – A – C)								
Smoker	60	−4,041	−2,861	−1,519	−6,581	−7,360	−5,367	−6,549
Never smoker	4,527	0	0	1,999	90	0	0	22

Note: 2000 dollars, 3% discount rate.
1. Calculations by marital status not shown.
2. Assumed independent of the spouse's marital status.
3. Weighted average per smoker.

Table 6.8

Net Effect of Smoking on Social Security for Retirement at Ages 62 and 65 (2000 Dollars)[1]

	Retirement at Age 62		Retirement at Age 65	
	Females	Males	Females	Males
(A) Effect on OASI Contributions				
Smoker	−26	−3,097	−238	−3,827
Never smoker	0	0	0	0
(B) Effect on OASI Benefits				
Smoker	−1,594	−10,775	−2,739	−12,609
Never smoker	2,449	29	1,999	22
(C) Effect on SSDI Contributions				
Smoker	−4	−446	−4	−446
Never smoker	0	0	0	0
(D) Effect on SSDI Benefits[2]				
Smoker	978	1,787	978	1,787
Never smoker	0	0	0	0
(E) Net Effect (B + D − A − C)				
Smoker	−586	−5,445	−1,519	−6,549
Never smoker	2,449	29	1,999	22
Net effect per smoker[3]	−574	−3,871	−1,509	−5,264

Note: 2000 dollars, 3% discount rate.

1. Assumes that both spouses retire at the same age.

2. Assumed independent of the spouse's marital status.

3. Smokers' net benefit reduction (private losses) are partially offset by increases in survivor benefits (quasi-external "gains") of $10 and $1,285 per female and male 24-year-old smoker, respectively, for retirement at age 65, and $12 and $1,574, respectively, for retirement at age 62.

Although not all earnings have been subject to the Social Security income taxation, most earnings are included. Using these data, we assessed the impact of smoking at age 24 on earnings over much of the life cycle.

For women, there were very minor differences in earnings between women who smoked at age 24, nonsmoking smokers, and never smokers (fig. 6.1).[8] By contrast, men who smoked experienced decreased earnings, particularly after about age 50. Discounted to age 24, men who smoked at age 24 lost nearly $39,000 in lifetime Social Security taxable earnings for this reason (table 6.9). Women lost less than $1,000. Differences in part reflect higher mortality attributable to smoking among males.

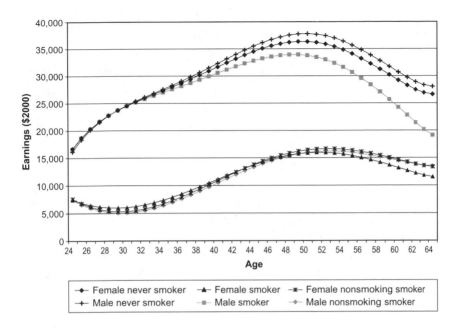

Figure 6.1
Predicted earnings by age, gender, and smoking status ($2000).

Discussion

Overview of Key Findings

Social Security receipts and outlays over a lifetime were strongly related to smoking patterns. Smokers, due to higher mortality rates, obtained lower lifetime benefits compared to never smokers, even after
accounting for their smoking-related lower lifetime contributions. The
effects of smoking on lifetime Social Security benefits were $1,519 for
24-year-old female smokers, and $6,549 for 24-year-old male smokers.
These are the private costs of smoking.

Married male smokers incurred the greatest benefit reduction due to
smoking-related early mortality ($6,581 to $7,360), followed by single
male smokers ($5,367) and female smokers married to never smokers
($4,041). Female never smokers who were married to smokers, on the
other hand, financially benefited from their spouses' early mortality,
since they received greater widow benefits at an earlier age. Relative to
the effects of smoking, effects of differences between smokers, former
smokers, and never smokers in observable characteristics other than

Table 6.9
Estimated Effects of Smoking on Lifetime Earnings (2000 Dollars)

	Actual Earnings	Counter-factual	Effect of Smoking	Percent
Female smoker	264,532	265,163	−631	−0.2
Female never smoker	257,202	257,202	0	0.0
Male smoker	689,565	728,131	−38,566	−5.6
Male never smoker	743,921	743,921	0	0.0

Note: Discounted at 3% per year to age 24.

smoking, such as education, risk preferences, and demographic characteristics, were relatively minor determinants of Social Security contributions and benefits over the life cycle.

Our analysis makes evident the importance of accounting for differential mortality prior to age 65. In terms of contributions, smokers were at a disadvantage because of their higher mortality rates. This factor had a more important effect than did the lower contributions of smokers to Social Security during the years they were alive. The magnitude was substantial: among nonsmoking males as a group, lifetime contributions per survivor increased by nine percent as a consequence of contributions by other nonsmokers who died prior to age 65. By contrast, for smokers, the corresponding increase per surviving smoker was 25 percent. If public health initiatives succeed in achieving their objectives, it will be necessary for policymakers to find alternative sources for safeguarding the financial viability of the Social Security pension program.

Comparison of Our Results with Previous Literature

Our estimates closely match those of the cost of smoking to Social Security reported by Shoven, Sundberg, and Butler (1989). Shoven and his coauthors' estimates for the reduction in benefits experienced by smokers, for couples in which only the wife smokes was $15,575 versus our estimate of $15,821 (inflated to age 65, year 2,000 dollars). Similarly, Shoven and his coauthors' estimate of $48,918 in two-earner couples in which both spouses smoke compares to our estimate of $47,260, with other household configurations falling in between these estimates. A very notable difference between our analysis and theirs relates to our inclusion of contributions by deceased smokers and the inclusion of SSDI contributions and benefits.

Our estimates are not directly comparable to those of Manning et al. (1991), who estimated a net external cost of smoking for retirement pensions at $3,300 to $44,000 per person (year 2000 dollars), using zero percent and, alternatively, five percent discount rates. These are the most important differences between their and our analysis. First, Manning et al. evaluated the cost to all retirement pensions, not just Social Security, and estimated benefit differentials of $25,000 and $256,000, respectively. If they had used a three percent rate, their estimates would likely appear somewhat small compared to our Social Security effects. Second, contributions to Social Security were not calculated separately in their study; the authors used a much broader measure, taxes on earnings. Manning et al.'s earnings tax differentials ranged from $68,000 to $550,000 (year 2000 dollars), depending on the discount rate. Our estimates are much more refined, in that they pertained directly to Social Security contributions, rather than to earnings broadly defined. Nevertheless, by any measure, Manning et al.'s estimates appear implausibly high.

Unlike our study, Manning et al. did not have longitudinal data on contributions and did not focus specifically on Social Security. They also did not account for contributions by smokers who did not survive to age 65. It is evident from our analysis that the negative externalities to Social Security contributions from smokers are more than offset by the net losses incurred by smokers due to their reduced benefit receipt.

Strengths of Our Analysis of Effects of Smoking on Social Security Contributions and Benefits

Our analysis has several important strengths. First, our results were derived from a nationally representative sample, allowing for a specific estimate of the total, national effect of lifetime smoking patterns in this cohort on Social Security. Linking a unique database of Social Security earnings records for a forty-one-year period to individual behaviors and demographic characteristics allowed us to estimate differential earnings profiles by smoking behavior for almost the entire work life of our cohort, holding other characteristics, including alcohol consumption and risk preferences, constant. Information on characteristics of respondents' spouses allowed us to control for the possibility of married spouses' matching by risk behaviors, by age, or by earnings levels. Second, our results were robust to changes in the specification of smoking variables, changes in variable specification in random effects models of contributions and earnings, the use of alternative life tables, and changes in the retirement age from 65 to 62. Third, to our knowledge, ours is the most comprehensive study to assess impacts of smoking patterns specifically on Social Security.

Especially compared to other databases, the HRS is rich in data on behaviors, such as alcohol consumption, which is correlated with smoking (Picone and Sloan 2003), preferences, and in such respondent characteristics as education. For this reason, we were able to include many of the most important determinants of earnings that have not been included in previous studies.

Limitations of Our Analysis

In spite of the strengths, several important limitations should be acknowledged also. First, and foremost, we were not able to measure age of onset of smoking habits, or changes in smoking intensity over the life cycle. In our study, we measured smoking based on self-reports at wave one. However, smoking is initiated after age 24 only rarely. Thus, our lack of information on timing of initiation of smoking is not a serious limitation. Smoking intensity varies over time. If anything, by the early 1990s, smokers in the 1931–1941 cohort probably smoked less than they had earlier in their lifetimes. Furthermore, some of the very heavy smokers from this birth cohort may have not survived to be included in the Health and Retirement Study. Adjustments based on 1990s' data may underestimate the effects of smoking, yielding, in this chapter, conservative estimates of the effect of smoking on Social Security contributions and benefits. By classifying recent quitters (those who quit within five years of the HRS interview) as current smokers, we reduced the potential effects of endogeneity of quitting as a result of poor health and its effects on earnings.

Second, earnings may be influenced by smoking and/or smoking could be correlated with an earnings determinant that we did not measure (see, e.g., Viscusi and Hersch 2001). Under several circumstances, earnings could be endogenous. For example, stresses related to a poor job match or unemployment may cause a person to smoke, or smokers may be less productive and experience higher rates of unemployment. Regarding potential confounding, a noteworthy point is that, although earnings differences by smoking status were largest after age 40, annual earnings began to diverge at younger ages. Differences in earnings at such early ages, especially between never smokers and former smokers, may reflect differences in earnings determinants correlated with smoking behavior, not smoking per se, that were not observed by us researchers.

Third, cohort effects may influence both the interpretation and generalizability of the results. In particular, Social Security tax rates and amounts subject to taxation have changed appreciably over time and differ substantially from those of other cohorts. These changes primarily affected contributions—benefit formulas have not changed meaningfully since the 1950s. Total contributions and absolute differences between consumption categories probably have been larger in later cohorts. Due to the redistributive nature of benefits, there is likely no large impact on benefit levels over time. However, later cohorts will be affected by the gradual increase in the normal retirement age from 65 to 67, with simultaneous declines in the present value of benefits. Other unique characteristics of this cohort may help identify more clearly the relationship between smoking and earnings. In particular, recreational drug use has been mentioned as a correlative of smoking and alcohol consumption and a determinant of earnings. Drug use was less prevalent on average in this than in later cohorts.

Fourth, we had to take marital status at the date of the interview as given; some respondents will have divorced subsequently, changing their and their spouses' expected benefit receipt. However, remarriage will affect eligibility for receipt of spouse and survivor benefits as well. If so, our estimated effect of smoking may be slightly upward biased.

Fifth, we did not have information on former spouses of divorced or widowed respondents. Respondents may be eligible for higher benefits based on their former spouses' earnings records, and, similarly, divorced spouses may be eligible for a benefit based on respondents' earnings records, even after their deaths. Due to the lack of information on the earnings history and characteristics of these persons, our estimates are necessarily incomplete. Smokers are more likely to be divorced in late middle age than nonsmokers (our unpublished analysis based on HRS). Thus, if anything, our results overestimate the effect of smoking on the benefit amounts paid on the smoker's earnings record. For example, a nonsmoker divorced from a smoker would be expected to continue benefit receipt on the smoker's earnings record for some period after the smoker's death.

Sixth, our analysis allowed effects of smoking to vary by gender and by age. A general specification would have included more interactions. However, allowing for differential returns to individual characteristics by smoking category would have been computationally infeasible in our analysis.[9] Also, with our sample sizes, there was the risk of over-fitting with a very general specification.

Seventh, we assumed that everyone retires at age 65 and did not in-corporate the effect of smoking on the onset of benefit receipt in our analysis. To the extent that smokers and former smokers retire earlier than never smokers, benefits may be higher for such individuals than our estimates imply. Early retirement, in the form of lower earnings, was accounted for in the analysis of smoking-attributable reductions in Social Security contributions. In analyses based on an assumption of universal retirement at age 62, we found that the Social Security pro-gram's reductions in benefit amounts for early retirees, are, if at all, actuarially fair only at a zero percent discount rate. At three percent, mean lifetime benefits in this cohort were always lower for retirement at age 62 than at age 65. Therefore, early retirement is likely associated with a net reduction in the present value of Social Security benefits. Consequently, our results are likely not very sensitive to the assump-tion of similar retirement behaviors for persons with different smoking behaviors. If every smoker retired at age 62 rather than 65, the effect would be to reduce the net savings from smoking by 62 percent for women and 26 percent for men.

Policy Significance

Our findings have important implications for public policy regarding smoking prevention and cessation, taxation, and the financing of Social Security. Our results can provide the basis for an important argument in antismoking campaigns, by making smokers aware of the Social Se-curity cost associated with their lower life expectancy. The knowledge that smokers, due to early mortality and reduced earnings, lose Social Security benefits, may induce many to quit earlier, and may induce some others not to start smoking. On the other hand, this finding also provides ammunition to the tobacco companies, who are fighting nu-merous legal battles about reimbursements for the cost of smoking to states and the federal government. It can be argued that smoking saves the federal government additional Social Security dollars due to smokers' early mortality, and hence should be held liable only for cost estimates of smoking that account for these "savings." To quote Gravelle (1998): "The fact of savings from government transfers due to premature death does not imply that there is a social gain from premature death; there is clearly a loss that accrues to the smoker who is part of society. Nevertheless, in a straight-forward accounting for costs, the government in its role as provider of certain services will experience financial savings from premature death, which must be considered in determining how different parties fare because of smoking" (p. 3).

Based on findings that smokers subsidize nonsmokers, one could infer that smokers are due compensation, or that Social Security contribution rates should be reduced for smokers. However, it is widely acknowledged that Social Security provides large cross-subsidies between subgroups of the population: the high and low earners, males and females, unmarried and married persons. As actuarial fairness is not one of the goals pursued by Social Security, such a change in contributions or benefits does not appear to be a likely consequence of this study. In fact, following one of the rationales for cigarette taxation listed by Viscusi (1999), the results of this study may even suggest that a greater taxation of cigarettes may be optimal. If "sin taxes" on tobacco are imposed to discourage behavior associated with inefficient decisions such as smoking, which reduces the lifetime benefit amount from Social Security, then this study may serve as an impetus to raise taxes to encourage individual behavior that maximizes the expected value of lifetime benefits from Social Security.

From a broader and especially longer-term perspective, however, this study provides another important implication for public policy. It will be necessary to tap additional revenue sources to pay for Social Security benefits of a population that, to an increasing extent, consists of nonsmokers. The long-term reduction in smoking rates will have drastic effects on Social Security contributions and benefit payments. Fewer persons will make contributions without reaching retirement age. More persons will become eligible for Social Security benefits. The average retirement age may increase with decreasing rates of disability, resulting in greater monthly benefit amounts. And the average life expectancy will increase by several years, resulting in a longer benefit duration.

Under current contributions and benefits schemata, reduced smoking rates will translate into increased expenditures for Social Security. These expenditures have to be offset by additional revenues. Sources for these revenues could be from higher tax rates on wages or general revenue sources transferred to the Social Security trust fund. To determine the precise impact that changes in smoking initiation rates and quit rates will have on the trust fund, additional studies will be necessary to develop estimates of marginal life expectancy gains from quitting at various ages as well as estimates of lag times between changes in smoking behavior and measurable changes in population-level life expectancy and earnings patterns.

**Private Pensions: Do the
Cross-Subsidies Mirror
Those for Social Security?**

Private pensions provide an important source of income support for the elderly. They have become increasingly important since World War II. Social Security retirement provides a safety net, but benefits do not provide sufficient funds for many retirees to maintain the lifestyles to which they had been accustomed prior to retirement.

In 1996, annual median private pension income was $5,803 among elderly pension recipients (year 2000 dollars) (U.S. House of Representatives Committee on Ways and Means 1998). Private pensions in general and provisions of pensions in particular have been linked to important decisions that individuals make in later life, including retirement and savings decisions.[1] Availability of data from the Health and Retirement Study (HRS) has helped stimulate new empirical research on pensions and their behavioral effects.[2]

Individuals obtain private pensions through their employers. Such pension plans fall into two general categories: defined-benefit (DB) and defined-contribution (DC) plans. The latter type of plan has become increasingly common in the past three decades (Brown 2001), but DB plans remain more prevalent (Gustman, Mitchell, and Steinmeier 1995). The DB plans share many common features with Social Security. Benefit levels are based on a formula, which varies among employers. The formula accounts for such factors as an employee's age, wage, and years of service. Payment is in the form of an annuity. By rewarding years of service, the intention is to encourage employee loyalty and reduce turnover. Eligibility for benefits from DB plans is affected by federally mandated vesting rules. Employers hold assets for paying retirement benefits in various types of securities, such as equity and various debt instruments. But employers, not the employees entitled to benefits from DB plans, bear the risk of fluctuations in the value of such assets.

Survivor benefits vary among plans. Some DB plans offer payment only in the form of a current or future benefit flow, but an increasing fraction of such plans offer the option of a lump-sum distribution at the time of job separation. Yet according to Hurd, Lillard, and Panis (1998), who used data from the Health and Retirement Study (HRS), a DB pension holder's taking the lump-sum distribution upon job separation is rare. The 1984 Retirement Equity Act protects spouses of deceased workers who are either retired or vested in their private plan. DB plans must offer a qualified preretirement survivor annuity if a married participant with a vested interest dies before receiving benefits; the benefit payment after retirement of the surviving spouse must be a qualified joint-and-survivor annuity in which survivor benefits are between 50 and 100 percent of worker benefits.

In DC plans, the employer makes a monetary contribution to a fund, which may also require a dollar contribution from the employee. Pension benefits are financed from individual retirement accounts to which employers and employees contribute. At any point in time, the employee's DC plan has a specific cash value, which varies according to dollar contributions and the performance of investments in the plan. With DC plans, vesting is immediate or nearly so. On leaving the employer, the employee has possession of an asset that will pay benefits on a periodic basis proportionate to its value at retirement, as a lump sum at death, or in various combinations of payment methods (but always based on the asset's market value).

With DC plans, the possibilities for cross subsidies are more limited than with DB plans. The value of the employee's DC plan is payable to survivors on the employee's death. In this sense, there is no cross subsidy, at least not one based on employee health behavior, such as engaging in smoking or heavy alcohol consumption. Also, retirees who smoke may have a greater propensity to annuitize the amounts in their accounts because of their lower life expectancy if annuity payments do not fully reflect this difference.

In contrast, DB plans entail potential transfers from smokers to nonsmokers, the main reason being the shorter longevity of smokers. The extent of such transfers depends on vesting provisions as well as survivor benefits. Further, the payment formula may be nonlinear in earnings, meaning in this context that payments do not rise proportionately with contributions to the plan. Rather, higher earners who have made greater contributions over their work lives received a lower fraction of what they contribute. This factor tends to work to the advantage of smokers enrolled in DB plans.

Whereas DB plans more closely resemble Social Security, DC plans resemble individual retirement accounts or Keogh plans. DB plans contain incentives to retire at a certain age, a feature only rarely shared by DC plans (Anderson, Gustman, and Steinmeier 1999). The vast majority of DB plans pay benefits as an annuity and do not permit lump-sum distributions at retirement (Brown 2001).

In this chapter, we limit our empirical analysis to DB plans. Given the similarities of DB plans and Social Security, our suspicion at the outset was that nonsmokers are subsidized by smokers, given the lower life expectancy of persons in the latter group. In fact, this is what we found. Since the potential for cross subsidies is much more limited for DC plans, we did not assess cross subsidies related to smoking for such plans.

New Empirical Evidence

Data

As its name implies, a key goal of the Health and Retirement Study has been to gather data on retirement and retirement benefits. The HRS collects a substantial amount of information on respondents' retirement expectations and attitudes, and, more pertinent to this chapter, information on benefits anticipated at retirement (Gustman, Mitchell, and Steinmeier 1995). The HRS collected self-reported information from respondents as well as information directly from the respondent's employer on the person's retirement plan. To accomplish the latter, respondents were asked to identify their employers, and the University of Michigan Institute for Social Research, the survey organization responsible for HRS, collected benefit plan reports from various sources.

The HRS is unique in providing data on private pensions from both self-reports and employers. Comparisons of the two types of data have shown that people often have inaccurate perceptions about their retirement benefits (see e.g., Johnson, Sambamoorthis, and Crystal 2000). Thus, for many purposes, especially for gauging behavioral responses to differences in provisions of retirement plans, having data on plan characteristics from firms is clearly preferable.

However, we based this chapter's empirical analysis on self-reported data for one major reason. Plan descriptions were available for only two-thirds of HRS respondents who reported being covered by a pension on their current or last job, and for even fewer HRS respondents covered by a pension on jobs held earlier than this (Gustman and Steinmeier 1999a,b). The loss in sample size due to missing values would have made it difficult to stratify the data by smoking status and gender, as we have done elsewhere in our study. Also, the aim of our analysis was to estimate a cross subsidy. For this purpose, having much detail on specific provisions of pension plans that would have been available from the employers' databases was not important.

We used responses to employment-related questions at wave 1 of the HRS to analyze the association between smoking and private pensions. Respondents who worked for pay at the survey date were asked about their participation in up to three retirement plans, as well as detailed questions about contributions to and expected benefits from each plan. Respondents who were not working then but had previously worked for pay were only asked about their participation in up to three plans and the benefits they expected to receive. Data on contributions were available only for the employed. We used information from both groups to estimate probabilities of participation in a plan, but information from only the employed group was used to assess associations between contributions and benefits.

Identifying Persons Enrolled in DB Plans

We identified respondents participating in DB retirement plans from a question asking whether the respondent was enrolled in or had previously been enrolled in DB, DC, or both types of plans. Any respondent who said that he or she was, or had been, enrolled in a DB or combination of DB and DC plans, was considered to be in a DB plan in our analysis.

Participants in DB plans who were employed at HRS wave 1 were asked about their contributions to these plans, as either an amount per time period or percent of pay. Using information on pay, we converted all responses to percent of pay. Total contributions to up to three DB or DB/DC plans were calculated as the sum of contributions to each plan. Thus, the estimates included DB plans from previous as well as current employment, assuming the person had vested benefits in a plan with a previous employer at the time of the HRS interview.

Box 7.1
Analysis of Participation in DB Pension Plans

Covariates in the multinomial logit analysis with a trichotomous dependent variable included: our basic specification (chapter 2); and the industry in which the respondent was working at wave 1 (agriculture/mining, manufacturing, transportation, financing, professional and related services, public administration, other). The distinction between former smokers who quit by age 40 and those who quit at later ages followed the method used to assess contributions to Medicare and Social Security in previous chapters. The split between former smokers based on quitting age allowed us to gauge the effect of smoking on the person's past earnings more precisely.

Respondents were asked the age at which they expected to start receiving benefits from each plan and the expected retirement benefits. From the information provided, we could express retirement benefits as a fixed amount per time period or percent of pay at retirement. We converted these estimates to a common measure, percent of pay at wave 1.

Analysis

We estimated the probability of participation in DB pension plans using multinomial logit analysis. There were three mutually exclusive groups: (1) respondent participated in a DB plan, (2) respondent participated in a DC plan only, and (3) respondent did not participate in a pension plan (box 7.1).

The next step was to analyze the probability that employees contributed to a DB plan and, conditional on making a contribution, the amount contributed. Many participants in DB plans reported zero employee contributions to their plan, that is, the plan was fully employer funded. We assessed the role of smoking and other factors on the probability that the employee contributed to a DB plan. The dependent variable in the logit analysis was equal to one if the employee contributed to the DB plan and zero if the employee made no contributions to the plan. Using the results, we predicted probabilities of nonzero contributions for participants in DB plans by age, gender, and smoking status, at the gender- and smoking-status-specific means of all other covariates. For those who contributed, we assessed effects of

Box 7.2
Estimating Lifetime Contributions to DB Pension Plans

Predictions were generated at the gender- and smoking-status-specific means of all other covariates. We adjusted for differential survival according to smoking history and converted predictions conditional on survival to expected contributions, conditional on smoking status and survival to age 24. The discounted (at three percent) sum of annual expected contributions gave the estimated mean lifetime contribution, by gender, of a representative person in each smoking category.

smoking and other factors on employees' contributions as a percentage of pay, using ordinary least squares regression.

Expected annual contributions were defined as the product of (1) the probability of participation in DB retirement plans, (2) the probability of a nonzero contribution to the plan, (3) the conditional level of contributions as percent of earnings, and (4) the expected earnings at each year of age.

Estimates of employees' lifetime contributions to DB pensions were based on estimates of their earnings histories, the duration of participation in DB plans, and variations in their contribution levels. We estimated gender- and smoking-status-specific earnings profiles as in chapter 6. Using age-, sex-, and smoking-status-dependent predicted earnings, predicted probabilities of participation in pension plans, predicted probabilities of nonzero contributions, and conditional contributions, we calculated expected mean contributions for every age between 36, the average starting age for contributions in the sample, and age 62 (box 7.2).

Expected annual benefits were the product of the annual benefit amount multiplied by the probability of survival to ages 62 to 100, given survival to age 24. The benefit amount was defined as a fixed percentage of mean annual pay between ages 36 and 62. For respondents who contributed to their retirement plan, the mean benefit level was 51.4 percent of their pay at retirement; for respondents with zero contributions, the expected benefit level was 40.4 percent. These values represent means among respondents with a DB plan and some expected benefits. Preliminary analysis showed no statistically significant difference in expected benefit levels by smoking status. We assumed benefit levels remained constant until death, after which we assumed a zero benefit (in our basic specification).

Box 7.3
Calculating Values of Contributions to and Benefits from DB Plans

Employee contributions, employer contributions, and pension benefits were recalculated for nonsmoking smokers by substituting counterfactual nonsmokers' earnings profiles, survival probabilities, probabilities of participation in DB plans, and the probability of nonzero employee contributions, for those of current and former smokers, accounting for differences in other covariates including race, education, industry, and marital status (see chapter 2 for a more detailed description of the nonsmoking smoker calculations). In sensitivity analysis, we compared the robustness of our findings to alternative assumptions about age of retirement—62 versus 65—and about smoking and pension plan participation, contributions, and benefits.

We computed lifetime employee pension benefits as the discounted sum of survival-adjusted expected annual benefit amounts between ages 62 and 100. Employer contributions were defined as the difference between lifetime benefits and lifetime employee contributions. Returns from assets held by employers in retirement accounts were reflected implicitly in employer contributions.[3]

To evaluate the effects of smoking on contributions to and benefits from DB plans, we computed counterfactual estimates for the hypothetical nonsmoking smoker (box 7.3). The counterfactual estimates were then subtracted from the estimates for actual smokers to determine smoking-attributable contributions and benefits for DB plans.

Defined-benefit plans vary in spousal survival benefit provisions; such provisions potentially affect cross-subsidies between smokers and others. Thus, we also analyzed the effects of alternative spousal survivor benefit provisions. A priori, survivor benefits were expected to reduce the effect of smoking on lifetime benefit payments, as spouses of smokers continue to receive benefits even after smokers die early. However, for DB plans with survivor benefits, smoking spouses of never smokers would potentially benefit from quitting, partially offsetting these effects.

The Health and Retirement Study (HRS) data contained no information on spousal benefits. We therefore estimated the effect of varying spousal survivor benefits, using data from the Social Security analysis in chapter 6.

We used previously estimated Social Security monthly benefit amounts (primary insurance amounts, or PIAs) for each spouse to

Box 7.4
Sensitivity Analysis

> We estimated lifetime benefits from alternative retirement plans with
> survivor benefits of 0, 50, 75, and 100 percent. To accomplish this, we
> calculated benefit multipliers for each scenario and for every combina-
> tion of smoking status for husband and wife, as the ratio of benefits
> under the 50, 75, and 100 percent scenario relative to the scenario with
> 0 percent survivor benefits. We used these multipliers to estimate the
> effect of smoking on lifetime DB benefits amounts for each scenario.

describe the effects of spouse benefits on a respondent's expected
monthly pension benefit on retirement at age 62. The main difference
between the Social Security benefit analysis and the (hypothetical) DB
pension benefit analysis was that in the latter, a spouse became eligible
for benefits on the other spouse's earnings record only upon death of
that spouse, and that the benefit was, unlike in Social Security, not
related to his or her own pension receipt.[4] We evaluated the sensitivity
of our results to varying levels of survivor benefits (box 7.4).

We also estimated contributions and benefit receipt, as well as the
effect of survivor benefits, for retirement at age 65 (versus 62 in the
base case).

Results

Smoking Status and Participation in a DB Plan

At wave 1, of 12,052 respondents who had ever worked for pay, 33.2
percent had a DB plan, 13.7 percent only had a DC plan, and 53.1 percent had neither type of plan (table 7.1).

There were substantial differences in participation by smoking status. Current smokers were significantly less likely to have a DB plan
and more likely to lack a private pension plan of any kind than were
never smokers. To the extent that smokers cross-subsidize nonsmokers
by their earlier mortality, smokers face a disincentive to demand coverage by DB plans. But then proportionately more smokers should be
covered by DC plans, and this pattern was also not observed. Former
smokers were more likely to have been included in a DB plan than
were never smokers and were more likely to have a private pension of
some sort.

Table 7.1
Descriptive Statistics: Participation in Pension Plans, Employee Contributions, and Expected Benefits

Variables	Smoking Status			
	Current	Former	Never	Total
Participation in pension plans				
Number of respondents	4,233	3,321	4,498	12,052
Percent with:				
Defined benefits plan (DB)	29.9***	37.2***	33.2	33.2
Defined contributions plan only (DC)	12.5*	14.8	14.1	13.7
No plan	57.6***	47.9***	52.6	53.1
Plan characteristics: Employees with DB Plans[1]				
Number of respondents with data on contributions	326	379	550	1,255
Nonzero contributions (%)	50.0	50.4*	43.8	47.4
Percent of pay if contributions > 0	16.8	6.8	17.4	14.2
Mean starting age	37.2	35.5	36.5	36.4
Data on contributions and benefits (N)	216	264	363	843
Zero employee contributions (%)	48.1	48.9	41.6	45.6
Expected benefits (% of pay)	39.2	41.4	40.5	40.4
Nonzero employee contributions (%)	51.9	51.1	58.4	54.4
Expected benefit (% of pay)	50.7	54.0	49.8	51.2
Mean expected age of benefit receipt	61.1	61.3	61.5	61.3

1. Employed respondents with DB Plan and nonzero pay. Excludes data from mixed plans, such as those with DB and DC components.
*, **, and *** refer to statistically significant differences in means relative to never smokers, at the 0.05, 0.01, and 0.001 levels, respectively.

Fewer than half of respondents (47.4%) with a DB plan made direct contributions to the plan. Those who contributed allocated a rather large share of their pay to pension contributions (14.2%). Overall, very few differences in plan characteristics by smoking status were statistically significant.

In regression analysis, smokers were not significantly less likely to participate in DB plans, controlling for other covariates, including age, race, education, marital status and industry (not shown). Smokers did not tend to favor DC plans, although, in view of their lower life expectancy, they might have done so. But of course, the plans were employer based, and employees in a given job were generally unlikely to

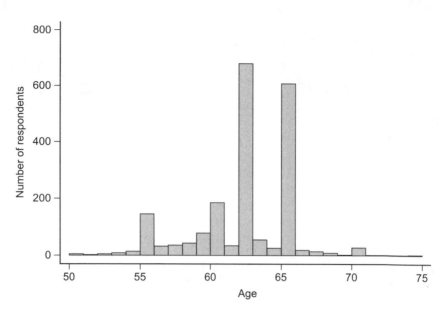

Figure 7.1
Expected starting age for benefit receipt from a defined-benefit plan.

have had a choice between a DB and a DC plan. There are many reasons that people have for selecting particular employers.

Expected Benefits as a Share of Pay

Respondents expected to receive benefits from their plans at 61, on average. Benefit levels varied with employee contributions to the plan. Respondents who did not contribute to their plans expected to receive 40 percent of their pay at retirement, and those who contributed expected to receive 51 percent of pay. Anticipated retirement ages spiked at 62 and 65 (fig. 7.1). Virtually no one anticipated retiring after age 70, and few thought they would do so after 65. Given the sharp decline in the stock market following early 2000, some people may have decided to continue working and some persons, having retired, may have reentered the work force.

Lifetime Contributions by Smoking Status

For women who smoked at age 24 and retired at age 62, the expected value of lifetime contributions to private pensions by female smokers

Table 7.2
Present Value of Expected Lifetime Private Pension Contributions (2000 Dollars)

	Retirement at Age 62		Retirement at Age 65	
	Females	Males	Females	Males
(A) Actual Smoking Status				
Smoker	7,541	15,333	8,437	16,807
Never smoker	8,151	17,288	9,214	19,267
(B) Nonsmoking Smokers				
Smoker	7,563	16,982	8,513	18,895
Never smoker	8,151	17,288	9,214	19,267
(C) Difference (A) − (B)				
Smoker	−22	−1,650	−77	−2,088
Never smoker	0	0	0	0

Note: 2000 dollars, 3% discount rate.

was $7,541, on average, compared to $8,151 for women who did not smoke at this age (table 7.2). Contributions were much higher for males. Male smokers contributed $15,333, on average, over their lifetimes, compared to $17,288 for male never smokers. Assuming retirement and beginning of receipt of pension benefits at age 62, female nonsmoking smokers would have contributed an additional $22 over their lifetime. Their male counterparts would have contributed an additional $1,650, relative to smokers with otherwise identical characteristics. The difference arose from a combination of participation, earnings, and survival differences attributable to smoking.

For retirement at age 65, the contributions differential increased to $77 and $2,088. Increasing the assumed retirement age by three years had only a very small influence on contributions to the retirement plan. Recall that these values are discounted back to age 24. Nominal contributions would have been considerably higher.

Lifetime Expected Benefits by Smoking Status

Estimated lifetime private DB pension benefits for female smokers retiring at 62 were $18,974 on average, compared to $22,210 for female never smokers (table 7.3). Benefits for male smokers were appreciably higher, $35,542 for smokers, and $47,395 for never smokers. Smoking was costly to men, reflected in a more than $11,000 differential in expected lifetime benefits between smokers and nonsmokers. We estimate

Table 7.3
Present Value of Expected Lifetime Private Pension Benefits (2000 Dollars)

	Retirement at Age 62		Retirement at Age 65	
	Females	Males	Females	Males
(A) Actual Smoking Status				
Smoker	18,974	35,542	15,719	28,064
Never smoker	22,210	47,395	18,856	39,009
(B) Nonsmoking Smoker				
Smoker	20,461	47,071	17,260	38,651
Never smoker	22,210	47,395	18,856	39,009
(C) Difference (A) − (B)				
Smoker	−1,487	−11,529	−1,542	−10,586
Never smoker	0	0	0	0

Note: 2000 dollars, 3% discount rate. Only includes benefits of persons employed at interview date.

that, if the male smokers never smoked, their expected lifetime benefits actually would have been almost identical to that of never smokers, with $47,071 in anticipated benefits, the effect of smoking being $11,529. Although still substantial, effects of smoking on expected benefits for female smokers were considerably lower at $1,487. For retirement at age 65, the benefit differential was somewhat greater for women, $1,542, and somewhat smaller for men, $10,586.

The net effect, accounting for both smoking-attributable contribution and benefit differences, was a $1,464 reduced net benefit from private DB plans for female smokers, and a $9,879 reduced net benefit for male smokers, assuming retirement at age 62 (table 7.4). With retirement at 65, reductions in net benefits were nearly identical for women, and slightly lower for men.

The estimated effects of smoking in tables 7.3 and 7.4 are based on an assumption that pension benefits were nontransferable; that is, benefit payments terminated with the death of a smoker. In calculations presented in table 7.5, we evaluated the effect of varying levels of survivor benefits on overall benefit payments. The effect of different transferability of benefits varied substantially by gender and with the spouse's smoking status. In view of their longer life expectancy, allowing for survivor benefits had a much larger impact on estimated net benefit for women than for men. We present estimates for never smokers since such persons may be married to smokers.

Table 7.4
Net Effect of Smoking on Private Pensions (2000 Dollars)

	Retirement at Age 62		Retirement at Age 65	
	Females	Males	Females	Males
(A) Effect of smoking on contributions	−22	−1,650	−77	−2,088
(B) Effect of smoking on benefits	−1,487	−11,529	−1,542	−10,586
(C) Net effect (B) − (A)	−1,464	−9,879	−1,465	−8,498

Note: 2000 dollars, 3% discount rate.

Women married to smokers are the chief beneficiaries of surviving-spouse eligibility for the deceased husband's DB plan benefits. For example, if all pension plans were to provide 50 percent survivor benefits, benefits would have increased by 48.5 percent on average for female smokers married to smokers. The corresponding increase for being married to a nonsmoking smoker was 32.0 percent. The *absolute* increase in benefits is positively related to the benefit amounts of the spouse and the probability of outliving the spouse. By contrast, the *percentage* increase in benefits is inversely related to the beneficiary's own benefit amount, and directly related to the probability of outliving the spouse. Never smokers can expect to outlive their spouses by a larger number of years relative to smokers, raising their *absolute* gains from pensions' greater survivor benefits. However, never smokers' own benefit amounts are also greater, reducing the *percentage* increase in benefits derived from pensions' survivor benefits. Thus, although the percentage increases were similar for female smokers and never smokers, the base amounts as well as the gains were higher for the latter group. In absolute terms, the benefit increase due to survivor benefits was greatest for female nonsmokers married to smokers. At 75 percent and 100 percent retention of benefits, the increase in benefits was correspondingly higher.

For men, estimated benefits were insensitive to the assumptions made about survivor benefits from private pension plans. This means that how the survivor benefit is structured had little influence on the cross-subsidy that male nonsmokers realized.

Irrespective of the percentage effects, the estimated effects of smoking on benefits were insensitive to alternative assumptions about

Table 7.5
Percent Increase in Present Value of Expected Lifetime Social Security Benefits under Various Survivor Benefit Scenarios

Survivor Benefit	Scenario	Smoking Status	Females		Males	
			Married to Smoker	Married to Nonsmoker	Married to Smoker	Married to Nonsmoker
0%	(Reference)		.	.	.	.
50%	(A) Actual	Smoker	48.5	30.4	5.8	3.7
		Never smoker	49.9	32.5	6.0	3.9
	(B) Counterfactual	Nonsmoking smoker	32.0	31.3	4.5	4.0
		Never smoker	33.0	32.5	4.4	3.9
75%	(A) Actual	Smoker	72.8	45.6	8.7	5.6
		Never smoker	74.9	48.8	9.0	5.9
	(B) Counterfactual	Nonsmoking smoker	48.1	46.9	6.8	6.1
		Never smoker	49.5	48.8	6.7	5.9
100%	(A) Actual	Smoker	97.1	60.8	11.6	7.5
		Never smoker	99.8	65.1	12.0	7.8
	(B) Counterfactual	Nonsmoking smoker	64.1	62.6	9.0	8.1
		Never smoker	66.0	65.1	8.9	7.8

Note: Estimated survivor benefits are assumed additive, i.e., in addition to own benefits.

Table 7.6
Sensitivity of the Estimated Effect of Smoking on Benefits to Various Assumptions Regarding Survivor Benefits (2000 Dollars)

Earnings Base for Benefit Computation	Percent of Benefit Retained by Surviving Spouse	Retirement at Age 62		Retirement at Age 65	
		Females	Males	Females	Males
Average earnings	0	−1,487	−11,529	−1,542	−10,586
	50[1]	−406	−11,773	−703	−10,833
	75	135	−11,892	−284	−10,955
	100	675	−12,012	136	−11,077
Maximum earnings	0	1,813	−12,251	−1,788	−11,131
	50	−532	−12,497	−786	−11,375
	75	109	−12,620	−285	−11,498
	100	750	−12,742	216	−11,620

Note: 2000 dollars, 3% discount rate.
1. Considered the "best estimate." In this scenario, smokers' net benefit reductions (private losses) are partially offset by increases in survivor benefits (quasi-external "gains") to nonsmokers of $295 and $687, on average, per female and male 24-year-old smoker, respectively.

retirement age and on whether or not benefits are based on average earnings over the period during which contributions were paid or on maximum earnings with the employer (table 7.6).

At midrange—50 percent of benefit retained by surviving spouses, a 62-year retirement age, and benefits based on average earnings, the cross-subsidy in benefits was $406 if the smoker was a woman and $11,773 for male smokers. After accounting for contributions differentials, the corresponding net cross-subsidies were $383 and $10,123, respectively (not shown). Varying the assumed retirement age had little influence on the estimated smoking effects on private pension benefits. For women, the net effect decreased by about $300; for men, net losses due to smoking decreased by about $1,000.

Discussion and Conclusions

Private pensions are of policy interest for several reasons. First, they are an important source of financial support for the elderly. Second, provisions of retirement plans affect labor market decisions of mature individuals (see e.g., Gustman, Mitchell, and Steinmeier 1994). Given the increased life expectancy in the United States and hence both the number of persons in retirement and the number of years each individual can be expected to be in retirement, the thrust of public policy in recent years has been to encourage later retirement.

Our analysis of defined benefit private pensions applied essentially the same methodology we used for Social Security OASI in the previous chapter. Qualitatively, the conclusion is much the same. In the context of such private pension plans, smoking causes a transfer to nonsmokers and possibly improved financial solvency of private pension plans. The main source of the transfer is smokers' lower probability of receiving pension benefits due to their worse survival prospects, the same reason that the cross-subsidies occurred for Social Security. The subsidy of nonsmokers is much larger for men ($10,123) than for women ($383). But in general, women have much lower pension wealth than men (see e.g., Hardy and Shuey 2000).

To the extent that people can be persuaded to quit smoking, the transfer will be diminished. Also, greater longevity of a group of employees would generate an unanticipated pension liability of employers, which may reduce the market value of private enterprises.

One important limitation of our results is that the analysis was based on information that was self-reported by respondents to the Health and Retirement Study. Also, a difference between our analysis of Social Security and our analysis of pensions is that rules for calculating Social Security benefits are known and do not vary among individuals (see e.g., Anderson, Gustman, and Steinmeier 1999 for discussion of this point).

In recent years, several studies have compared responses obtained directly from persons interviewed with actual features of the same person's pension plan, reporting discrepancies. One major weakness is in understanding specific features of the plans, such as spikes in benefits. Errors in reporting can occur with features as basic as whether the person was enrolled in a defined-contribution or in a defined-benefit plan.

A comparison of self-reported and employer-provided data on private pensions indicated that among workers linked to provider data on DB plans, 16 percent reported that they participated only in DC plans. Misreporting of plan type was even greater among those linked to DC plans supplied by providers (Johnson, Sambamoorthis, and Crystal 2000). To the extent that such errors exist, they would affect the accuracy of the cross-subsidy as reported here.

In this chapter, we only considered cash benefits offered as a fringe benefit upon retirement. Another fringe benefit is retiree health benefits, which after age 65 provide supplemental coverage to Medicare. This is a major source of private health insurance coverage for persons age 65. Effects of smoking on private health insurance coverage were reported in chapter 5. The dollar equivalent value of retiree health insurance is dwarfed by the value of employer-provided private pensions (Gustman and Steinmeier 2000). For younger retirees not yet eligible for Medicare, employer-provided health insurance is a higher-valued fringe benefit.

8   Do Nonsmokers Cross-Subsidize Smokers in the Market for Life Insurance?

In a competitive insurance market, the expected payment by insurers equals the payment by policyholders to insurers plus a competitive return on expenditures by the insurer on inputs.[1] Under these circumstances, when a person purchases insurance, the individual trades a cash flow of premiums for a cash flow of payments from the insurer of an almost equivalent amount. Also included are administrative expenses (loading), which in a competitive market should reflect the minimum cost of marketing policies and processing claims, as well as the user cost of capital. Risk-averse persons are willing to pay such cost to gain greater certainty in future cash flows. Persons who incur the insured loss lose by buying insurance after the fact (ex post) and those who do not incur the insured loss realize a loss ex post. Since everyone dies eventually, life insurers pay benefits; here, the transfer is from those who die late to those who die early.

But before the loss is incurred (ex ante), the identity of persons who will and will not incur a loss is unknown and, within a risk class, insured individuals are homogeneous with respect to the probability of incurring a loss. Thus, if insured persons within risk classes pay premiums nearly equal to the actuarial value of the loss, no cross subsidies occur within or between risk classes.

A competitive outcome might not occur for several reasons, and cross-subsidies arise as a consequence. The first reason is imperfect information on both the supply and demand sides of the market. Asymmetric information may occur because potential policyholders know more about their probabilities of future loss than do insurers. For insurance whose payment is related to the health and longevity of policyholders, such asymmetric information may reflect health habits of insured persons or genetic or family history, which may be costly for insurers to monitor. Shoppers for insurance may be foreclosed from seeking out the lowest-cost alternatives because of prior contractual obligations or ignorance about price differentials.[2]

Second, premiums might not be actuarially fair as a consequence of practical difficulties in developing a good risk classification system.[3] Classifying factors used to establish rating categories for purposes of setting premiums need to be demonstrably good predictors of future loss, that is, the factors must be statistically related to losses across a credible base of experience.[4] Some factors, for example, certain types of medical injuries or thefts in a high-income neighborhood, occur rarely, and for this reason, a credible experience base may be lacking. Other factors occur frequently, but the link to future loss has not been statistically established.

The classification system should achieve separation in anticipated losses across the various classifications it creates. "Separation in anticipated losses" means that the difference in two adjacent insurance risk classes should be sufficiently large to warrant charging the two groups different premiums. Thus, the members of a class should naturally cluster together in their predicted experience, and each class should be noticeably distinct from its neighbors. The variables used to define risk classes should be reliable predictors, not subject to gaming or outright falsification. Risk-classifying factors should motivate policyholders to prevent losses.

Third, risk classification may conflict with specific policy objectives or ethical concerns (see, e.g., Abraham 1986; Harrington and Doerpinghaus 1993). Race is the prototypical example of a factor that may be an actuarially sound predictor of loss but socially impermissible as a classifying factor. In some contexts, prior health, family history, or geographic location ("red-lining") would be impermissible as well. Patient-protection laws prohibit release of medical information that may be potentially useful to employers and others.

To what extent do these impediments pertain to life insurance and smoking? Many of the impediments to a good risk classification system do not exist in the context of smoking and life insurance or, at least, are not as important as for other lines of insurance. For life insurance, but generally not health insurance, applicants answer questions about their medical histories and often undergo physical examinations. Results of such examinations are shared among insurers. Also, life insurance, especially whole-life or cash policies as whole-life policies are often called, are purchased early in life when a person generally is healthy.[5] For these reasons, adverse selection is less likely to be problematic for life insurance than for other types of insurance, especially those for which policies are purchased on a regular basis, such as once a year.

Although the association between life expectancy and smoking was unknown until about the middle of the last century, the association now has been well established for several decades. Furthermore, smoking is a commonplace event, not a rare one; in this sense, assembling a credible experience base is very feasible. Because smoking has a substantial effect on survival (chapter 4), placing smokers in a risk class achieves separation of loss.

The reliability of smoking information provided by applicants for life insurance as a predictor of longevity is more questionable. Smokers may lie about their habit when they apply for insurance coverage. A recent quitter would be at an elevated risk for early mortality, but biochemical markers may not reveal whether the person quit not long ago. Insurers could question associates of the applicant to determine whether the person's statements on the application are truthful, but such monitoring is likely to be costly.[6] Also, smoking status changes over time, particularly as smokers make attempts to quit.[7] Payments can be disallowed if the insurer can demonstrate that the person made misrepresentations on his or her application, but the time allowed for contesting statements on applications typically is limited.

In contrast to health insurance, and auto liability insurance to a lesser extent, risk classification in life insurance is based on health and health behaviors in context with social norms.[8] Society seems willing to allow the market to penalize an individual for "bad" genes in the market for life insurance. A cancer victim, for example, would typically pay a higher life insurance premium (if the person can be insured at all).

In health insurance, basing premiums on health and health behaviors is widely viewed as unethical. In the case of automobile liability insurance, being able to drive is viewed by many as a "right," since ability to drive is linked to access to a livelihood; thus, although drivers with bad driving records may have to pay higher liability insurance premiums, insurance is typically available. Cross-subsidization seems to be variable; for example, Puelz and Snow (1994), using data from the state of Georgia, find no evidence of cross subsidization of risks in the auto liability market, but it seems unlikely that this result generalizes to states with large insurance pools for high-risk drivers.

Evidence from trade journals, such as *National Underwriter (Life and Health, Financial Services edition)* and *Broker's World*, suggests that risk

Box 8.1

To Smoke or Not to Smoke

From a 1972 article on smoking and life insurance rates: "Despite the potential impact of smoking as a new risk factor for insurability, very few life-insurance companies have considered it feasible to adopt a history of cigarette smoking as a major underwriting criterion. The reason is in the drastic effect this would have in separating smokers from nonsmokers into separate policyholder groups. Nonsmokers would have about 75 percent of the standard mortality table mortality rate while smokers would have a mortality ratio of about 150 percent. Smokers would become a huge new rated class. Besides problems in verification on applications, most insurance executives are hard pressed to justify rating up to 90 percent of now standard risk when smoking is still socially acceptable" (Singer 1972, p. 50).

classification on the basis of smoking status has been widespread in life insurance (see Schwartz 1992 and Bell 1996 for references to articles in the trade literature), but this is a relatively new phenomenon. Until recently, it was thought that recognizing smoking as a risk factor would result in premium differentials that were too large (box 10.1). The main impediment now is lack of reliability—that is, the ability of insurers to distinguish smokers from others.

To the extent that smokers pay actuarially justified premium surcharges for life insurance, cross-subsidies of smokers by nonsmokers should be minimal. The empirical question in this chapter is to determine whether this is indeed so.

New Empirical Evidence: Methods

At every wave of the Health and Retirement Study (HRS), respondents were asked whether they were covered by one or more life insurance policies. Follow-up questions about the type of coverage, face value of the policies, and the cost of coverage varied considerably across waves (table 10.1). We combined information from all waves to estimate effects of smoking on the probability of having term life insurance and cash value ("whole-life") policies, face values of these policies, and the contributions made over respondents' lifetimes. Selection into HRS was based on respondents' ages in 1991 (ages 51–62), but, as explained below, we extrapolated our results to other ages.

Table 8.1
Life Insurance Variables in Waves 1 through 5 of the Health and Retirement Study

	Wave 1	Wave 2	Wave 3	Wave 4	Wave 5
Term Life and/or Cash Policy	×	×	×	×	×
—Face value			×	×	×
—Cost of insurance					
—Duration of coverage			×	×	
Term Life Insurance	×	×			
—Face value	×	×			
—Cost of insurance	×	×			
—Duration of coverage	×	×			
Cash Value Policy	×	×			×
—Face value	×	×			×
—Cost of insurance	×				×
—Duration of coverage	×				

At wave 1, respondents were asked whether they were covered by term life insurance policies, with a follow-up question on whether their group term insurance policies were obtained through an employer. Respondents were also asked about the face value and cost of any cash-value policies, as well as how long they have had cash policies. Wave 2 asked similar questions, but omitted questions about the cost of cash policies and how long respondents had been covered by these policies. At waves 3 and 4, no distinction was made in the survey between term life and cash-value (whole-life) policies, and no questions were asked about the cost of coverage. At wave five, respondents were asked about the total face value of their life insurance coverage, both term-life and cash policies, as well as about the face value and the cost of cash policies. We could thus calculate the face value of term life insurance coverage. At wave 1, one respondent per household was asked to answer questions for both spouses if married; at subsequent waves, each respondent was asked separately.

We used responses from all waves to estimate the probability of having any life insurance coverage, and data from waves 1, 2, and 5 to predict individual probabilities of being covered by term life and cash policies.

We estimated lifetime benefits from life insurance policies using predicted probabilities of coverage and face values, and life tables (from chapter 4). Methodological detail is provided in box 8.2.

Box 8.2

Analysis of Probability of Having Any Life Insurance Coverage and Face Values (Amount) of Coverage for Persons with Such Coverage

Using random effects logit, we estimated equations for life insurance coverage with a dependent variable of 1 if the respondent reported coverage and 0 otherwise. We included these covariates: smoking status, drinking status, history of problem drinking, body mass index (BMI), age, gender, race, education, risk aversion, and the financial-planning horizon.* In addition, we included binary variables for currently working, a more detailed description of respondents' marital status than we used in the analysis reported in the other chapters, any children in the household, any children living outside the household, mother alive, father alive, proxy interview, and binary variables for waves 2 through 5. Multiple observations on individuals entered the sample repeatedly at each wave. We adjusted standard errors for correlated errors among repeated observations on the same individual. As in analysis for other chapters, observations were weighted by their sampling weights to ensure that estimates are representative of the U.S. population.

Face values were highly skewed in linear form but were approximately normally distributed when the variable was expressed in natural log form (fig. 8.1).

Using random effects regression, we assessed variation in the log dependent variable, including the same explanatory variables as in the analysis of the probability of having life insurance, with one exception: in the analysis of face value, we also included a binary variable for group life insurance coverage. Combining parameter estimates from the logit and linear regression models, using Duan's (1983) smearing correction, we calculated predicted life insurance coverage for each person and year between the ages of 24 through 100. Most respondents had acquired their life insurance coverage many years before the HRS wave 1 interview (fig. 8.2).

We predicted the starting age for each respondent using estimates from a linear regression model of starting age for cash value policies at wave 1 against the same covariates as described above.

*See chapter 2 for descriptions of these variables.

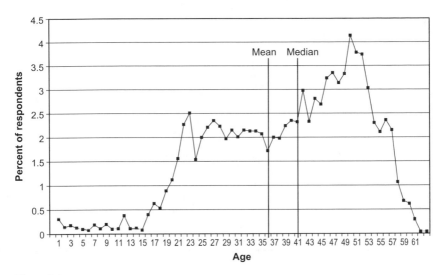

Figure 8.1
Age at which health and retirement study respondents obtained cash value life insurance policies.

With this information, we predicted payouts from life insurance policies at each year of age from 24 to 100. We accounted for differential survival probabilities according to the individual's smoking status. Expected lifetime payouts of persons at 24 were calculated as the sum of annual predicted payments between 24 and 100, discounted at 3 percent per year.

We estimated lifetime premium payments using self-reported premiums at each wave, the reported duration of respondents' coverage, the predicted face value of term-life and cash-value policies, and respondents' life tables (box 8.3).

New Empirical Evidence: Results

Life insurance was very common (table 8.2). Sixty-eight percent of current smokers had some form of life insurance coverage. Former and never smokers were somewhat more likely to have a life insurance policy then were current smokers: 76.5 and 70.9 percent, respectively. Men were more likely to be covered than were women.

The face value of life insurance policies was considerably higher for men than for women, for never than for current smokers, and for term life insurance than for cash-value policies. Never smokers reported the

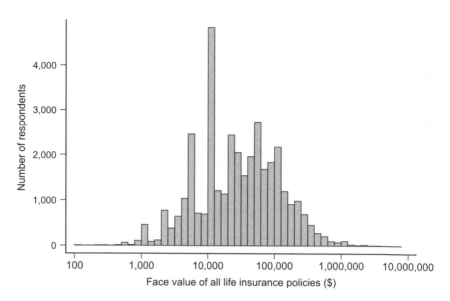

Figure 8.2
Distribution of face values of life insurance policies.

Box 8.3
Analysis of Probability of Any Employee Contributions to Any Life Insurance
Plans and of Face Values Conditional on Any Employee Contributions

As with our analysis of lifetime benefits, we used a two-part model, estimating the probability of any employee contributions using a random
effects logit model, and the conditional log annual premium per $10,000
of coverage, using random effects regression. We calculated the cost of
coverage using self-reported annual payments for term life insurance
policies in waves 1 and 2, and for cash-value policies in waves 1 and
5. We used the same equation specification as in the analysis of the
face values. We used parameter estimates from these models to predict
annual age-specific contributions. We also used ordinary least squares to
analyze determinants of the age at which respondents first obtained
their coverage. We performed counterfactual calculations to determine
the effects of smoking on life insurance premium payments and payouts (see chapter 2 for the conceptual explanation of the nonsmoking
smoker).

Table 8.2
Life Insurance Coverage by Smoking Status, Health and Retirement Study, Wave 1

| | Any Policy | | Cash Value Policy | | | | | Term Life Policy | | | | | |
	Has Life Insurance (%)	Mean Face Value ($)	Covered (%)	Mean Face Value ($)	Zero Premium (%)	Premium per $10K[1] Mean ($)	Median ($)	Starting Age (Years)	Covered (%)	Mean Face Value ($)	Zero Premium (%)	Premium per $10K[1] Mean ($)	Median ($)
Females													
Current	63.6	32,567	26.7	26,478	16.0	554	240	39	43.7	29,867	38.5	1332	192
Former	66.6	38,745	29.1	27,018	25.8	596	192	38	44.0	39,243	40.7	962	120
Never	65.6	41,914	28.5	31,797	22.0	422	240	38	44.3	40,517	36.8	256	120
Males													
Current	72.2	92,111	33.5	62,881	15.7	624	214	38	53.5	82,142	35.8	670	100
Former	82.9	119,873	45.1	82,478	15.7	259	175	39	61.0	101,899	37.2	229	65
Never	80.8	168,791	46.0	119,920	19.0	302	170	38	60.3	136,681	33.3	156	60
Total													
Current	68.0	65,462	30.2	47,351	15.8	594	221	38	48.7	59,708	37.0	953	120
Former	76.5	92,502	38.8	66,298	18.7	356	180	38	54.3	81,757	38.3	456	77
Never	70.9	94,645	34.7	74,213	20.6	364	200	38	49.9	81,830	35.3	213	82

1. Given nonzero premiums.

highest face values, on average, followed by former and then current smokers. The distribution was very skewed with a long right tail, with means being much higher than median values, the former being substantially influenced by a few high values.

Slightly more than one-third of term life insurance policyholders did not pay premiums at the interview date for these policies; between 15 and 20 percent of cash policyholders did not pay premiums. Respondents' median cost per $10,000 of coverage was about twice as high for cash-value policies than for term life insurance policies, and higher for women than for men.

Differences in median premiums per $10,000 of coverage between never and current smokers were relatively small. The patterns suggest that risk classification based on smoking status was by no means universal at the time the middle-aged persons first interviewed by HRS in 1992 had purchased their life insurance policies. Differences in mean premiums by smoking status were appreciably larger, suggesting that some smokers paid substantial surcharges.

At least two factors plausibly underlie this lack of variation in median premiums by smoking status. First, many respondents obtained their policies when risk rating on the basis of smoking status was unusual; on average, respondents obtained their cash policies between the ages of 38 and 39. Second, we defined smoking status as of wave 1; some persons we classified as former smokers were current smokers when they purchased their policies. Although HRS asked the age at which the respondent obtained cash-value policies, it did not request comparable information for term life insurance policies. Thus, we defined smoking status as of wave 1 for both types of insurance.

In multivariate analysis, being a current smoker was not a statistically significant predictor of having life insurance coverage, but such persons were less likely to have a cash-value policy than were never smokers, plausibly because premium surcharges for smoking are much more widespread for cash than term policies (appendix to chapter 8). On average, holding other factors constant, current smokers reported a lower face value of their life insurance policies relative to never smokers, especially for term life insurance policies. The difference in coverage amounted to about 10 percent.

Based on our computation of expected lifetime premium payments by smoking status and gender (table 8.3), female smokers, on average, paid $10,615 for term life insurance, and male smokers paid $21,835.

Table 8.3
Lifetime Expected Premiums Payments by Smoking Status (2000 Dollars)

	Term Policy		Cash Value Policy	
	Female	Male	Female	Male
Actual				
Smoker	10,615	21,835	6,940	28,471
Never smoker	12,327	26,944	9,086	42,246
Counterfactual				
Nonsmoking smoker	11,152	24,265	8,219	34,699
Never smoker	12,327	26,944	9,086	42,246
Net Effect				
Smoker	−538	−2,430	−1,278	−6,228
Never smoker	0	0	0	0

Never smokers paid $12,327 and $26,944 on average. Female and male smokers, on average, paid $6,940 and $28,471, respectively, and never smokers paid $9,086 and $42,246, respectively, for cash-value policies.

Female nonsmoking smokers would have paid $538 more for term life insurance over their lifetime, while male nonsmoking smokers would have paid $2,430 more than actual smokers. For cash-value policies, the differences were larger, $1,278 for women and $6,228 for men. Our analysis controlled for risk tolerance. Thus, the difference reflects greater demand for coverage by nonsmokers because they faced lower premiums than smokers (at least sometimes). Much of the increase in contributions reflects longer life expectancy of nonsmoking smokers than for actual smokers.

Female never smokers had the lowest expected value of lifetime benefits from life insurance policies, $1,262 (table 8.4); male smokers had the highest mean expected values, $7,175. Expected payouts were greater from term life insurance policies than cash-value policies, despite much greater lifetime contributions for the latter. Smoking substantially increased the expected payouts, especially for males. The expected lifetime benefits from life insurance policies for 24-year-old smokers were over 11 percent greater for female smokers and over 43 percent greater for male smokers, relative to counterfactual never smokers. If they had never smoked, expected payouts from life insurance policies would have been $150 lower for term insurance policies purchased by female smokers and $53 for cash policies. For males,

Table 8.4
Lifetime Expected Life Insurance Benefits by Smoking Status (2000 Dollars)

	Term Policy		Cash Value Policy	
	Female	Male	Female	Male
Actual				
Smoker	1,386	7,175	649	3,851
Never smoker	1,262	5,689	629	3,466
Counterfactual				
Nonsmoking smoker	1,236	4,864	596	2,806
Never smoker	1,262	5,689	629	3,466
Net Effect				
Smoker	150	2,311	53	1,045
Never smoker	0	0	0	0

Table 8.5
Net Effect of Smoking on Life Insurance Premium Payments and Benefits (2000 Dollars)

	Females			Males		
	Marginal Effect on		Net	Marginal Effect on		Net
	Premiums	Benefits	Cost	Premiums	Benefits	Cost
Term Life Insurance						
Smoker	−538	150	688	−2,430	2,311	4,740
Never smoker	0	0	0	0	0	0
Cash Policy						
Smoker	−1,278	53	1,331	−6,228	1,045	7,273
Never smoker	0	0	0	0	0	0

expected payouts would have been $2,311 lower from term and $1,045 from cash-value life insurance policies.

Combining reduced premium payments and increased benefits, we found that smoking imposes a substantial net cost on life insurance companies (table 8.5). Term life insurers faced additional costs of $688 for each female and $4,740 for each male smoker. Expected costs to cash-value life insurance policy issuers were $1,331 per 24-year-old female smoker and $7,273 for each male smoker, relative to non-smoking smokers of each gender. These costs are in effect transfers from nonsmokers to smokers as cross-subsidies are needed to finance this shortfall.

Conclusions and Implications

At least over the period we examined, a cross-subsidy from life insurance purchases benefited smokers at the expense of nonsmokers. The subsidy was $2,019 per female 24-year-old smoker and $12,013 per male 24-year-old smoker. This subsidy would not have occurred if insurers had universally charged smokers the actuarial value of the loss in death-contingent payments that smoking causes. Until the 1950s and 1960s, failure to charge a premium differential for smoking reflected lack of knowledge about the mortality effects of smoking. This was followed by a period of reluctance on the part of insurers to impose an actuarially fair surcharge on smokers. More recently, surcharging by life insurers has become more common.

Failing to surcharge has caused two major distortions. First, it has affected the composition of the insured, increasing the demand for life insurance among smokers and decreasing it among nonsmokers. Second, it has resulted in a subsidy of personally harmful behavior, which may encourage the activity.

Because purchase of life insurance is a private decision and possessing a life insurance policy is clearly not a universal "right," the appropriate role of the public sector is debatable. One view with which we have some sympathy is to write the cross-subsidies off as an artifact of our history. Surcharging appears to be increasingly more common, a trend that suggests no new public role.

A somewhat limited role for regulation would be to inform potential purchasers who are nonsmokers that particular insurers do not impose a surcharge. A more activist policy is premium regulation requiring insurers to impose a specific surcharge. The case for such intervention is the high cost to consumers of searching for life insurance. The case against it is the view that the market should take care of such discrepancies in premiums: a firm that surcharges should be able to attract nonsmoking policyholders from firms that do not.

Employer-provided life insurance is a special case. As with health insurance, which is a much larger fringe benefit, employers make no distinction between smokers and nonsmokers or on the basis of smoking history. Presumably, nonsmokers buy such insurance because they have no choice or because the load on such policies is so low relative to individual policies. Here, the policy issues are embedded in a larger set of policy issues related to employer provisions of fringe benefits and the favorable tax treatment of such benefits. That life insurance should be singled out as a special case seems doubtful.

Finally, several limitations of our analysis should be noted. First, our results pertain only to individuals past the age of 50. As noted previously (chapter 4), some excess smoking-related mortality occurs in the under-50 group, but excess mortality attributable to smoking is much higher in absolute terms for persons older than 50. Second, some of the persons classified as former smokers in our analysis were undoubtedly current smokers at the time they obtained their life insurance policies. However, the effect of this error in measurement is to distort the difference in subsidies between former and current smokers. Our calculations of loss are between never smokers and the others, and these differentials should not have been affected. Third, our calculations describe the historical record. Since life insurance premium-setting practices appear to have changed, smokers reaching age 50 in the future will not benefit from a cross subsidy as large as those who preceded them.

Fourth, our predictions in tables 8.3 and 8.4 show relatively large differences between lifetime contributions and lifetime benefits. There are several reasons for this discrepancy. (1) We used 1998 life tables for our predictions of mortality and probabilities of benefit receipt, but premiums were set much earlier when beneficiaries acquired their policies. Between 1980 and 1998 the life expectancy of a 40-year-old female increased by 1.3 years, that of a 40-year-old male by 2.8 years (U.S. Department of Commerce 2001, table 97), although it is not clear to what extent this may differ by-smoking status. (2) We measured premium payments per $10,000 of coverage at one point in time, and had to assume that premiums were constant throughout the duration of coverage. If premiums were lower at younger ages, which would often be true of term but not cash value life insurance, those contributions discounted by the smallest factor are overstated. (3) Finally, some of the difference between contributions and benefits may reflect the loading factor on the policies.

Appendix to Chapter 8

Table 8.A.1 shows parameter estimates from our logit analysis of having life insurance, ordinary least squares analysis of the natural logarithm of face values of life insurance, policies, and ordinary least squares estimates for starting age for cash policies.

Table 8.A.1
Results of Regression Analysis of Probability of Life Insurance Coverage and Amount of Coverage in Those with Coverage

| | | Parameter Estimates | |
Dependent Variable	Model	Current Smoker	Former Smoker
Has any life insurance (OR)	Logit[1]	1.08 [0.91; 1.27]	1.36*** [1.16; 1.60]
Has term life insurance policy (OR)	Logit[1]	1.02 [0.93; 1.12]	1.03 [0.94; 1.13]
Has cash value insurance policy (OR)	Logit[1]	0.85* [0.73; 0.99]	1.05 [0.90; 1.22]
Log face value of all policies	OLS[2]	−0.11*** (0.03)	−0.05* (0.02)
Log face value of term policies	OLS[2]	−0.12*** (0.03)	−0.05 (0.03)
Log face value of cash value policies	OLS[2]	−0.08* (0.04)	0.04 (0.04)
Starting age for cash policies (years)	OLS[2]	0.54 (0.51)	0.89 (0.51)

1. Odds ratios (OR) with 95% confidence intervals.
2. Parameter estimates with standard errors in parentheses. The models controlled for smoking, drinking, body mass index, age, working status, education, race, sex, risk preferences, marital status, kids in the household, parents alive, group policy, industry, proxy answer, and wave indicator variables. Only results for smoking variables presented.
*, **, and *** indicate statistical significance at the 0.05, 0.01, and 0.001 levels, respectively.

9

Effects of Smoking on Morbidity, Disability, and Work Loss

The health effects of smoking was a highly studied topic in the medical and public health fields during the twentieth century. The topic could be considered "mature" as we have moved into the twenty-first century.

Because our study is about the private and social cost of smoking, we are concerned about effects of smoking on morbidity, disability, and death mainly to the extent that these health outcomes influence such cost. The effects of smoking on mortality and morbidity are well known. Effects on disability are much less well established. Conceptually, the effect of smoking on the number of years a person spends in a disabled state is unclear. On the one hand, from what we know, smoking hastens the onset of disability (Sloan, Smith, and Taylor 2003). On the other hand, since smoking decreases longevity, smokers may spend less time with disabilities than do nonsmokers. This at least seems to be the hope of many smokers—to have a quick and painless death, even if death comes at a younger age (see Sloan, Smith, and Taylor 2003).

A central question in this chapter is, do smokers spend fewer or more years of life with functional impairments? And if so, what is the present value of the loss, which could be a loss or gain, the latter if smokers spend fewer years with disabilities because they die earlier?

We first review evidence on the effects of smoking on morbidity, work disability, and functional status. We then provide new evidence on the effects of smoking on morbidity and disability. Next, we describe studies that have attempted to gauge the cost of disability and morbidity. No method for valuing such loss is generally accepted; nor does a single value serve as the gold standard. With estimates of the effect of smoking on disability based on our analysis of data from the Health and Retirement Study (HRS) and the life tables of chapter 4, we quantify losses from disability. Finally, we analyze the effect of smoking on work-loss days and quantify the dollar value of such loss, conditional on the person being employed.

Previous Literature

Evidence on the Influence of Smoking on Morbidity and Functional Status

Although the strong, detrimental effects of tobacco smoking on longevity and on mortality are well known, the effect of smoking on functional status, including disability, has been less frequently studied. Furthermore, among the studies that have been done, findings are mixed.

Current and former smoking have been identified as risk factors for functional status decline (Branch 1985; House et al. 1994; Liu et al. 1995). Lacroix et al. (1993) found loss of mobility, measured in terms of ability to climb stairs and walk a half mile, after four years of follow-up to be more likely among current smokers. Nusselder et al. (2000), using data from Holland and from the American National Longitudinal Study of Aging, demonstrated compression of morbidity among nonsmokers; they live longer overall and live a shorter time with disability than do smokers. Reed et al. (1998) found not smoking cigarettes to be a predictor of "healthy aging" (surviving and remaining free of major chronic illnesses and physical and cognitive impairments). A follow-up study based on data from Sweden found that rates of hospitalization and disability resulting in governmental income support were double in smokers relative to nonsmokers; exsmokers had disability rates between the two other groups (Lannerstad 1980).

The Alameda County (California) study has provided some of the best longitudinal information regarding predictors of ill health and disability among persons age 65 and older, but for a small sample (n = 356) in a single location. However, current (relative to former or never) smoking was only slightly associated with a decline in physical functioning. After controlling for other health conditions, the effect of smoking was even smaller (Strawbridge et al. 1996). The authors concluded that this was not surprising because, by the end of the follow-up period, most smokers had either died or quit; they suggested that a healthy survivor effect explained the lack of findings.

An analysis from the Established Populations for Epidemiologic Studies of the Elderly (EPESE) (Ferrucci et al. 1999) found that never smoking and exercise were associated with longer overall life expectancy; however, never smoking was also associated with more years of disabled life expectancy. Another Scandinavian follow-up study (Biering–Sorensen et al. 1999) reported that lack of physical activity and smoking at baseline were both significant predictors for subsequent receipt of disability pension.

Smoking does not occur in a vacuum, and ample evidence indicates that other modifiable risk factors are also important in explaining ill health and disability. In an extensive systematic literature review, Stuck et al. (1999) concluded that there was evidence for a relationship between smoking, low physical activity, no alcohol consumption (relative-to-moderate use) and increased and decreased body mass index (BMI) on the one hand and decline in functional status on the other.

The results for tobacco and alcohol consumption differed from the MacArthur studies of successful aging (Seeman et al. 1994, 1995), which found that although, in a sample of high-functioning elderly aged 70–79, lower education, and lack of emotional support were related to a decline in physical function, smoking or alcohol intake were not.

A limitation of earlier studies including these modifiable risk factors lies in the specialized nature of the samples used (e.g., members of a runners' club). Differences in the sample characteristics might explain why the effects of smoking, exercise, body mass index, and alcohol consumption on the one hand, and various indicators of ill health on the other, are quite variable. Small study samples and different ways of reporting smoking, alcohol consumption, and especially exercise also explain some of this variation. Measures of morbidity, functional decline, and disability also have varied (Stuck et al. 1999). Finally, most earlier studies of disability have focused on older rather than middle-aged individuals. Due to premature mortality of smokers, samples of older persons are likely to contain proportionately more never smokers and long-term quitter and current smokers who are relatively less vulnerable to the ill effects of smoking.

Specific Diseases

The evidence of linkage between smoking and specific diseases is well known. Thus, we only provide a brief overview of the evidence here. Tobacco is particularly linked to both onset and death from numerous types of cancer and for cardiovascular disease. Even though the consensus on the negative health effects of smoking is strong, there are differences in the published literature on the magnitude of the effect or relative risk of death or disease from smoking (van de Mheen and Gunning-Schepers 1996).

Numerous cancers have been linked to smoking or exposure to tobacco smoke, including lung cancer, head and neck cancers (including cancers of the esophagus, larynx, tongue, salivary glands, lip, mouth, and pharynx), urinary bladder and kidney cancers, uterine, cervix, breast, pancreas, and colon cancers (World Health Organization 2003). The etiological fractions, the proportions of cancers attributable to smoking, vary by type of cancer, as do the relative risks of developing a cancer for smokers relative to nonsmokers.

Smokers are five to ten times more likely to develop lung cancer, 12 times more likely to develop laryngeal cancer, 27 times more likely to develop oral cancer, two to three times more likely to develop bladder cancer, twice as likely to develop colon cancer, and 60 percent more likely to develop breast cancer. Tobacco use is responsible for 80 percent of all lung cancer cases and 40 to 70 percent of bladder cancer cases in the Western world, 30 percent of cervical cancer deaths, and 30 percent of pancreatic cancer (World Health Organization 2003).

Cardiovascular disease also has been closely linked to cigarette smoking. Recently, Jacobs et al. (1999) found strong dose-response relationships between smoking and mortality from cardiovascular diseases. Smoking larger numbers of cigarettes per day increased the likelihood of both onset of disease and of death from heart disease. Doll, Peto, and Wheatley (1994) found cardiovascular mortality to be significantly affected by the smoking habits in a forty-year follow-up study of more than 30,000 British doctors, illustrating the linkage between smoking and cardiovascular disease using a longitudinal perspective. Recent declines in cardiovascular disease mortality over the decade 1980–1990 have been attributed, at least in part, to reductions in smoking prevalence among adults (Hunink et al. 1997).

Although cancer and heart disease are the leading causes of death in the United States and have been closely linked to cigarette smoking, other diseases and conditions also occur more commonly among smokers compared to nonsmokers. These other diseases range from increased occurrence of gum disease to other serious and life-threatening diseases such as chronic obstructive pulmonary disease (COPD).

Work Disability and Functional Status in Middle Age: Evidence from the HRS

Using the Health and Retirement Study, Sloan, Smith, and Taylor (2003) assessed effects of smoking and other factors on five binary (0–1) dependent variables: at least one activity of daily living (ADL) limitation; being work disabled; in fair or poor health; difficulty in climbing more than one flight of stairs; and difficulty in walking several blocks. They controlled for several other factors: age, race, marital status, education, body mass index, exercise, and alcohol consumption. The analyses were conducted separately for men and women. Because several of these variables also may have been affected by smoking (for example, amount of exercise), the estimated effects of smoking on these measures were probably conservative.

Relative to never smokers, male never smokers were 42 percent as likely to be work disabled as were current male smokers. Female never smokers were 64 percent as likely to have been work disabled as their current smoker counterparts. Never male smokers were 55 percent as likely to have an ADL limitation than were current male smokers. For females, the corresponding value was 52 percent, although this result was not statistically significant at conventional levels. For both genders, current smokers were at least twice as likely to be in fair or poor health, report difficulty in climbing more than one flight of stairs, and have difficulty in walking several blocks than were never smokers, who otherwise were comparable on several important observable characteristics.

In sum, Sloan, Smith, and Taylor's (2003) analysis of the effect of smoking on disability and health suggested that smoking is an important cause of disability, especially for men. This conclusion was strengthened because disability tended to decrease with the number of years since the person had quit smoking. In fact, disability rates of former smokers who had quit ten or fewer years before 1992 (1982–1992) tended to be more similar to disability for rates persons who said that they smoked at the time of the 1992 HRS interview; for those who had quit before 1982, disability rates more closely resembled those for never smokers.

Morbidity Attributable to Smoking: New Empirical Evidence from the National Health Interview Survey

Smoking has a long latency period, and we expected the effects of smoking to vary over a smoker's lifetime, becoming more evident in middle and old age. To assess effects both before and after age 50, we used the 1998 National Health Interview Survey (NHIS).[1] The NHIS is based on a different sample each year. By using the NHIS, coverage of all age groups was gained at a cost of losing the panel feature. Many of the health and disability variables are common to NHIS and other data sets.

Not surprisingly, morbidity rates were much higher in older age categories than for the youngest age group (table 9.1). For example, the probability of being in fair or poor health among persons aged 24–50 was 0.07. For persons in the 51–64 and the 65+ age groups, the corresponding probabilities were 0.17 and 0.26, respectively. Age-related differences for specific diseases were even greater. Affirmative responses to the question "has a doctor ever told you that you had coronary heart disease?" were almost 20 times higher for the oldest than for the youngest age group.

In the multivariate analysis (results presented in the appendix to chapter 9), current smokers were about twice as likely to be in fair or poor health than were never smokers. The probability of having emphysema was about 20 times as high for current as for never smokers aged 24–50. The probability of current smokers having emphysema was substantially elevated in the other age groups, but the relative effects between current and never smokers were half as large or less than this. Smoking had the smallest effects on the probability of having cancer, but the cancer category contained many cancers that have not been linked to smoking as well as smoking-attributable cancers. Almost without exception, risks of adverse health outcomes for current smokers were higher than for former smokers.

Based on our multivariate analysis, we estimate that 4.6 million adults aged 24+ were in fair or poor health because of their smoking in the United States in 1998 (table 9.2). 2.1 million persons had emphysema for this reason. Most of the cancers attributable to smoking occurred before age 65. Only 34,000 excess cancers were attributed to

Table 9.1
Prevalence of Fair/Poor Health and Selected Illnesses by Age, 1998 National Health Interview Survey

	Weighted Rate per 1,000	
	All Persons	Never Smokers
Age 24 through 50 (N = 17,554)		
Fair/poor health status	69.9	48.2
Ever been told by a doctor:		
—you had cancer	28.6	23.8
—you had emphysema	4.1	0.4
—you had a heart attack	8.0	4.0
—you had a stroke	4.9	2.9
—you had coronary heart disease	7.2	3.7
Age 51 through 64 (N = 5,637)		
Fair/poor health status	170.1	134.1
Ever been told by a doctor:		
—you had cancer	92.5	76.1
—you had emphysema	24.9	5.1
—you had a heart attack	48.9	21.4
—you had a stroke	31.1	24.4
—you had coronary heart disease	53.2	30.7
Age 65 and over (N = 6,289)		
Fair/poor health status	261.0	232.8
Ever been told by a doctor:		
—you had cancer	177.6	173.4
—you had emphysema	50.8	15.1
—you had a heart attack	115.6	88.8
—you had a stroke	82.5	75.3
—you had coronary heart disease	134.3	104.8

current smokers over age 65; for former smokers, there were 54,000 excess cases of cancer attributable to smoking.

Our analysis implies that 1.8 million persons among current smokers aged 24–50 were in fair or poor health because of their smoking habit in 1998. For current smokers aged 51–64, the number in fair or poor health was elevated by 1.1 million for this reason. Among current smokers 65+, nearly 700,000 persons were in fair/poor health because they smoked.

Among current smokers who were aged 24–50 in 1998, 172,000 had experienced a stroke and 383,000 had cancer because they smoked. In

Table 9.2
Persons in the United States in Fair/Poor Health and with Major Chronic Conditions because They Smoked

	Current Smokers	Former Smokers
Age 24 through 50	N = 35,844,168	N = 12,581,425
Fair/poor health status	1,841,516	122,316
Ever been told by a doctor:		
—you had cancer	383,124	80,629
—you had emphysema	361,471	31,193
—you had a heart attack	296,948	54,631
—you had a stroke	172,291	5,441
—you had coronary heart disease	256,577	66,718
Age 51 through 64	N = 9,881,525	N = 9,618,982
Fair/poor health status	1,098,237	163,914
Ever been told by a doctor:		
—you had cancer	404,080	302,375
—you had emphysema	490,192	160,910
—you had a heart attack	528,359	338,366
—you had a stroke	186,414	3,037
—you had coronary heart disease	409,994	294,782
Age 65 and over	N = 4,691,511	N = 11,681,167
Fair/poor health status	659,501	671,357
Ever been told by a doctor:		
—you had cancer	34,244	53,908
—you had emphysema	545,699	546,915
—you had a heart attack	195,629	457,661
—you had a stroke	151,237	60,313
—you had coronary heart disease	116,951	636,022

the 51–64 group, smoking-attributable disease ranged from 186,000 for stroke to 528,000 for heart attack, and for persons over age 65, the effects ranged from 34,000 for cancer to 546,000 for emphysema. Among persons 65+, there was more smoking-attributable disease among former smokers than among current smokers for emphysema, heart attack, and coronary heart disease. We found the same pattern for persons in fair or poor health at the interview date among those 65+. In many cases, the persons had probably quit following onset of the disease (Sloan, Smith, and Taylor 2003) or smokers had died from a smoking-related disease before reaching age 65.

Combining data on disease prevalence from the National Health Interview Survey with life table estimates, we calculated extra life years

Table 9.3
Extra Life Years with Illnesses Attributable to Smoking

	Female Smoker		Male Smoker	
	Expected Value	Effect of Smoking (%)[1]	Expected Value	Effect of Smoking (%)[1]
Panel A. Life Years with Condition				
Fair/poor health status	10.41	2.69 (25.8)	7.92	1.41 (17.8)
Ever been told by a doctor:				
—you had cancer	5.95	0.46 (7.7)	3.92	−0.45 (−11.4)
—you had emphysema	1.85	1.48 (79.9)	1.82	1.36 (74.5)
—you had a heart attack	2.54	0.80 (31.5)	3.59	0.80 (22.2)
—you had a stroke	1.91	0.17 (9.1)	1.90	−0.20 (−10.4)
—you had coronary heart disease	2.93	0.79 (26.8)	3.88	0.65 (16.7)
Panel B. Discounted Value (Years)				
Fair/poor health status	3.83	1.27 (33.0)	3.13	0.90 (28.7)
Ever been told by a doctor:				
—you had cancer	2.10	0.37 (17.7)	1.22	0.04 (2.9)
—you had emphysema	0.56	0.47 (83.2)	0.57	0.45 (79.1)
—you had a heart attack	0.71	0.28 (39.7)	1.10	0.37 (34.0)
—you had a stroke	0.54	0.11 (19.4)	0.55	0.02 (3.5)
—you had coronary heart disease	0.79	0.27 (33.9)	1.12	0.31 (27.2)

1. Percent of expected value.

with illnesses attributable to smoking from the vantage point of a 24-year-old person. In table 9.3, we show the extra life years, not discounted, and alternatively discounted at three percent.

On average, 24-year-old women who smoked could have expected to spend 10.41 years in fair or poor health before death (zero discount rate). Smoking at age 24 extended time in fair or poor health by 2.69 years, which is 25.8 percent of the total time spent in fair or poor health.

Since fair or poor health is much more likely to be reported by older persons, discounting makes quite a difference. Thus, for women, the discounted effect of smoking at age 24 on years in fair or poor health was only 1.27 years over a lifetime, about half the undiscounted estimate, but 33 percent of the expected time in fair or poor health for a 24-year-old female smoker. For men, the corresponding estimate was an added 0.90 years or almost 11 months in fair or poor health. Clearly, being in fair or poor health often precedes death. For smokers, death occurs earlier on average, but time in bad health is not much extended beyond that for persons who do not smoke at 24.

Smoking extended particular types of morbidity by three years or less and mostly less than a year. For example, female smokers at age 24 could have expected to spend 1.48 years extra with emphysema because they smoked, undiscounted, or 0.47 of a year, discounted. At first glance, this seems like a small effect, but for women, this effect of smoking represented 80 percent of the expected value for all women who smoked at age 24. Although emphysema onset was highly related to smoking, the prevalence of this disease was not high and thus, even smokers can expect not to spend much of their lifetimes with this disease. For men, the undiscounted extension in life with emphysema as a result of smoking was about 15 months. On a discounted basis, a 24-year-old male smoker could expect extra life with emphysema to be only about six months. For all of the diseases, the extended time with the disease resulting from being a smoker was less than a year (discounted values).

Disability Attributable to Smoking: New Empirical Evidence from the National Health Interview Survey

The NHIS requests information on various dimensions of disability. Among these, the most severe measure of disability is limitations in activities of daily living (ADLs), which involves needing help with such personal activities as bathing, dressing, eating, toileting, and so on. For persons in the 50-and-under age group, results from regression analysis indicated that the effect of smoking on the probability of getting an ADL limitation was not statistically significant at conventional levels (appendix to chapter 9). But at this age, ADL limitations were very rare (probability = 0.0052) (table 9.4). For the other age groups, being a current smoker about doubled the risk of getting an ADL limitation.

Current smokers in all two of the three age groups (24–50 and 51–64) were more likely to need help with chores, shopping, and so on —often termed "instrumental activities of daily living limitations" (IADLs) than were never smokers. For this calculation, we excluded persons with an ADL limitation. For persons 65+, results were not quite statistically significant at conventional levels. Being a former

Table 9.4
Prevalence of Persons with Limitations by Age, NHIS 1998

	Weighted Rate per 1,000	
	All Persons	Never Smokers
Age 24 through 50		
ADL limitation	5.2	4.2
IADL limitation (no ADL)	9.9	7.0
Any other limitation (no ADL or IADL)	75.0	52.7
Age 51 through 64		
ADL limitation	12.8	8.9
IADL limitation (no ADL)	29.7	23.5
Any other limitation (no ADL or IADL)	172.5	137.8
Age 65 and over		
ADL limitation	49.0	47.6
IADL limitation (no ADL)	86.4	106.2
Any other limitation (no ADL or IADL)	275.2	247.7

smoker tended to increase the probability of having IADLs, but not by as much as for current smokers.

We also assessed the effect of smoking and other factors on the probability of having any other limitations, a much more frequent occurrence than either ADL or IADL limitations (table 9.4). Smoking generally raised the probability of having a limitation other than an ADL or IADL, with the exception of former smokers 24–50 and former smokers 65+. This category of limitations included difficulties in performing any activities because of physical, mental, or emotional problems, other than ADL and IADL limitations.

In aggregate terms, based on results from our regression analysis, relative to the total adult U.S. population aged 24 and over, the effect of smoking on the number of persons with ADL limitations was rather small (table 9.5). Slightly over one-half million persons had ADL limitations due to smoking. Slightly under one-half million persons suffered an IADL attributable to smoking. Almost four million persons had limitations other than ADLs or IADLs attributable to smoking.

Valuing Losses from Disability and Morbidity

Our next step was to value loss due to disability. In contrast to death, there is virtually no empirical evidence on the topic of how much

Table 9.5
Number of Persons with Limitations because They Smoked

Limitations	Current Smokers	Former Smokers
Age 24 through 50	$N = 35,844,168$	$N = 12,581,425$
ADL limitation	77,417	1,061
IADL limitation (no ADL)	211,499	34,931
Any other limitation (no ADL or IADL)	1,776,749	114,200
Age 51 through 64	$N = 9,881,525$	$N = 9,618,982$
ADL limitation	112,511	15,371
IADL limitation (no ADL)	172,265	73,950
Any other limitation (no ADL or IADL)	815,592	227,890
Age 65 and over	$N = 4,691,511$	$N = 11,681,167$
ADL limitation	108,787	222,469
IADL limitation (no ADL)	78,571	(118,489)
Any other limitation (no ADL or IADL)	347,267	522,759

people would be willing to pay to avoid the nonpecuniary loss associated with permanent disability. A few studies have investigated the cost of disability measured in a form of loss that is readily valued in pecuniary terms, such as for medical and nursing care, equipment, and for caregiving (e.g., Trupin, Rice, and Max 1996; Rice et al. 1989). We assessed the cost of medical and nursing home care attributable to smoking in chapter 5.

Pecuniary loss cannot plausibly reflect the entire cost of disability. People care about inconvenience, dependence on others for support, inability to provide support and companionship to others, and embarrassment, all concomitant features of disability not as readily valued.

Perreira and Sloan (2002) investigated the nonpecuniary value of disability in late life, focusing on limitations in ADLs common to several diseases or conditions, such as stroke, hip fracture, and dementia. Respondents to the survey used for the analysis were asked to exclude pecuniary loss in their answers to a survey the authors constructed. Using a contingent valuation approach (see, e.g., Freeman 2003), they estimated that people would be willing to pay between $50,000 and $70,000 for each year of disability avoided after age 62 (inflated to year 2000 dollars). The same study reported a median estimate of value of life of $13 million, which is within the range of past value-of-life studies, but far above the estimates from the metanalysis studies briefly described in chapter 2. For this reason, we used the lower bound estimate of $50,000 for the nonpecuniary loss associated with limitations in ADLs in 1998 for purposes of calculating the value of the loss associated with added years of disability attributable to smoking.[2]

In our empirical analysis, we gauged additional time spent with an ADL, IADL (for persons without ADL limitations), or other limitation attributable to smoking (table 9.6). Smoking extended one's life with an ADL limitation slightly: by 0.43 years for women and by 0.12 of a year for men (undiscounted values). Smoking did not increase time with an IADL limitation. Smoking increased years of life with limitations other than ADLs or IADLs: 2.08 years for women and 0.83 for men.

Assuming the loss associated with each person with at least one ADL limitation at $50,000 per annum, a 24-year-old smoker faced an expected loss attributed to this habit (in present value terms) of $6,303 if a woman and $3,096 if a man.

For IADL limitations, we assumed an annual loss of $25,000 for each year the person has this type of limitation. This value seems plausible but not based on a prior study as was the assumed value of a year with an ADL limitation.[3] For women, the expected discounted value of the loss for smokers at age 24 was $1,735. For men, such loss was only $296. With a 3 percent discount rate, due to discounting, losses reflect when the onset of limitation occurs during the life cycle. Such limitations occur earlier in life for smokers. Losses due to any limitation other than ADLs and IADLs were $11,315 for female and $7,640 for male smokers, respectively. In total, the loss from smoking-attributable to disability was $19,353 for women and $11,032 for men.

We did not perform a comparable analysis for losses associated with morbidity. Much of such loss should be reflected in our calculations for the effect of smoking on loss due to disability, especially any limitation other than an ADL or IADL limitation variable.

Work Loss Days of Employed Persons

Mortality, morbidity, and disability from smoking result in lost output, both in households and in the workplace. Some persons discontinue work. Others continue to work, but miss work and are less productive on the job when present. Expectations of higher absenteeism among smokers may reduce smokers' employment opportunities or wages, or may result in smokers' self-selection into jobs with specific sick leave coverage (see, e.g., Viscusi and Hersch 2001). This selection process may occur prior to or after the onset of smoking-related illnesses. Work may be missed because of acute illness and chronic conditions.

Table 9.6
Extra Life Years with Disability Attributable to Smoking

	Loss per Year	Females		Males	
		Expected Value	Effect of Smoking (%)[1]	Expected Value	Effect of Smoking (%)[1]
Panel A. Life Years with Disability					
ADL limitation		1.77	0.43 (24.5)	0.97	0.12 (12.7)
IADL limitation (no ADL)		3.14	−0.32 (−10.2)	1.25	−0.35 (−27.9)
Any other limitation (no ADL or IADL)		11.16	2.08 (18.7)	8.45	0.83 (9.9)
Panel B. Discounted Value ($)					
ADL limitation	50,000	22,392	6,303 (28.1)	14,706	3,096 (21.0)
IADL limitation (no ADL)	25,000	22,012	1,735 (7.9)	10,399	296 (2.8)
Any other limitation (no ADL or IADL)	10,000	41,031	11,315 (27.6)	33,086	7,640 (23.1)
Total		85,435	19,353 (22.7)	58,192	11,032 (19.0)

1. Percent of expected value.

Previous Research

Numerous studies have documented a positive association between smoking and absenteeism. Several studies appeared within 10 years of the first surgeon general's report on smoking and health (U.S. Department of Health, Education, and Welfare 1964). Most of this research, including Lowe (1960), Coates, Bower, and Reinstein (1965), National Center for Health Statistics (1967), Smith (1970), Holcomb and Meigs (1972), Schmidt (1972), Wilson (1973), and Ferguson (1973), was reviewed by Athanasou (1975). Estimates of the effect of smoking included: 19 percent of lost work days (U.S. Public Health Service 1967); a 7 to 83 percent differential in sick days, depending on the smoking status and frequency (U.S. Public Health Service 1967; Wilson 1973); 44 percent more days restricted to bed (Ferguson 1973); a 3.8 calendar-day differential per smoker per year (Strnad, Fingerland, and Mericka 1969); and a 2 percent productivity differential due to lost work days (Strnad, Fingerland, and Mericka 1969).

Later studies confirmed these results. Parkes (1983) reported 56 to 91 percent more absent episodes for smokers relative to nonsmokers. Parkes (1987) analyzed the joint effects of obesity and smoking and found that smokers of optimal weight had higher rates of absence than 90 percent of nonsmokers. Bertera (1991) estimated 0.9 excess illness days per smoker per year, relative to nonsmokers, in a study of more than 45,000 employees. Leigh (1995) estimated 59 to 79 percent higher absence rates among male smokers and 11 to 36 percent higher absence rates for female smokers relative to never smokers. Bush and Wooden (1995) reported 66 percent increased probabilities of absence for male smokers and 23 percent for female smokers. Additional years of smoking increased the probability of absence by 1.2 percent per year. Vistnes (1997) found that female smokers were 28 percent more likely than never smokers to be absent some time during calendar year 1987, but male smokers were not significantly more likely to have been absent.

Quitting smoking reversed the effects of smoking on absenteeism over time (Bush and Wooden 1995; Wooden and Bush 1995). Former smokers who quit 20 or more years ago were 4.5 times less likely to be absent from work compared to persons who quit smoking in the previous year. With the exception of Parkes (1987), all previous studies of smoking and absenteeism used cross-sectional data in their analyses.

Table 9.7
Effect of Smoking on Work Loss and Absenteeism

	Female Smoker	Male Smoker
Panel A. Undiscounted (days)		
Actual work loss	201	450
Nonsmoking smoker	157	171
Effect of smoking	45	280
Panel B. Discounted at 3% to age 24		
Actual work loss	112	99
Nonsmoking smoker	85	70
Effect of smoking	27	29
Value of work loss[1]	$2,658	$3,747

1. Daily earnings of $98.20 for females, and $129.20 for males.
Source: Median 2000 values from U.S. Department of Commerce, 2002, table 613.

Effects of Smoking on Worker Absenteeism: New Findings Based on the National Health Interview Survey

Based on findings from our regression analysis (see appendix to chapter 9), we estimated that a man who smoked at age 24 would have a total of 450 work loss days between 24 and 64 of which 280 lost days were attributable to smoking (table 9.7). This large number of smoking-attributable days was highly concentrated in the later working years. Discounted at three percent, the present value of these work loss days was only 99, and the effect of smoking was only 29 days. The total number of workdays lost by women was less than half that for males but was concentrated at younger ages. Overall, for adult women, the discounted marginal effect was almost identical to that for men, 27 days.

We valued work days lost at the mean earnings per hour in 2000 (U.S. Department of Commerce 2002).[4] We did not use different wage rates of men and women. In present-value terms, the discounted loss at age 24 from work absences was $2,658 for women and $3,747 for men. If we had distinguished between male and female wage rates, the differences would have been larger but still quite small relative to some of the other smoking-attributable losses, including earnings losses.

Discussion and Conclusions

As with mortality, the impact of smoking on occurrence of chronic diseases is well researched. But to our knowledge, no prior study has assessed effects over the life cycle. By contrast to mortality and morbidity, relatively little research has been conducted on the effects of smoking on disability and on work-loss days. In this chapter, we reviewed the research that had been done and presented findings from our own research.

These are this chapter's major findings. At all ages, being a smoker increased the probability of self-reporting that one is in fair or poor health. Although this is a self-report, people who state that they are in fair or poor health are more likely to experience adverse health events in the future, including higher mortality (Idler and Kasl 1995). We found that being a current smoker led to higher rates of various chronic conditions, including cancer, emphysema, and various forms of cardiovascular disease. In absolute terms, smoking has more serious effects later in the life cycle. Effects are long lasting, as demonstrated by the large impacts on the numbers of former smokers over the age of 65 who had various smoking-related illnesses.

Although the finding that smoking is bad for you is "old hat," to our knowledge, no previous study calculated the impacts of smoking on extra years with particular forms of morbidity. Because smoking also decreases survival, it is possible that a smoker spends less time with particular chronic conditions than does an otherwise comparable non-smoker. In fact, smoking did increase life years with particular chronic conditions. Among the indicators we studied, the largest increase was for years in fair or poor health, three years on a discounted basis for women and about a year for men. Overall, effects of smoking on years with specific smoking-related diseases were trivial—much less than an extra year. Being in fair or poor health is a much more general measure and may capture symptoms before a definitive diagnosis is made. Discounting at three percent reduced the present value of smoking-attributable years with a chronic condition. Some researchers have concluded that people apply much larger discount rates to health risks (see e.g., Moore and Viscusi 1990a,b). Using a discount rate above three percent would have reduced the present values below those reported in the chapter.

Similarly, smoking increased the probability of having a limitation in activities of daily living, or in instrumental activities of daily living, or having any other limitation in market or in household work. Relationships were more distinct for current than for former smokers. For men, smoking increased the various forms of disability by less than a year over the life cycle. For women, by contrast, female smokers at age 24 could expect an increase in limitations other than limitations in activities of daily living and in instrumental activities of daily living of about two years on average.

We computed the present value of the loss attributable to disability caused by smoking. We interpreted loss associated with increased disability as a nonpecuniary loss. According to our calculations, a female smoker at age 24 could expect a loss due to disability of about $19,000 on average. For men, the loss was about $11,000.

Of course, these losses reflect the assumptions we made about the value of a life year. Readers who are more comfortable with other assumptions can easily compute alternative values. Doubling the underlying dollar values per life year would double our estimates and so on.

In chapter 6, we reported as attributable to smoking about a $38,000 loss in Social-Security-taxable earnings up to age 65 for men and a trivial amount of loss (about $600) for women. In this chapter, we reported estimates of the effects of smoking on days lost from work. For men, the estimated loss from such sick days was less than a tenth the estimated loss in taxable earnings. For women, the loss from sick days, though higher than for taxable earnings loss, was not large either, about $2,000 over the working life course.

In chapter 11, we will use these estimates to compute the private and social cost of smoking. Our results on the influence of smoking on morbidity and disability have other potential applications as well.

In focus groups of smokers and former smokers (Sloan, Smith, and Taylor 2003), some of us found that messages about the harmful effects of smoking on disability and on the burden to others were more salient than was information about adverse effects of this behavior on survival. Smokers did not seem to dread premature mortality, especially if death were quick and painless. However, they did dread the prospect of living in a nursing home or living in the community but being dependent on others for performing basic personal tasks, such as bathing and eating.

If we had found that smoking increased life years with ADL limitations, this result might have been used in formulating information messages to encourage smoking cessation. That smoking increases ADL dependencies by less than a life year would probably not make a very effective message. Because we required empirical evidence over the life course, we combined cross-sectional estimates of the effects of smoking on ADL dependencies and other limitations from the National Health Interview Survey with our life tables showing effects of smoking on longevity. In the future, as the initial Health and Retirement Survey sample ages, it should be possible to obtain more accurate longitudinal information on the effect of smoking on dependencies. But in the meantime, our estimates serve to warm antismoking advocates that, although smoking is bad for you, it is not necessarily bad for you across the board.

Appendix to Chapter 9

Using logit analysis, we assessed effects of smoking on health limitations and self-reports of health in the adult population, defined as 24 and over. We stratified the sample into three age groups, 24–50, 51–64, and 65 and over. The dependent variables for health were: (1) fair or poor health versus good-to-excellent health; and (2) ever told by a physician that person had cancer, emphysema, heart attack, stroke, or coronary heart disease (table 9.A.1). Virtually all of the odds ratios for the current smoker variable were statistically significant at conventional levels. Most of the odds ratios for former smoker were statistically significant at conventional levels. With one exception (out of 18 regressions), the odds ratio for current smoker exceeded its counterpart for former smoker. The exception was for coronary heart disease among person over age 65. As noted at the bottom of the table, we controlled for other potential determinants of fair/poor health and prevalence of chronic diseases.

Table 9.A.1
Odds of Poor Health and Selected Illnesses by Age and Smoking Status

	Odds Ratios Relative to Never Smokers	
	Current Smokers	Former Smokers
Age 24 through 50 (N = 17,554)		
Fair/poor health status	2.11***	1.26
	[1.79; 2.49]	[0.98; 1.64]
Ever been told by a doctor:		
—you had cancer	1.49**	1.27
	[1.17; 1.89]	[0.90; 1.81]
—you had emphysema	19.66***	5.71*
	[6.86; 56.37]	[1.45; 22.47]
—you had a heart attack	2.63***	1.77
	[1.65; 4.20]	[0.95; 3.29]
—you had a stroke	2.35**	1.14
	[1.33; 4.16]	[0.53; 2.45]
—you had coronary heart disease	2.73***	2.05*
	[1.71; 4.36]	[1.01; 4.13]
Age 51 through 64 (N = 5,637)		
Fair/poor health status	2.25***	1.20
	[1.84; 2.76]	[0.94; 1.53]
Ever been told by a doctor:		
—you had cancer	1.73***	1.51**
	[1.31; 2.28]	[1.16; 1.96]
—you had emphysema	9.46***	3.97***
	[4.82; 18.57]	[1.93; 8.14]
—you had a heart attack	3.45***	2.55***
	[2.38; 5.00]	[1.70; 3.83]
—you had a stroke	1.75**	1.01
	[1.17; 2.61]	[0.67; 1.53]
—you had coronary heart disease	2.44***	1.98***
	[1.73; 3.43]	[1.40; 2.80]
Age 65 and over (N = 6,289)		
Fair/poor health status	2.19***	1.44***
	[1.80; 2.66]	[1.22; 1.71]
Ever been told by a doctor:		
—you had cancer	1.06	1.03
	[0.83; 1.34]	[0.86; 1.23]
—you had emphysema	8.47***	3.97***
	[5.73; 12.52]	[2.75; 5.75]
—you had a heart attack	1.54**	1.46**
	[1.18; 2.01]	[1.16; 1.84]
—you had a stroke	1.53**	1.07
	[1.16; 2.03]	[0.84; 1.38]
—you had coronary heart disease	1.28*	1.58***
	[1.00; 1.64]	[1.28; 1.95]

Note: Odds ratios with 95% confidence intervals from logistic regression models controlling for age, gender, race, marital status, education, income less than $25,000 per year, alcohol consumption, and body mass index.
*, **, and *** indicate statistical significance at the 0.05, 0.01, and 0.001 levels, respectively.

Table 9.A.2
Odds of Functional Limitations by Age and Smoking Status

	Weighted Rate per 1,000		Odds Ratios Relative to Never Smokers	
	All Persons	Never Smokers	Current Smokers	Former Smokers
Age 24 through 50				
ADL limitation	5.2	4.2	1.44 [0.90; 2.30]	1.03 [0.47; 2.25]
IADL limitation (no ADL)	9.9	7.0	1.72** [1.20; 2.47]	1.43 [0.73; 2.77]
Any other limitation (no ADL or IADL)	75.0	52.7	1.95*** [1.69; 2.24]	1.21 [0.96; 1.52]
Age 51 through 64				
ADL limitation	12.8	8.9	2.21* [1.18; 4.16]	1.20 [0.52; 2.78]
IADL limitation (no ADL)	29.7	23.5	1.81** [1.24; 2.65]	1.45 [0.91; 2.30]
Any other limitation (no ADL or IADL)	172.5	137.8	1.83*** [1.51; 2.22]	1.24* [1.01; 1.53]
Age 65 and over				
ADL limitation	49.0	47.6	1.95** [1.30; 2.93]	1.71*** [1.27; 2.30]
IADL limitation (no ADL)	86.4	106.2	1.32 [0.99; 1.76]	0.82 [0.63; 1.06]
Any other limitation (no ADL or IADL)	275.2	247.7	1.56*** [1.28; 1.90]	1.32*** [1.12; 1.56]

Note: Odds ratios with 95% confidence intervals from logistic regression models controlling for age, gender, race, marital status, education, income less than $25,000 per year, alcohol consumption, and body mass index.
*, **, and *** indicate statistical significance at the 0.05, 0.01, and 0.001 levels, respectively.

Table 9.A.3

Parameter Estimates from Two-Part Models Predicting Work Loss Days per Person per Year[1]

	Ages 24–50		Ages 51–64	
	Females	Males	Females	Males
Probability of Any Work Loss (Odds Ratios)				
Current	1.08	1.22***	0.95	0.93
	[0.97; 1.21]	[1.09; 1.36]	[0.77; 1.17]	[0.71; 1.20]
Former	1.19	1.30**	1.16	0.86
	[0.99; 1.42]	[1.08; 1.56]	[0.90; 1.48]	[0.67; 1.10]
Conditional Number of Days (Log) (Parameter Estimates)				
Current	0.27***	0.29***	0.28*	0.40**
	(0.04)	(0.05)	(0.12)	(0.13)
Former	0.02	0.07	0.18	0.26
	(0.07)	(0.07)	(0.15)	(0.14)

1. Relative to never smoker.

*, **, and *** indicate statistical significance at the 0.05, 0.01, and 0.001 levels, respectively.

Government intervention is widely accepted for the markets in which externalities are present. In this context, potential externalities of concern are the adverse effects of smoking on the health of others as well as the financial externalities, described in chapters 5 through 8. Here our focus is on externalities in the health domain, although such externalities, through their effects on health and longevity, may also generate financial externalities.

In general, economists treat costs imposed on others within the same household as internal. The implicit assumption is that members of the same household arrive at some mutually beneficial solution through explicit or implicit bargaining (see Manser and Brown 1980; McElroy and Horney 1981; Chiappori, Fortin, and Lacroix 2002). In this sense, the costs of smoking as well as other "bads" are internalized.

Family members, especially spouses, routinely engage in trades. For example, the husband may want a new sports car. The wife may want to travel to Florida with an old college roommate. Myriads of trades are made over the course of a marriage. Even if a habit such as smoking by one spouse negatively affects the other, there are probably other trades that compensate for this loss.[1] If marriage partners have better outside options net of the cost of dissolving the marriage, the marriage dissolves.

Alternatively, rather than engage in trades, spouses take account of each other's behavior, but decisions are made separately in noncoordinated fashion. How smoking enters the decision depends in large part on the nature of smoking's external effect. A spouse may derive pleasure from smoking with one's spouse. A nonsmoking spouse may hate the smell or fear adverse health effects and therefore spend less time at home. Altruistic individuals may be concerned about the welfare of their spouse. For example, individuals may be concerned about the health or life expectancy of their spouses. Such pure consumption externalities (the husband gains utility from the wife's health and conversely) should directly affect one's own decisions about consumption of addictive goods, such as tobacco.[2]

Clearly, there are many possibilities. Currently, there is no empirical evidence on this topic, especially as applied to addictive goods. But the bottom line is that, in general, economists regard the costs and benefits of smoking within a household as internal. This position seems more untenable in the case of children, particularly unborn children who are in no position to bargain or even to act noncooperatively, unless perhaps one argues that a parent represents the interests of the child.

The view that costs and benefits of smoking within households are internal is not shared by some others outside the economics profession. A law review article by Hanson and Logue (1998) provides some humor on this point, perhaps not intentionally (box 10.1).

Economists could argue that Hanson and Logue exclude the possibility of bargaining among spouses to the extent that smoking by one spouse has bad effects on the other. Or in some cases, the spouse may enjoy the conversation with the smoking spouse over a cup of coffee.

Box 10.1
Are Costs of Smoking Incurred by Family Members Internal?

"Even if the assumption that family costs are fully internal to individual decision makers were plausible with respect to other types of costs, it is implausible with respect to the costs of smoking. If the costs and benefits of smoking were truly internalized across members of a family, one would expect nonsmoking members of a family to be more encouraging of those family members who smoke. Yet one does not hear statements of the following sort from family members of smokers: 'It's fine that my spouse (or child or parent) smokes. In light of the fact that she has taken into account the costs to herself, to me, and to other family members, it must be that she is benefiting greatly from the cigarettes. I would not want to deprive her of that tremendous pleasure. Indeed, given the net benefits, I am glad that she smokes.' Similarly, it would be astonishing to hear a smoker say: 'It's worth it to me to smoke even when I consider the costs to my loved ones of my dying earlier than I otherwise would and of their dying earlier than they otherwise would.' It is likely that neither nonsmokers nor smokers frame the matter in those terms because smokers do not, in fact, fully internalize the costs that they impose on others" (Hanson and Logue 1998, p. 1238).

On the other hand, society may have a negative view of the adverse health effects of smoking on spouses and other family members, rejecting the notion that such effects are private matters. First, society at large shares in the costs of caring for individuals inflicted with smoking-related diseases. Second, people may be altruistic. When a man or women dies prematurely or a child is permanently impaired by a mother's smoking during her pregnancy, people may feel worse off.

A few activities, particularly smoking in the workplace and other public places, impose externalities, but the most important effects on others are likely to be on members of the same household. Such persons are likely to spend more time with the smoker than do coworkers or customers in a restaurant, bar, or other public place. Given the controversy about whether secondary smoke involving spouses is external or internal, we will take an agnostic approach—estimating such cost and considering it as a mixed category somewhere between external and internal, classifying it as "quasi-external cost."

We have three objectives in this chapter. First, we briefly review empirical evidence on the health harms of secondhand smoke or "environmental tobacco smoke" (ETS). Second, we present new results on effects of smoking on others within the same household, using data from the Health and Retirement Study (HRS). The HRS is unique in providing identical information on both spouses/partners. Thus, even though the sample is limited to mature adults, this feature more than offsets the limitation for an analysis of effects of secondary smoke on adults. Third, following approaches described for mortality (chapter 4) and disability (chapter 9), we quantify losses associated with secondhand smoke within households. Since HRS data are unique in providing identical information on both spouses, it is not possible to conduct a parallel analysis with other data on younger persons.

What Is ETS?

Mainstream and Sidestream Smoke

ETS is a mixture of sidestream smoke and mainstream smoke. Mainstream smoke is the smoke inhaled and exhaled by the smoker. Sidestream smoke is the smoke emitted from a smoldering cigarette between puffs. On average, ETS is approximately 85 percent sidestream and 15 percent mainstream. Although the former type is diluted compared the latter, it contains most of the same toxic and carcinogenic compounds as mainstream smoke, some in even higher concentration. The major cited reasons for the higher concentration of some toxins are (1) sidestream smoke is not filtered, (2) a lower burning temperature during the generation of sidestream smoke results in a less complete combustion of tobacco, and (3) oxygen deficiency during smoldering results in a strong reducing environment (U.S. Department of Health and Human Services 1991). Furthermore, exposure to ETS can have disproportionate health consequences because it continues for the entire duration of a person's presence in a contaminated environment. By contrast, a smoker's exposure to mainstream smoke is limited to the time it takes to smoke a cigarette. However, people exposed to environmental smoke may receive a lower dose of contamination per unit of time to which they are exposed than do smokers.

Exposure

Most epidemiological studies identify exposure from self-reports, and limit the measurement to broad categories, such as whether a person lives with a smoking spouse or is exposed to ETS at work. Few studies have inquired specifically about duration of exposure. Some studies have used biomarkers, particularly nicotine and its metabolite cotinine, to determine the presence and amount of exposure (Ney and Gale 1989). Cotinine is used in the National Health and Nutrition Examination Survey (NHANES); however, due to its short half-life, only very recent exposure is detected, and its measurement thus cannot be used to evaluate chronic exposure. Survey responses to questions about any exposure within the family or at work remain the most widely used measures of ETS exposure.

Pirkle et al. (1996) published national estimates of ETS exposure from the third NHANES (NHANES III, conducted in 1988–1991). According to this study, exposure to ETS is very widespread, but estimates differ substantially, depending on whether survey responses or biomarkers are used to measure exposure. Although 63 percent of nonsmokers reported no exposure at either home or work, 88 percent of nonsmokers had detectable levels of serum cotinine, suggesting that almost 90 percent of the nonsmoking public has been exposed to levels of tobacco smoke that are detectable through this biomarker. Although most exposure measurements have focused on exposure in the home, a recent review of empirical evidence (Jaakola and Samet 1999) concluded that mean exposure levels at work are relatively similar to mean exposure levels at home, but that maximum exposure levels are higher at the office. Unfortunately, none of the studies of exposure levels at work derived its results from a representative sample of the U.S. population, making it difficult to determine the generalizability of these results.

The Health Effects of ETS

Evolution of ETS as a Public Policy Concern

The link between ETS and poor health has been established more con-clusively in recent years, but relationships were noted in the early 1970s, not long after the first report of the surgeon general on smoking and health (U.S. Department of Health, Education, and Welfare 1964). Attention to ETS increased as evidence mounted that tobacco smoke had negative health consequences not only for smokers but also for nonsmokers. Official pronouncements suggesting that policy interven-tion was warranted began in the 1970s. In 1971, the U.S. surgeon gen-eral called for a national "Bill of Rights for the Nonsmoker"; the 1972 surgeon general's report was the first report to review the effects of ETS; in 1973, Arizona passed the first statewide ban on smoking in public places; and by 1975, ten states had passed legislation regulating smoking in public places (see U.S. Department of Health and Human Services 2000a for a historical review).

Two major reports on ETS were released in 1986 after several studies in the 1970s and early 1980s documented an association between ex-posure to ETS and various health outcomes. The National Research Council released "Environmental Tobacco Smoke: Measuring Expo-sures and Assessing Health Effects" (National Research Council 1986) and the eighteenth surgeon general's report on smoking and health, *The Health Consequences of Involuntary Smoking*, highlighted the risks of ETS (U.S. Department of Health and Human Services 1986). This re-port resulted from a review of the empirical evidence available at the time, concluding that the increased risk of lung cancer for nonsmokers as a result of exposure to ETS was nearly 30 percent above their risk in the absence of ETS. Both reports concluded unambiguously that pas-sive smoking is a cause of lung cancer as well as other diseases in otherwise healthy nonsmokers.

Since the release of these two landmark reports, numerous studies have analyzed and quantified the extent of the exposure, health consequences, and made estimates of the cost of ETS more precise. This has become a major research and policy issue for the tobacco industry, antismoking lobbyists, and economists interested in the social cost of smoking. Passive smoking has become the "true battleground" in the public relations and policy war surrounding tobacco (Hirschhorn 2000), because it represents the realization of harm by persons who did not themselves smoke. The evidence indicated that secondary smoking-related harms were not only a result of lifestyle choices but also constituted a contagion in the classic public health sense. Most studies concluding ETS is not harmful to health were written by authors with tobacco industry affiliations (Barnes and Bero 1998).

Specific Adverse Health Effects of ETS

The primary effects of ETS established in the empirical literature to date have been on rates of lung cancer and heart disease, adverse reproductive outcomes, and other negative health effects on young children.

The first adverse health outcome attributed to ETS was lung cancer (U.S. Department of Health, Education, and Welfare 1972), which also has been the most frequently studied health effect of ETS. In a recent reanalysis of the epidemiological evidence on passive smoking and lung cancer, Hackshaw, Law, and Wald (1997) summarized results of 39 studies published from 1982–1997. They reported an increased risk of lung cancer for lifelong nonsmokers who lived with a smoking spouse—24 percent for women and 37 percent for men—relative to never smokers who did not live with a smoking spouse. The article focused on women, whose risks had been examined by the vast majority of studies. They also reported a dose-response relationship between the amount of exposure and the risk of lung cancer—a 23 percent increase in the probability of contracting lung cancer for every 10 cigarettes smoked per day by the husband, an indication of the effects of ETS intensity. Similarly, increased duration of exposure raised the risk of lung cancer; every 10 years of exposure increased the risk by 11 percent.

ETS exposure at work also leads to an elevated risk of lung cancer. Wells (1998) reviewed 14 studies; based on the five that satisfied minimum criteria on study quality, the combined relative risk for persons exposed to ETS at work was 1.39. Another review, by Brown (1999), based on a review of 14 studies of ETS and lung cancer, placed the risk of workplace exposure at a somewhat lower level—a 25 percent elevated increased risk at the mean and a 91 percent increased risk at the ninety-fifth percentile.

These reviews, and most individual empirical studies, support a 1992 report by the U.S. Environmental Protection Agency (EPA) that concluded that ETS is a known human carcinogen responsible for about 3,000 lung cancer deaths per year in nonsmokers (U.S. Environmental Protection Agency 1992) out of about 145,000 lung cancer deaths that year in the United States. However, the strength of the evidence regarding the effect of ETS on lung cancer differs by gender. The surgeon general's report entitled, *Women and Smoking*, concluded that "exposure to ETS is a cause of lung cancer among women who never smoked." (U.S. Department of Health and Human Services 2001). To date, the evidence on lung cancer in men has not been sufficient to warrant the same conclusion.

In recent years, the focus of studies on effects of secondhand smoke has shifted to heart disease. Taken as a group, heart diseases are much more prevalent than lung cancer, and even slightly elevated risks may translate into a much larger number of affected persons. While the 1986 surgeon general's report on smoking and health (U.S. Department of Health and Human Services 1986) concluded that insufficient evidence was available to establish a relationship, the 2001 *Women and Smoking* report, based on more recent evidence, found a causal relationship between spousal ETS exposure and coronary heart disease mortality among female nonsmokers.

A review by He et al. (1999) of 18 epidemiological studies concluded that nonsmokers exposed to ETS had a 25 percent greater risk of coronary heart disease then did nonexposed nonsmokers. The authors also found a significant dose-response relationship; that is, the risk of heart disease was higher when nonsmokers were exposed to the smoke from a pack or more daily as compared to less than a pack per day. The risk also increased according to the duration of exposure.[3] Law, Morris, and Wald (1997) evaluated the relative risk of ischemic heart disease and found that, at age 65, exposure to ETS increased the risk of ischemic heart disease by 30 percent, an effect slightly smaller than that from actively smoking one cigarette per day. Controlling for differential dietary habits of persons living with smokers, the increased risk fell from 30 to 23 percent.

Based on 17 case control and cohort studies investigating the relationship between spousal ETS exposure and coronary events and mortality, Thun, Henley, and Apicella (1999) found very similar effects on nonsmoking spouses, in analysis of effects separately by gender, type of study (cohort or case control), type of outcome (fatal or nonfatal), and country (United States or other countries). In most cases, risks increased with the spouse's smoking frequency, and risks were greater when spouses continued to smoke than when they quit smoking.

Of two similar reviews of studies on workplace exposure and cardiovascular disease, one derived comparable conclusions (Steenland 1999), although another did not (Kawachi and Colditz 1999). Even though five of six studies reviewed in the latter article showed elevated risks, none of the differences were statistically significant. Steenland's estimate of added risk translates into an excess risk of death by age 70 of 7 per 1,000, and 1,710 excess ischemic heart disease deaths per year among nonsmoking U.S. workers aged 35–69.

Howard and Wagenknecht (1999) investigated mechanisms underlying harmful effects of ETS. They summarized effects of ETS on several important determinants of incident coronary events, finding a significant association between ETS and the thickness of the carotid artery, arterial endothelial function, and the presence of silent cerebral infarctions.[4]

Other diseases and conditions linked to exposure to ETS include various negative reproductive outcomes; respiratory illnesses and reduced lung function, particularly in exposed young children; and tissue irritation of the eyes, nose, throat, and airway. Passive smoking also has subtle but substantial effects on the respiratory health of nonsmoking adults, including coughing, phlegm production, chest discomfort, and reduced lung function (U.S. Department of Health and Human Services 1986; U.S. Environmental Protection Agency 1992). You et al. (1999) reported findings of an increased risk of ischemic stroke for spouses of smokers compared with spouses of nonsmokers.

Effects on Children

The literature contains a considerable body of research on effects of passive smoke on infant birth weight, providing some evidence of a harmful effect. Low birth weight (LBW) is caused mainly by intrauterine growth retardation (Chiriboga 1993). Dejin–Karlsson et al. (1998) found that nonsmoking women exposed to passive smoke early in pregnancy are at double the risk of delivering a small-for-gestational-age (SGA) infant. Rebagliato, Florey, and Bolumar (1995) found that infants' mean birth weight was 87.3 grams (g) lower for infants of mothers with cotinine levels greater than 1.7 nanograms/ milliliters (ng/mL) as compared to those with cotinine levels of 0–0.5 nanograms/milliliters. The study also found a negative association with the duration of maternal passive smoke exposure in public places. Fortier, Marcoux, and Brisson (1994) found a relationship between SGA and passive smoke exposure at work but not at home.

Studies also have been performed that examine the specific risk caused by paternal passive smoke. Martinez, Wright, and Taussig (1994) found that, on average, newborns of nonsmoking mothers whose fathers smoked more than 20 cigarettes per day were 88 grams lighter than infants not exposed to smoking. Zhang and Ratcliffe (1993) found a 30 grams deficit after adjustment for gestational age, parity, maternal age, and occupation.

Low birth weight has important long-run effects. Recent empirical research by Behrman and Rosenzweig (2003) has established a link between birth weight and various outcomes as a adult. For example, persons who were LBW babies earned lower wages as adults.

Although these studies appear to support a harmful effect of paternal passive smoke, some researchers have proposed other theories. Paternal smoking before conception may cause male germ cell mutations, and some drugs can also be transmitted in seminal fluid. These possibilities may complicate the studies of passive smoke and birth weight (Olshan and Savitz 1995), especially because smokers are more likely to use illicit drugs.

The danger posed to a fetus by exposure to tobacco smoke does not end once it leaves the womb. Exposure to tobacco smoke both before and after birth has been irrefutably shown to cause Sudden Infant Death Syndrome (SIDS) in children of smokers. SIDS is the diagnosis given to the sudden, inexplicable death of a seemingly healthy infant, usually between the age of one week and one year. Although the incidence of SIDS has steadily decreased in recent years, it still affected 6 in 10,000 infants in the United States in 1998, down from 15 in 10,000 in 1980 (American SIDS Institute 2001).[5]

Controlling for socioeconomic status and other risk factors, maternal smoking has been consistently shown to be one of the leading causes of SIDS. In one review of 34 studies, 33 found elevated probabilities of SIDS associated with maternal smoking (Cooke 1998). Conservative estimates are that smoking doubles the risk, but more extreme findings claim infants of smoking mothers are at nearly five times the risk for developing SIDS.

Paternal smoking also increases the risk of SIDS to the infant, as does smoking by anyone in the household (Mitchell et al. 1993; Klonhoff–Cohen et al. 1995; Blair et al. 1996). Paternal smoking in isolation (after adjustment for maternal smoking and other factors) has been shown to increase the risk of SIDS by a factor of between 37 and 246 percent. These are similar to the odds ratios associated with an infant's risk of SIDS with a smoking father and nonsmoking mother (Nicholl and O'Cathain 1992; Mitchell et al. 1993; Blair et al. 1996). A biological gradient directly relating the number of cigarettes smoked by members of the household to risk of SIDS to the infant has established a dose-response relationship (Mitchell et al. 1993). Klonhoff–Cohen et al. (1995) concluded that infants exposed to more than 20 cigarettes per day from any household smoker are 22.7 times more likely to die of SIDS than infants in nonsmoking households.

Studies conducted as early as 1974 confirmed the connections between incidences of infant pneumonia and bronchitis and parental smoking (Charlton 1994). Studies of the relationship between exposure to ETS (recently measured by cotinine levels in the blood rather than parental reports) have associated passive smoking with conditions ranging from asthma to middle-ear disease to low weight-for-age. The widespread and involuntary exposure of children in particular to ETS has been shown to induce and aggravate many conditions, most of them respiratory. Since 43 percent of American children are exposed to ETS in their own homes (Pirkle et al. 1996), and nearly all are exposed outside of their homes, the health effects of ETS on morbidity are large.

Respiratory complications associated with passive smoking are not only harmful but also expensive. Although not all of these cases are attributable to tobacco smoke, the aforementioned U.S. Environmental Protection Agency report estimated that between 150,000 and 200,000 lower respiratory tract infections in children under the age of 18 months are caused annually by ETS, with between 7,500 and 15,000 of them leading to hospital stays (U.S. Environmental Protection Agency 1992).

Asthma affects almost 9 percent of children (National Center for Health Statistics 2003) and has been linked to passive smoking by many studies (Charlton 1994). Asthmatic children who are exposed to ETS have emergency room visits for acute exacerbations of their asthma with greater frequency than those who are not commonly exposed to ETS; they also display an increase in airway reactivity and decrease in pulmonary function (Chilmonczyk et al. 1990). Wheezing affects half of all children by the age of 6 through either asthma or wheezy bronchitis (Csonka et al. 2000). Another study found that the incidence of wheezing (attributed to wheezy bronchitis) increased by 14 percent when the mother smoked more than four cigarettes per day and by 49 percent when the mother smoked more than 15 cigarettes (Neuspiel et al. 1989).

Even though the aggravation of childhood respiratory conditions by passive smoking is generally accepted, the question of whether passive smoking can cause such conditions has not been quite so conclusive. Soyseth, Kongerud, and Boe (1995) found that postnatal maternal smoking induced asthma in some children, but did not induce (only aggravated) other respiratory conditions, such as bronchial hyper-responsiveness. Other studies have also concluded that exposure to ETS may put children at a greater risk for developing asthma (Weiss et al. 1980; Weitzman and Sobol 1990; Martinez, Cline, and Burrows 1992).

Passive smoking has nonrespiratory consequences as well. Having a smoking parent has been shown to put a child at greater risk for requiring surgery for otitis media, an inflammatory process in the inner ear, and a very common reason for seeking ambulatory care (Hinton 1989). As early as 1985, a study found that two-thirds of 2-to-3-year-olds with three or more attacks of otitis media had smoking parents, yet only one-third of children with no attacks had parents who smoked (Pukander et al. 1985). Etzel et al. (1992) estimated that one-third of all cases of otitis media with effusion in children are caused by parental smoking.

Passive smoking has also been associated with reduced weight and slowed growth. One study of children with cystic fibrosis (who, due to their existing chronic pulmonary disease, were expected to have a more pronounced reaction to ETS) compared their health upon entry to and exit from a two-week smoke-free summer camp (Rubin 1990). The study found that the children who came from homes in which they were exposed to ETS gained significantly less weight than their counterparts who came from smoke-free homes, implying that passive smoking had been impeding their weight gain. Other studies have also established the connection between exposure to ETS and weight reduction as well as growth retardation (Wingerd and Schoen 1974; Rona et al. 1981; Berkey et al. 1984; Rona, Chinn, and Florey 1985;

Dunn et al. 1976); for instance, children whose mothers smoked while pregnant are an average of 1 to 2 centimeters shorter than children whose mothers did not (Rush et al. 1992).

Finally, child health in general (as measured by days of school absence due to sickness) has also been associated with passive smoking. Data from National Health and Nutrition Examination Survey III (NHANES III) showed that high cotinine levels were associated with six or more days of school absence in the past year (Mannino et al. 2001). Furthermore, the presence of a pack-a-day smoker in the house has been shown to increase sick days by 20 percent (Ostro 1989).

ETS compounds also have been linked to cancers other than lung cancers, particularly in children. The 2001 surgeon general's report on *Smoking and Health* reviewed evidence on adverse pregnancy outcomes, including lower fetal length, lower birth weight, perinatal and neonatal mortality, and congenital malformations (U.S. Department of Health and Human Services 2001). The results are not very robust across studies, but suggest somewhat elevated rates of adverse events for women exposed to ETS relative to women who were not exposed.

Pathways

Because mainstream and sidestream smoke contain most of the same carcinogenic compounds (although passive smokers are exposed at much lower doses), most mechanisms for lung cancer, heart disease, and reproductive outcomes are similar or identical to those that cause disease in smokers. Several studies have measured urinary concentrations of tobacco-specific carcinogens to better quantify the exposure of nonsmokers to ETS.

Multiple mechanisms for the causal effect of smoking on SIDS have been suggested. Smoking during pregnancy is causally associated with LBW, which is in turn a risk factor for SIDS (DiFranza and Lew 1995). Exposure to smoke is causally associated with respiratory complications in children, and it has been proposed that smoke affects neuroregulation of breathing, which could lead to SIDS (Nicholl and O'Cathain 1992). Exposure to ETS may lead to a change in oxygen sensitivity of peripheral arterial chemoreceptors, leading to oxygen deprivation (Wisborg et al. 2000). Nicotine has been hypothesized to influence the maturation of cardiorespiratory control (leading to irregular heartbeat) and cause the lethal action of SIDS-associated bacterial toxins (Wisborg et al. 2000).

The physiological pathways for the effect of ETS on coronary heart disease were reviewed by Glantz and Parmley (1995). They concluded that passive smoking reduces the blood's ability to deliver oxygen to the heart, increases platelet activity, accelerates atherosclerotic lesions, and increases tissue damage following ischemia or myocardial infarction. These effects reduce exercise capability, can damage the lining of the coronary arteries, increase the development of atherosclerotic plaque, and increase the risk for recurrent or more serious (larger) myocardial infarctions. Adverse reproductive outcomes are partly attributed to carbon monoxide (CO) and nicotine; CO binds to hemoglobin in place of oxygen, thus limiting the oxygen supply, and nicotine has vasoconstrictive properties (U.S. Department of Health and Human Services 2001).

Despite the plausibility of the biological pathways, the magnitude of the estimated effects of ETS exposure on the risk of heart disease has been called into question, and doubts have been expressed about the validity of empirical studies that gave rise to these estimates (Howard and Thun 1999). The rationale is that nonsmokers' exposure to ETS, on average, is estimated as the equivalent of actively smoking 0.1 to 1 cigarette per day. Compared with an active smoker who smokes 10 cigarettes per day, the nonsmoker's exposure is only one to 10 percent. However, the ETS effects on nonsmokers in some studies suggest risks of up to 50 percent of the smoking-attributable risk to active smokers. Howard and Thun (1999) reviewed the extent to which various hypothesized methodological problems or biases may be responsible for this "discrepancy." They concluded that it appears biologically plausible that ETS could cause the substantial increase in coronary heart disease risk that has been observed in epidemiologic studies.

Glantz and Parmley (1995) also mentioned three reasons why nonsmokers may be even more vulnerable to the effects of ETS than active smokers themselves. First, there is a qualitative difference between ETS and mainstream smoke in that ETS contains some toxins at higher levels and others at lower levels as compared with the smoke inhaled by the smoker. Second, smokers might have already achieved the maximum physiological response to some toxins so that additional exposure does not increase their risk. Finally, because nonsmokers do not have the benefit of smokers' adaptation of their cardiovascular systems to compensate for all the effects of smoking, compared with active smokers, exposed nonsmokers are disproportionately affected by the adverse health effects of ETS.

Effects of Environmental Tobacco Smoke on Utilization of Personal Health Services

Several studies have documented an association between exposure to ETS and the utilization of selected health services; however, overall the empirical evidence on this issue is very sparse and generally limited to children or infants. Cunningham et al. (1996) found that children exposed to ETS were 60 percent more likely to go to a hospital's emergency room for wheezing. Chen, Li, and Yu (1986) studied children's hospital admission rates for respiratory illness in Shanghai and found a positive association with the number of cigarettes smoked in the children's families. Harlap and Davies (1974) found significantly higher hospital admission rates for bronchitis and pneumonia due to ETS.

New Research on the Effects of ETS in Households: Overview and Methods

Overview

Using the first five waves of the Health and Retirement Study (HRS), we analyzed relationships between spouses' exposures to ETS and several health outcomes. The large size and longitudinal character of this national data set allowed for conclusions regarding the intrafamily health and mortality effects of secondhand exposure to tobacco smoke in a well-defined age cohort of persons who were generally in middle age.[6] The HRS is unique in providing identical data on both spouses in a panel. Thus, we could measure smoking and adverse health effects in an identical fashion for both spouses. Other data sets typically contain considerable information on one member of the household but only summary measures of characteristics on other members.

In our analysis, exposure to ETS was defined simply as being married to a smoker. Thus, we neglected other sources of exposure to secondary smoke on which we had no information, such as from other persons in the household as well as exposures in the workplace and in other public areas. Apart from the number of cigarettes consumed by the smoker, we did not have any biomarker information to quantify levels of exposure to ETS. Even in view of these limitations, the HRS is an excellent source of information on effects of ETS on health because identical information on numerous variables is available for both spouses.

We focused our analyses on three types of outcome measures: (1) mortality; (2) fair or poor health; and (3) prevalence of specific smoking-related illnesses between waves 1 and 5, an eight-year time interval (1992–2000). We created a set of binary variables equal to one if respondents reported that a doctor had ever told the respondents that s/he had cancer, emphysema, a heart attack, a stroke, or coronary heart disease. We also created binary variables for the presence of any activity of daily living (ADL), Instrumental activity of daily living (IADL), or other limitation.

Methods

We selected all 4,673 married couples (9,346 individuals), responding to the first wave of the HRS. For each person, we identified his or her own as well as the spouse's smoking status at baseline. We defined three mutually exclusive smoking categories: current, former, and never. As elsewhere in this study, the current category included former smokers who had quit within five years before the interview.

Effects of the spouse's smoking behavior were estimated using logistic regression with each of the above outcome measures as dependent variables. Health effects were estimated using a pooled time series cross section for waves 2 through 5. Covariates were included as lagged variables. Mortality effects were estimated from information on death between two adjacent waves.

The key explanatory variables were smoking status of self and spouse. We defined smoking status of both spouses as current, former, or never smokers, with current and former defined as in previous chapters. We controlled for covariates other than own and spousal smoking (see chapter 2). These included other health behaviors, alcohol consumption, and body mass index that reflects the person's physical activity and diet, as well as risk preferences and financial horizon. Thus, if spouses of smokers tend to have poor health habits, engage in risky behavior, and/or be myopic, our analysis took account of this. Of course, it is never possible to know if one holds too little (or too much) constant in assessing the effects of a single behavior, in this case spousal smoking.

We used 1998 National Health Interview Survey data to estimate lifetime age-specific prevalence rates for each illness, limitation, and fair or poor health status. We used parameter estimates on spouses' current smoking from the logistic regression models to obtain age,

Table 10.1
Spouses' Smoking Status at Wave 1 (%)

| | Husband's Smoking Status | | | |
	Current Smoker	Former Smoker	Never Smoker	Total
Wife's Smoking Status				
Current smoker	16.0	9.2	4.3	29.5
Former smoker	5.2	12.1	4.9	22.2
Never smoker	12.1	19.3	16.9	48.3
Total	33.3	40.6	26.1	100.0

gender, and smoking-status-specific prevalence rates for each condition in a hypothetical unexposed population, and a population exposed to ETS. Using the HRS sample, we calculated the expected lifetime effect of ETS using respondents' actual exposure during their current marriage, a 25 percent probability of ETS exposure prior to the current marriage, and a one percent per year separation or divorce rate after 2000. Exposure ended when the spouse died or quit smoking. We used the same quit rates as in previous chapters, which were based on HRS. For persons in HRS who were not married, we assumed no exposure to ETS over their life cycle.

New Research on the Effects of ETS in Households: Empirical Results of Husband–Wife Smoking Status Combinations

Husbands were more likely to smoke at wave 1 than were wives—33.3 percent for husbands and 29.5 percent for wives (table 10.1). There were nearly twice as many never smokers among the wives (48.3 percent) than among the husbands (26.1 percent). The most common combination was former-smoking husbands married to never-smoking wives (19.3 percent), followed by couples who were both never smokers (16.9 percent). In 16.0 percent of cases, both spouses were current smokers.

We computed estimates of the number of years exposed to smoking (not shown). Wives of current smokers had been exposed to smoke from husbands for a mean of 25.3 years (median, 29). The corresponding estimate for husbands was 25.5 years (median, 28). The latter may be an overestimate, because many women started smoking later than men (U.S. Department of Health and Human Services 2001). Mean durations of exposure for spouses of former smokers were under half those for spouses of current smokers. These durations largely reflect the long time that most of the interviewed couples had been married at wave 1. Most respondents had been married for 30 or more years at wave 1; nearly 90 percent had been married for 10 or more years. The HRS provided no record of smoking behavior of spouses from previous marriages.

Effects of Smoking on Spouses' Mortality

Overall, the estimated effects on mortality were highly plausible, with own effects exceeding effects of spousal smoking (appendix A to chapter 10). Being a current smoker raised the probability of one's own death by 325 percent on average compared to a never smoker. By contrast, being the spouse of a current smoker raised the probability of the spouse's death by 27 percent if she or he was married to a current smoker. Being a former smoker raised the probability of one's own death by 94 percent compared to a never smoker.

On the other hand, being married to a former smoker was highly protective. Such persons experienced an eight percent decrease in the probability of death compared to a never smoker. Our analysis differed from an earlier analysis of survival (chapter 4) in being restricted to married persons in the HRS age cohort. Also, in this chapter's analysis, we combined male and female samples and limited the sample to married persons. We needed to make these adjustments because the sample size was smaller; by combining data for the two genders, we had enough statistical power to detect a mortality effect for spousal smoking.

On average, our results imply that 8,407 married persons died annually because their spouses smoked in the HRS age cohort, which overall consisted of about 17.5 million persons (table 10.2). By contrast, 70,580, over eight times as many persons with spouses/partners, died annually as a consequence of their own smoking.

Effects of Smoking on Prevalence of Spouse Morbidity and Disability

We computed prevalence estimates of health problems, pooling five waves of HRS (appendix to chapter 10). The advantage of pooling was to increase the statistical power of the analysis. Only four of the parameter estimates for being married to a current smoker were statistically significant at the five percent level or better: ever diagnosed with lung disease; ever had congestive heart failure; ever had

Table 10.2
Expected Number of Deaths (Married Persons Aged 53–70)

	Spouse Effects	Own Effects
Estimated Number of Deaths in Cohort		
—by 1994 (2 years)	14,344	105,964
—by 1996 (4 years)	37,453	308,447
—by 1998 (6 years)	52,117	489,885
Mean Number of Deaths per Year	8,407	70,580

Notes:
Number of married persons in age group: 17,492,694.
Estimated total number of deaths per year in age group: 113,822.
Expected number of total deaths per year in age group based on 1998 NCHS life table: 129,902.
Mortality rate—this sample: 0.00651.
Mortality rate—national estimate: 0.00743.

angina or chest pain; ever reported an ADL limitation. By contrast, all of the parameter estimates for being a current smoker were statistically significant at conventional levels.

Persons married to current smokers were 32 percent more likely to have been diagnosed with a lung disease (see appendix A to chapter 10). We estimate that 162,000 spouses had lung disease as a consequence of being married to a smoker (table 10.3). Not surprisingly, the effect of own smoking was to increase the probability of such a diagnosis by a much greater amount—185 percent.

The probability of ever having been diagnosed with congestive heart disease for spouses married to current smokers was elevated by 81 percent. Although this result is plausible, the corresponding own effect, surprisingly, was slightly lower than this. Similarly, the probability of having angina or chest pain was elevated by 36 percent for spouses of current smokers and by 38 percent for current smokers themselves.

On average, persons married to smokers were 21 percent more likely to report having at least one ADL limitation. We estimated that 115,000 persons aged 51–70 had an ADL limitation as a result of being married to a smoker. This contrasts to a 49 percent own smoking effect.

Extra Life Years with Morbidity and Disability Attributable to Secondary Smoke

We next assessed the extra life years that a person married to a smoker might expect to have in fair or poor health, with a particular chronic

Table 10.3
Effect of Smoking on Health and Disability among Married Persons Aged 53–70

	Weighted Rate per 1,000		Marginal Effect (Persons w/Condition)	
	All Persons	Married to Never Smokers	Spouse's Smoking Current	Own Smoking Current/ Former
Characteristics at Waves 1–5 (N = 15,480,514)				
Fair or poor health	189.1	182.3	110,746	298,127
Ever ...				
diagnosed with lung disease	99.4	80.0	162,054	322,746
had a heart attack	71.9	75.6	12,668	194,228
had congestive heart disease	23.8	17.2	78,793	42,220
had angina or chest pain	72.9	64.4	106,786	66,276
had any heart problem(s)	180.2	182.8	6,302	187,701
had a stroke	36.2	38.4	26,446	76,760
had cancer	86.1	75.9	10,840	90,116
reported an ADL limitation	120.0	108.2	115,396	141,019
reported limitation (work, home, other)	117.5	106.6	54,783	211,770

condition, or with an ADL, or an IADL, or other limitation (table 10.4). The effects of secondary smoke, both undiscounted and discounted, were negligible.

Valuing the Cost of ETS

On an undiscounted basis, an "average" woman married to a male smoker by age 24 (or who will do so over the life course) has a reduced life expectancy of 0.39 years if she too smokes or of 0.20 years if she does not smoke (table 10.5). For a corresponding "average" man, the corresponding reductions in life expectancy are 0.53 years if the man smokes and 0.19 if he does not, undiscounted. Discounted at three percent, the marginal effects are all under two months. The differences in life expectancy translate into losses of $13,734 for each female smoker and $28,973 for each male smoker.[7] The value of ETS-attributable limitations is $1,369 for each female smoker, and $800 for each male smoker.

Table 10.4
Extra Life Years with Illnesses Attributable to Exposure to Secondary Smoke among Married Persons Aged 53–70

	Female Married to Smoker		Male Married to Smoker	
	Expected Value	Effect of Spouse Smoking (%)	Expected Value	Effect of Spouse Smoking (%)
Panel A. Life Years with Condition (Undiscounted)				
Fair/poor health status	7.77	0.22 (2.8)	7.06	0.32 (4.4)
Ever been told by a doctor:				
—you had cancer	6.40	0.03 (0.5)	3.82	0.03 (0.8)
—you had emphysema	0.99	0.06 (5.2)	1.52	0.14 (8.9)
—you had a heart attack	2.02	0.01 (0.5)	3.46	0.03 (0.9)
—you had a stroke	1.69	0.03 (1.8)	1.81	0.06 (3.2)
—you had coronary heart disease	2.27	0.21 (9.0)	3.92	0.63 (15.9)
ADL limitation	1.19	0.02 (2.0)	0.98	0.05 (4.9)
IADL limitation	3.01	−0.03 (−1.0)	1.12	−0.02 (−2.2)
Any limitation	8.43	0.18 (2.1)	6.98	0.23 (3.3)
Panel B. Discounted Value (Years)				
Fair/poor health status	2.76	0.12 (4.3)	2.73	0.16 (5.6)
Ever been told by a doctor:				
—you had cancer	2.06	0.02 (0.8)	1.26	0.01 (1.1)
—you had emphysema	0.31	0.03 (7.4)	0.48	0.06 (11.1)
—you had a heart attack	0.55	0.00 (0.7)	1.03	0.01 (1.2)
—you had a stroke	0.46	0.01 (2.7)	0.51	0.02 (4.2)
—you had coronary heart disease	0.62	0.08 (12.9)	1.16	0.23 (19.9)
ADL limitation	0.27	0.01 (4.3)	0.29	0.02 (7.7)
IADL limitation	0.70	−0.01 (−2.0)	0.30	−0.01 (−3.5)
Any limitation	2.92	0.10 (3.2)	2.64	0.12 (4.3)
Value of limitations	60,168	1,201 (0.7)	48,148	2,024 (1.0)

Table 10.5
Life Years Lost and Value of Life Years Lost and Disability Due to Second-Hand Smoke

	Undiscounted			Discounted			Value of Life Years Lost
	Expected Value	Unexposed	Effect of Smoking	Expected Value	Unexposed	Effect of Smoking	
Female smoker	55.47	55.86	−0.39	27.01	27.12	−0.11	$11,329
Female never smoker	59.27	59.47	−0.20	27.82	27.88	−0.06	5,919
Male smoker	49.98	50.50	−0.53	25.59	25.75	−0.16	16,273
Male never smoker	56.20	56.39	−0.19	27.14	27.20	−0.05	5,383
Discounted value of lost life years and limitations per smoker							
—Value of life years lost among males, per female smoker (cost per female smoker)							13,734
—Value of life years lost among females, per male smoker (cost per male smoker)							28,973
—Value of limitations among males, per female smoker (cost per female smoker)							1,369
—Value of limitations among females, per male smoker (cost per male smoker)							800

Summary and Conclusions

Our analysis confirmed some adverse effects of environmental tobacco smoke (ETS) on general health status, mortality, and the prevalence and incidence of smoking-related illnesses among spouses of current and former smokers reported by others. Precise details differ among studies. Environmental tobacco smoke is an area for which the costs to society seem to be greatly in flux. Historically, people tended to be exposed to more smoking, but workplace smoking restrictions are now quite widespread. Moreover, even smoking in the home has decreased dramatically as smokers have become increasingly conscious of the need to avoid other household members being exposed.

The really new findings, using recent data that should reflect changes in smoking patterns within households, pertain to the effect of a person being married to a spouse who smokes throughout years of life with particular chronic conditions, and the estimates of present value of loss associated with decreased longevity. Overall, by late adulthood, effects of smoking on years with chronic conditions and with various functional limitations were small. However, the value of years lost was considerable, $14,000 per 24-year-old female smoker and $29,000 per 24-year-old male smoker. These values incorporate the probability of being married, even if the person was not married at age 24. Losses from limitations increase such cost by about $1,000. This cost accounts for the increased prevalence of smoking-related diseases only to the extent that they affect rates of limitations.

These amounts are appreciably larger than the effect of smoking on utilization of health services (see chapter 5), a relationship that has received much publicity, especially in the context of tort litigation in which the states sued tobacco manufactures for Medicaid outlays they attributed to smoking.

Of course, these estimates only represent the experience of married couples when both partners survived to middle age. These costs might not apply to other cohorts. A cohort's exposure and relative odds of dying due to ETS, although assumed constant, are likely to change over time. If smokers die prematurely, the nonsmoking spouse may outlive the smoking spouse. Similarly, the spouse may quit the habit after a health event or the onset of an illness. Both would reduce exposure over time. Similarly, over time, the health effects of ETS may decline relative to the health effects of old age, somewhat reducing the estimates of life years lost attributable to smoking.

Even more significantly, exposure to ETS is not limited to this age cohort or to intrafamily exposure. First, exposure at work and other places outside the home is potentially of even greater magnitude than exposure at home (Pirkle et al. 1996). Second, as discussed in chapter 3, exposure of infants and children can yield different, potentially even greater and more costly health effects. Third, although our analysis covered less than a decade in the lives of 51-to-62-year-olds, the results of the cross-sectional analysis indicate that much of the effect of ETS may materialize in poor health and increased prevalence of disease *prior to* age 50. Similarly, some effects might become even more pronounced among older persons that were included in our analysis.

Finally, it is possible that one or several risk factors for adverse health outcomes may be associated with being married to a smoker, and these factors rather than environmental tobacco smoke itself may account for the elevated risk of adverse outcomes among spouses of smokers relative to spouses of nonsmokers. As Thun, Henley, and Apicella (1999) suggested, the best method for assessing such potential confounding is to assess the extent to which the estimates of risk change when other risk factors are added or subtracted from the model. In general our results on smoking were robust to changes in equation specification.

Appendix 10.A.1: Mortality Effects of Own and Second-Hand Smoke among Married Persons in the HRS

Table 10.A.1 gives the odds ratios for mortality from own and second-hand smoke during the two-year period following an HRS interview. Being a current smoker raised the risk of one's own death by 325 percent on average compared to a never smoker. By contrast, being the

Table 10.A.1
Mortality Effects of Own and Second-Hand Smoke among Married Persons in the HRS

	Spouse Effects		Own Effects	
	Odds Ratio	[95% CI]	Odds Ratio	[95% CI]
Current smoker	1.27***	[1.26; 1.28]	4.25***	[4.22; 4.28]
Former smoker	0.92***	[0.92; 0.93]	1.94***	[1.93; 1.96]

Note: Other covariates included: alcohol consumption, problem drinking, risk tolerance, financial planning horizon, body mass index, age, race, education, number of years married, gender, and indicator variables for waves 2, 3, and 4.

spouse of a current smoker raised the risk of death by 27 percent. Being a former smoker raised the probability of one's own death by 94 percent compared to a never smoker. Spouses of former smokers had a reduced risk of death relative to spouses of never smokers. Thun, Henley, and Apicella (1999), summarizing the findings of three studies based on data from both spouses, reported a risk ration of 0.98 for spouses of former smokers.

Appendix 10.A.2: Association between Own and Second-Hand Smoke and the Prevalence of Health Problems among Respondents Married to Smokers in HRS

Table 10.A.2 gives the odds ratios for the prevalence of selected diseases for current and former smokers, and spouses of current and former smokers, relative to never smokers. Persons married to current

Table 10.A.2
Prevalence of Health Problems among Respondents Married to Smokers, HRS Waves 2–5 (Ages 53–70)

	Spouse's Current Smoking		Current Own Smoking	
	Odds Ratio[1]	[95% CI]	Odds Ratio[2]	[95% CI]
Characteristics at Waves 1–5				
Fair or poor health	1.13	[0.98; 1.32]	1.78***	[1.53; 2.08]
Ever ...				
diagnosed with lung disease	1.32*	[1.05; 1.65]	2.85***	[2.24; 3.63]
had a heart attack	1.03	[0.79; 1.35]	2.19***	[1.63; 2.95]
had congestive heart disease	1.81**	[1.17; 2.80]	1.76*	[1.12; 2.75]
had angina or chest pain	1.36*	[1.06; 1.76]	1.38*	[1.07; 1.77]
had any heart problem(s)	1.01	[0.84; 1.21]	1.41***	[1.17; 1.69]
had a stroke	1.13	[0.81; 1.57]	1.66**	[1.14; 2.41]
had cancer	1.03	[0.79; 1.33]	1.35*	[1.05; 1.73]
reported an ADL limitation	1.21*	[1.00; 1.46]	1.49***	[1.23; 1.82]
reported limitation (work, home, other)	1.09	[0.90; 1.31]	1.60***	[1.33; 1.94]

1. Odds ratios relative to persons married to never smokers.
*, **, and *** denote significance at the 0.05, 0.01, and 0.001 levels, respectively.
2. Odds ratios for own smoking presented for comparison; the analysis also controlled for own former smoking, results not shown.
3. Independent variables were measured one wave prior to the dependent variable. Only persons who survived to wave 2 entered this analysis.

smokers were 32 percent more likely to have been diagnosed with a lung disease. The effect of own smoking was to increase the probability of such a diagnosis by 185 percent. The probability of ever having been diagnosed with congestive heart disease for spouses married to current smokers was elevated by 81 percent. The probability of having angina or chest pain was elevated by 36 percent for spouses of current smokers. On average, persons married to smokers were 21 percent more likely to have reported having at least one ADL limitation. The elevated risk for the various forms of heart disease fall within the range of findings reported in a review of epidemiologic studies of fatal and nonfatal cardiovascular disease and exposure from spousal smoking by Thun, Henley, and Apicella (1999).

11   Summing Up

Good and Not-So-Good Uses of Cost Estimates

The view that smoking is harmful to one's health is now accepted by everyone, including the major tobacco manufacturers.[1] Yet millions of persons continue to smoke, and an appreciable share of the teenage population begins to smoke each year. It seems ironic that societies have implemented specific protections for various hazards, such as for prescription drug, occupational, and environmental dangers whose risks are often far lower than those from smoking.

Societies have adopted various methods for controlling behaviors deemed to be harmful. One type of approach involves command-and-control rules that ban certain activities and establish penalties for violation of these rules. Examples are national prohibition of alcohol production and sales and laws banning sale and consumption of narcotics. They may also include regulation of the information that commercial sellers provide. In the context of smoking, for example, a major issue has been allegations that tobacco companies have provided misleading information to consumers about the safety of their product (see e.g., Kessler 2001).

The command-and-control approach requires that regulators identify violations and violators, apprehend, and mete out punishment. Not only is such enforcement costly, especially for activities that are as common as smoking, but increasingly, it has been recognized that the command-and-control enforcers face incentives of their own, resulting in enforcement that may be incomplete and inconsistent.

An alternative is to rely on market-based incentives. This approach relies on prices to deter undesirable behaviors and to guide the parties to a socially optimal level of the activity. The public sector may affect prices by implementing taxes and subsidies, the latter for activities to be encouraged, such as tobacco control programs to prevent people from starting or tobacco cessation programs to assist quitting. In addition, the market-based approach may take the form of *ex ante* incentives to take due care, as in tort. Faced with the threat that a private party may sue if injured, tort *ideally* gives an incentive to sellers to exercise due care. Revenues raised may be used to compensate the victims of harmful acts.[2]

In the context of smoking, whether command-and-control or market incentives are used, it seems unlikely that the socially optimal level of consumption is zero. People do derive some personal benefits from smoking, such as relief from stress, enjoyment of the taste, having something to do with their hands, appearing rugged (Marlboro man) or lean and sophisticated (Virginia Slims) and for demonstrating their masculinity, femininity, or "maturity." Also, trying to achieve a smokeless society would bring with it various adverse side effects, such as smuggling as a result of the high prices and, at least in the short-run, substantial adverse effects on employment in the agriculture, manufacturing, and retail sectors.

The market approach can lead to optimal behaviors if a set of rather restrictive assumptions are not violated. People should have perfect information about the costs and benefits of smoking, not only currently but in the future as well. They should be forward-looking. Also, they should have time-consistent preferences. That is, preferences should not depend on the circumstances in which individuals find themselves or be mutable over time. No one would argue that these assumptions are fully satisfied in the context of smoking. At issue is the extent to which they are violated and whether alternative approaches would yield more socially desirable outcomes.

Both the command-and-control and the market approaches require at least a rough assessment of the optimal level of consumption, which also may be thought of as the amount of the harmful activity that should be tolerated. Of course, policymakers can rely on hunches about benefits and costs, as is typically done. However, basing public policy on hunches and anecdotes is at best a second-best alternative when sound information is lacking; more precise quantification is far preferable.

Unfortunately, one thing that a study of the private and social cost of smoking cannot do is to determine the socially optimal level of cigarette consumption. In particular, the optimum depends on both the private benefit as well as cost. We have not attempted to value the benefit in this study. Although, in principle, it would be possible to value benefits using techniques developed in economics and marketing, we would be left with the question of whether public policy should rely on private valuations of the benefits of such a harmful habit as smoking.

A major complexity in valuing the benefit of smoking is the addictive property of cigarettes. The Becker–Murphy (1988) model of rational addiction, which is based on assumptions of good information and forward-looking behavior, has been used in empirical research on cigarette demand (see e.g., Becker, Grossman, and Murphy 1994 and more generally Chaloupka and Warner 2000), but to our knowledge, never to address the normative issue of determining the appropriate rate of smoking and of tax subsidy policy needed to achieve optimal consumption levels. And its use in a normative application would be much more controversial than when used for the purpose of generating refutable hypotheses.

Some thought experiments provide insights nevertheless. First, to the extent that fully informed, rational, forward-looking, and time-consistent individuals' smoking decisions are motivated by private calculation of costs versus benefits, the benefits of smoking must be considerable. As explained more fully below, according to our calculations, at age 24, the present value of the life cycle stream of cost in 2000 dollars, including purchase of the cigarette product, is $86,000 for women who smoke at age 24, and $183,000 for men who smoke at this age. These amounts, especially for men, are equivalent to the price of a nice house in 2000. The sum for women could buy at least a condominium. If, in fact, the decision to smoke in young adulthood is motivated by a comparison of costs versus benefits, the benefits from smoking would have to be considerable indeed. In a way, it seems doubtful that the benefits could be this large.

Although this interpretation of our findings implies that smokers are irrational, especially in young adulthood, our findings are subject to alternative interpretations. A sizable portion of this consists of the willingness-to-pay value of mortality losses incurred by smokers. Thus, it is not a monetary loss to smokers, but something more intangible. These are implicit values based on actual actions that people take in the labor market. These actions are in the form of added compensation that employees obtain for working in riskier jobs (Viscusi and Aldy 2003).[3] Two counterexamples (box 11.1) suggest that at least for some smokers in early adulthood, the benefit may be as large as the

Box 11.1

An Alternative Interpretation: Two Thought Experiments

The following thought experiments suggest that smoking at age 24 may be a rational decision, at least for some individuals.

Thought Experiment #1

We state in chapter 1 that each pack of cigarettes costs two hours of life expectancy. Since each cigarette consumed probably takes about six minutes to smoke, this is equivalent to saying that smokers give up one minute of life for every minute spent smoking. This does not even take into account discounting: were we to do so properly, smokers probably give up 10–20 seconds of life per minute spent smoking. But leaving discounting aside, this formulation implies that smokers enjoy each minute spent smoking twice as much as each minute spent not smoking. A priori, this seems plausible on its face. That is, we presumably all can imagine certain activities so pleasurable that it might be worth trading some quantity of life to achieve higher quality of life. It becomes even more plausible once discounting is taken into account since it effectively implies that for smokers, a life in which smoking was denied might be worth only two-thirds to five-sixths as valuable as a life in which smoking was permitted.

Thought Experiment #2

The average smoker evidently smokes about 400 packs a year, which implies giving up 800 hours of future life expectancy or a little more than two hours a day. A minimum of one-sixth and possibly upwards of one-third or more of adults watch two or more hours of TV a day.[4]

Suppose we were doing a study on the private and social costs of TV watching. Leaving aside the multitaskers who might do other things while the TV is on, assume that each hour of TV watching is completely unproductive and therefore the cumulative loss of time to such activity can be monetized as if one had literally lost that many hours/years of life as a consequence. Thus, if we were to monetize the private costs of TV watching, we would derive aggregate figures very similar to smoking, that is, measured in hundreds of billions of dollars, and if we were to measure costs over the life cycle we would get figures much higher than for smoking, since people don't die prematurely from watching TV and since we treat each hour watched as if the person had "died" for that interval; hence we would be accumulating hours lost even at age 18, and so on. So suppose we end up with an average lifetime figure of $200,000 attributable to watching TV. Would we compare that to the cost

Box 11.1 (*continued*)

of a house and express bafflement that anyone could possibly give up so much of their precious lifetime in pursuit of this activity? The point is, we could take any lifetime activity that consumed about two hours daily—be it eating, reading, or any other hobby/activity—and it would have roughly the same social cost as smoking, that is, of eye-opening size, but does that necessarily mean that we have to conclude that humans are irrational or addicted to engage in them?

private cost, implying that the decision to smoke may be rational for some individuals. That the benefit may be high for some persons is more compelling than is the argument that we have overstated cost because we have included intangible loss.

Second, appreciable external costs are imposed on family members. As discussed in the previous chapter, we have considered effects of secondary smoke on the spouse and infant children as a "quasi-external" cost. These costs amount to $16,000 for each female smoker, and $29,000 for each male smoker.

We have also computed estimates of the "pure" external cost of smoking by gender, again from the perspective of a 24-year-old smoker. These costs, net of excise taxes, are $4,000 for females and $8,000 for males who smoke at age 24. Considering the number of persons who turn age 24 annually (population counts from the 2000 U.S. Census of Population), we estimate that the external lifetime cost from people who turn 24 and smoke each year at $7 billion. When adding quasi-external cost to this figure, the total external lifetime cost of 24-year-old smokers is $35 billion. This is an incidence estimate. Every year, there is a new $35 billion.

Adding private, quasi-external, and external costs yields estimates of the social cost of smoking. This amounts to $106,000 per woman who smokes at age 24 and about twice this amount for each male smoker of this age, $220,000. With each new cohort of smokers of age 24 in the United States, $204 billion of new lifetime cost is added.

As emphasized in chapter 2, very few persons may be expected to initiate smoking after this age, and many will quit subsequently (fig. 5.1). As others before us have found, using less in-depth methods than in our analysis, the external costs of smoking are *relatively* minor, certainly much lower than the private or internal costs (Manning et al.

1989, 1991; Viscusi 1999, 2002; Cutler et al. 2002; and chapter 3 more generally).

Thus, if external costs are small, some would conclude that less should be done by the public sector to discourage smoking than is currently done. However, we found that, especially with secondary smoking effects on spouses, social costs far exceeded federal and state excise tax payments. Thus, especially if cigarette taxes are to reduce adverse effects of secondary smoke on spouses, higher taxes would be justified.

Cigarette excise taxes have risen dramatically in recent years, as have cigarette prices (Orzechowski and Walker 2002). Price increases represent forward shifting of these excise tax increases as well as payments made by the major cigarette manufacturers pursuant to the 1998 Master Settlement Agreement (MSA), between the tobacco companies and state attorneys general in forty-six states, and independent settlements, between the companies and the four attorneys general in the remaining states (Mollenkamp et al. 1998).

Questions can be raised at several levels. At the most general level, one can ask why public policy is going in one direction, which is counter to the advice of some of the best academic studies of smoking cost (e.g., Manning et al. 1989, 1991; Viscusi 1995, 1999, 2002). It seems contradictory to assume that individuals smokers are rational, which is a standard assumption that economists make about human beings, but that voters and policymakers are totally irrational. In this sense, perhaps it is the scholars who are in error. Perhaps their view of the cost burden from smoking is too narrow. If there were no financial externalities in automobile insurance, would society be indifferent if it thought that 100,000 drunk drivers annually suffered self-inflicted deaths by running their cars into trees?

Society adopts many public policies to mitigate the rate of injury to self. The plausible reason is consumption externalities.[5] Self-inflicted wounds, even if inflicted by well-informed, forward-looking agents, become a matter of public interest because many citizens are made worse off when they occur. Certainly, if people are not well informed, do not foresee adverse consequences of their personal behavior, or lack self-control, for example, wanting to quit but can't, these arguments add force to the case for public intervention.

On the other hand, rather than guide public policy, an even less legitimate use of cost of smoking studies has been to justify demands for funds to support public antismoking programs and/or biomedical research to lead to cures of smoking-related diseases. The technique here is to find a number, which is "good," as long as it is large. Whether this has been the intent or not, this has been the effect of much of the analysis of smoking cost based on the cross-sectional methodology we described in chapters 2 and 3. This method does not adequately account for the mortality effects of smoking. To the extent that persons die prematurely, this will affect the number of participants in various public and private programs, especially those in which benefits are paid to elderly persons.

That mortality affects cash flow of these programs is a factual matter, not a moral one. This does not mean that mortality costs should not be counted, but it is appropriate to distinguish between total costs from those accruing to particular programs. Of course, once we admit the existence of consumption externalities, the issue of who is due compensation for costs attributable to smoking becomes much more complex, but the split between compensating individual smokers as victims versus taxpayers into such public programs as Medicaid becomes much less clear.

After reviewing our findings, we shall return to specific policy issues: setting excise taxes on cigarettes, payments to states under the MSA, and federal litigation against the tobacco companies.

Summary of Findings: Private, "Quasi-External," External, and Social Costs of Smoking

The Private Cost of Smoking

We found that the present value of the private cost of smoking to a 24-year-old smoker in 2000 was $141,181, $86,236 for women and $182,860 for men (table 11.1). On a per-pack basis, the private cost was $32.78. The national cost that 24-year-old smokers will impose on themselves over their life cycles is $168 billion. This seems like a large number, which it is, but it important to consider that this reflects costs 24-year-old smokers impose on themselves over about six decades.

Part of the private cost is the expected expenditures on cigarettes over the life course (box 11.2). To arrive at an estimate of $13,338 for cigarette expenditures over the life cycle, which is equivalent to $3.12 on a per-pack basis, we took lifetime cigarette excise tax payments—based on age-specific consumption from the 1998 National Health Interview Survey (NHIS), discounted by three percent per year, and

Table 11.1
Private Cost of Smoking to a 24-year-Old Smoker

| | Cost per Smoker | | | National Cost (Millions 2000 Dollars) | Cost per Pack |
	Female Smoker	Male Smoker	Mean Cost[1]		
Cost of cigarettes	13,033	13,570	13,338	15,916	3.12
Mortality cost	52,385	113,923	87,378	104,267	20.28
Disability cost	19,353	11,032	14,621	17,448	3.44
Medical care cost	951	1,110	1,041	1,243	0.24
Social Security outlays	1,519	6,549	4,379	5,226	1.01
Social Security taxable earnings	631	38,566	22,202	26,494	5.10
Defined benefit private pension outlays	383	10,123	5,922	7,066	1.36
Life insurance outlays	−2,019	−12,013	−7,702	−9,190	−1.78
Total private cost of smoking	86,236	182,860	141,181	168,469	32.78

Source of population data and data on adults by smoking status: U.S. Bureau of the Census, 2000 Census, summary file 1; and 1998 NHIS. Smokers include persons who quit less than 5 years ago.
Note: Number of 24-year-old smokers based on U.S. population aged 24, and smoking rates among 24-year-olds by gender.
1. Weighted average based on 514,733 female and 678,554 male 24-year-old smokers.

multiplied by the probability of survival to each year, for a typical 24-year-old smoker—and multiplied this estimate by the average price-to-tax ratio in the year 2000.

The largest component of private cost is mortality cost, $87,378 or $20.28 per pack, followed by losses in Social Security taxable earnings, $22,202 or $5.10 per pack. These estimates are based on assigning a value of $100,000 per life year. Alternative assumptions, higher or lower, would yield proportionally different estimates. It seems unlikely that the value of a life year is less than $100,000, and it might be considerably higher. Many life-saving interventions in widespread use cost far more than $100,000 per life year saved (Tengs et al. 1995).

The loss in Social-Security-taxable earnings for men at $38,566 is far more than for women. For the latter, this loss was trivial, $631. We only considered Social-Security-taxable earnings rather than total earnings. Again, our estimates are probably conservative, as smokers are probably underrepresented among very high earners. Including the

Box 11.2
Methods Computing Expenditures on Cigarettes and State and Local Excise Taxes

We calculated lifetime excise taxes on cigarettes paid by representative smokers who were 24-years-old in 2000 using annual excise taxes per cigarette (Orzechowski and Walker 2002), deflated to year 2000 dollars, and the expected number of cigarettes smoked over the smoker's life cycle. We assumed that tax rates after 2002 remained constant at 2002 levels, and thus underestimated lifetime tax payments for this cohort if excise taxes continue their recent trends. To estimate lifetime cigarette consumption, we used self-reported consumption data from the 1998 National Health Interview Survey. We regressed the average number of cigarettes smoked per day by current smokers against age and second- and third-degree polynomials of age, separately for males and females. We used parameter estimates from these models to calculate the expected number of cigarettes smoked per day for each age between 24 and 100. We combined these estimates with age-specific quit rates and mortality patterns to estimate the total number of cigarettes consumed over the smoker's life cycle. We obtained an estimate of lifetime excise tax payments by multiplying the expected annual number of cigarettes consumed by the relevant excise tax rate, discounting to age 24, and summing over the life cycle.

Lifetime costs of cigarettes were obtained using the average 2002 tax-to-price ratio for cigarettes, including both brand and generic cigarettes (Orzechowski and Walker 2002).

willingness-to-pay value and the Social-Security-taxable earnings loss is not double counting since the willingness-to-pay value represents the consumption benefit of a life year that is independent of one's earnings.

Private disability cost is about as high as are expenditures on cigarettes, $14,621 or $3.44 per pack. Since nonsmokers subsidize smokers' life insurance premiums, there is a private cost offset of $7,702 or $1.78 per pack.

Our calculations did not consider that the real price of cigarettes is likely to rise further. Our estimates of the cost of cigarettes over the life cycle are conservative in that they do not consider that the real price of cigarettes has risen in recent years. Also, we did not quantify all possible private costs. For example, without indicating the source of the information, Brigham (1998, p. 178) included an annual expenditure of $310–$520 as the annual cost of extra cleaning bills for a smoker versus a nonsmoker.

The one estimate that we may have overstated is the subsidy accruing to smokers from life insurance purchases. Increasingly, insurers seem to be surcharging for smoking. To the extent this occurs, smokers should expect less of a cost offset from life insurance than the estimate we report in table 11.1. The medical care cost to the smoker is quite small, about $1,000 on average. This cost reflects higher out-of-pocket payments and increased taxes borne by smokers (as well as by non-smokers) to finance higher cost of public health insurance programs.

The Quasi-External Cost of Smoking

Quasi-external costs mainly represent the costs imposed on the spouse when his or her marriage partner smokes. There is also a small component for infant deaths.

The quasi-external cost of smoking is $23,407 over the life cycle or $5.44 per pack (table 11.2). Given the higher rates of smoking for men

Table 11.2
Quasi-External Cost of Smoking Caused by a 24-Year-Old Smoker

	Cost per Smoker			National Cost (Millions 2000 Dollars)	Cost per Pack
	Female Smoker	Male Smoker	Mean Cost[4]		
Spouse mortality cost[1]	13,734	28,973	22,399	26,729	5.20
Spouse disability cost	1,369	800	1,045	1,247	0.25
Social Security survivor benefits	−10	−1,285	−735	−877	−0.17
Private pension spouse benefits	−295	−687	−518	−618	−0.12
Infant deaths[2]	597	622	611	730	0.14
Medical expenditures[3]	590	615	604	721	0.14
Total quasi-external cost of smoking	15,985	29,037	23,407	27,932	5.44

Source: U.S. Bureau of the Census, 2000 Census, summary file 1; and 1998 NHIS. Smokers include persons who quit less than 5 years ago.
Note: Number of 24-year-old smokers based on U.S. population aged 24, and smoking rates among 24-year-olds by gender.
1. Value of lost life years per smoker.
2. Based on 599 male and 409 female deaths, valued at $100,000 per lost life year, discounted at 3%, for a total cost of $3.036 billion.
3. $3 billion per year; see table 3.3 in chapter 3.
4. Weighted average based on 514,733 female and 678,554 male 24-year-old smokers.

than for women historically, the cost per male smoker is $29,037. The cost per female smoker is only half this, $15,985. The national cost of spousal smoking, again for the 24-year-old who smokes, is $28 billion. The estimates exclude additional medical care attributable to spouse smoking.

The External Cost of Smoking

The external costs are much smaller than either their private or quasi-external counterparts, $6,201 per 24-year-old smoker, $3,829 for female and $8,001 for male smokers at this age, net of federal and state cigarette excise taxes paid by smokers (table 11.3). On a per-pack basis, the external cost is $2.20 in contrast to $0.76 in excise taxes paid per pack. Net of taxes, the per-pack external cost of smoking is $1.44.

This implies that even with a narrow definition of external cost, one that excludes the quasi-external costs, cigarette excise taxes are too

Table 11.3
External Cost of Smoking Caused by a 24-Year-Old Smoker

	Cost per Smoker			National Cost (Millions 2000 Dollars)	Cost per Pack
	Female Smoker	Male Smoker	Mean Cost[4]		
Work loss (sick leave)	2,658	3,747	3,277	3,911	0.76
Medical care cost not borne by the smoker	2,806	1,501	2,064	2,463	0.49
Social Security outlays[1]	−1,509	−5,264	−3,644	−4,348	−0.84
Income taxes on Social Security taxable earnings[2]	126	7,713	4,440	5,299	1.02
Defined benefit private pension outlays	−88	−9,436	−5,404	−6,448	−1.24
Life insurance outlays	2,019	12,013	7,702	9,190	1.78
Productivity losses[3]	984	1,024	1,007	1,201	0.24
Total external cost of smoking	6,996	11,299	9,443	11,268	2.20
Federal excise taxes	−1,489	−1,550	−1,523	−1,818	−0.36
State excise taxes	−1,678	−1,748	−1,718	−2,050	−0.40
Net external cost of smoking	3,829	8,001	6,201	7,400	1.44

1. Accounts for the effect of smokers' early death on their spouses' benefit receipt.
2. Assumes an average income tax rate of 20% on the marginal earnings.
3. $5 billion per year, see chapter 3.
4. Weighted average based on 514,733 female and 678,554 male 24-year-old smokers.

low. However, the $2.20 figure is driven by the $1.78 cross subsidy of life insurance premiums. To the extent that cross subsidies from non-smokers to smokers no longer occur, it appears that cigarette taxes are about equal to the external cost per pack. One might also argue that life insurance policies are inherently a private decision. To the extent that nonsmokers are sufficiently risk averse to pay a substantial load on private life insurance policies, they still may be better off sub-sidizing smokers and having life insurance than doing without such coverage.

Work loss and medical care cost not borne by the smoker amount to $1.48 per pack. However, this cost is more than offset by the cross subsidy to nonsmokers from smokers' Social Security contributions attributable to smokers' earlier mortality and the cross subsidy from defined-benefit private pension programs.

We estimate that over the life course, a 24-year-old woman who smoked would pay $3,167 in federal and state excise taxes, and a man would pay $3,297. Again, these estimates are conservative, in that they reflect past tax rates through 2002, and do not account for the substan-tial increases in cigarette excise taxes that are occurring (National Gov-ernors Association and National Association of State Budget Officers 2002).

Considering all the elements of external costs and the number of people who turn 24 each year and smoke, the national external and quasi-external lifetime cost per year is $13.8 billion for females and $32.8 billion for males.

The Social Costs of Smoking

The social cost is the sum of purely private, quasi-external, and external cost. In table 11.4, we show the social cost of smoking attributable to persons who smoke at age 24—$170,789 on average or $39.66 per pack. For female smokers, about 81 percent of social cost is private cost. For males, about 83 percent of social cost is private. Men contribute about three times the amount to the social cost of smoking than women.

Surprising and Not-So-Surprising Findings of Our Research

Surprising Findings

Although the totals just described are interesting, many other results are interesting in their own right. Along the way, we have studied

Table 11.4
Social Cost of Smoking Caused by a 24-Year-Old Smoker

	Cost per Smoker			National Cost (Millions 2000 Dollars)	Cost per Pack
	Female Smoker	Male Smoker	Mean Cost[1]		
Private cost	86,236	182,860	141,181	168,469	32.78
Quasi-external cost	15,985	29,037	23,407	27,932	5.44
External cost	3,829	8,001	6,201	7,400	1.44
Social cost	106,050	219,899	170,789	203,801	39.66

1. Weighted average based on 514,733 female and 678,554 male 24-year-old smokers.

effects of smoking on quite a number of outcomes. Several of our results are surprising, and some not so surprising.

Smoking Kills but Does Not Extend Life with Major Disabilities

Perhaps the most surprising result is that smoking extended life years in a very disabled state only slightly, far less than its impact on longevity. Smoking leads to earlier occurrence of disability, but severe disability is a precursor to death almost equally for smokers as for nonsmokers. Limitations *other* than for activity of daily living and instrumental activity of daily living, which presumably are more minor, and time in self-reported fair or poor health, were extended more than were the more severe forms of disability. This finding is important at two levels, one general and the other directly pertinent to the design of smoking-cessation interventions.

At a general level, this implies that if we were able to achieve much lower rates of smoking, we would realize an improvement in the population's health and functioning temporarily, but eventually these nonsmokers would contract nonsmoking-related diseases, become disabled, and eventually succumb from these diseases as well. There would only be a slight contraction in life years with disability. At the same time, pressures on some public budgets would increase, such as for Social Security, as longevity is extended. This does not mean that promoting smoking cessation is not worthwhile, only that statements to the effect that 400,000+ persons die annually from smoking is somewhat misleading. Although we confirmed the much-publicized estimate in our own research (see chapter 4), the estimate is misleading in the sense that if death rates due to smoking-attributable diseases fell, death rates from other causes would rise, albeit at a later date. And time is money. From our results, we do not anticipate that a massive decline in smoking rates would lead to a major compression of time in disability.

This pattern of results is also important for the design of smoking-cessation interventions. Focus groups that some of us conducted with smokers and former smokers in the Health and Retirement Study (HRS) age cohort for an earlier study revealed that smokers were likely to be impressed by information that their smoking would lead to disability and dependence on others than they were with the prospect of an earlier death (Sloan, Smith, and Taylor 2003). The focus group participants did not seem to mind a quick and painless death.

Perhaps the ends justify the means. If information messages that smoking extends time in disability are salient to smokers, does it matter if the messages are truthful? Most of us would prefer truthful messages. Our research for this book implies that, although smokers may be adverse to living with severe disabilities, they have no more to fear than others, except, of course, that their disabilities will occur sooner in life. Perhaps even a truthful message can be designed to be salient. The mature smokers in the Health and Retirement Study age range may not spend much more time with severe disabilities than others, but such disabilities occur sooner on average for smokers. Thus, we can say that some smokers will miss active interactions with grandchildren and enjoyment from retirement if they become prematurely disabled.

Smoking-Attributable Mortality Remains High Even with Better Controls for Other Health Behaviors and Other Characteristics of Smokers

For years, tobacco manufacturers and their lobbyists were critical of the claims of the epidemiologists and public health experts. For reasons that are partly explained by the tobacco settlements with the state attorneys general in 1998, the manufacturers have changed their historical position and now agree that smoking is harmful.[6]

The companies' critique of those who warned of harms of smoking prior to the late 1990s was based on two arguments. The first was that epidemiological evidence does not prove causation. To prove causation, it is necessary to conduct randomized controlled trials (RCTs). As RCTs to measure the harms of smoking would be unethical, the companies could know that smoking could never be shown to cause death, disability, and morbidity if the evidence had to be based on an RCT. In an RCT, some persons would be randomly assigned to a smoking group. Others would be randomly assigned to a nonsmoking control group. The smokers in this idealized experiment would agree to continue smoking, no matter what the circumstances were (e.g., onset of chronic bronchitis). Persons in the control group would agree not to smoke, no matter how great the cravings were or how stressful their lives were. Randomization would serve two purposes: (1) It would ensure that quitting would not occur when the person experienced health shocks, a major source of endogeneity—bad health affects smoking as well as the reverse. (2) It would ensure that characteristics of smokers were the same as nonsmokers in dimensions both easy and difficult to measure. Absent randomization, there is a risk that the estimated effects of smoking are biased due to confounding.

Our analysis did not deal with the endogeneity issue, that is, that expected longevity, health, and disability may affect tobacco consumption, except that with a panel, smoking behavior was measured prior to the observed outcomes. Having a panel is a major step forward, but it does not completely eliminate the threat of endogeneity. Also, whereas the Health and Retirement Study is a panel, the National Health Interview Survey, which we also used, is a single cross section. In principle, we could have dealt with endogeneity of smoking using an instrumental variables (IVs) approach, but there would have been several problems with this, such as having weak IVs[7] and knowing that other health behaviors (e.g., heavy and problem drinking and those reflected in body mass index) plausibly are also endogenous, making correcting for endogeneity a very complex process.

Compared to previous research, we took many precautions to reduce the likelihood of confounding, particularly when we used the HRS. Not only did we include health behaviors other than smoking, but we also controlled for such factors as education, risk preferences, and financial time horizon. Thus, if confounding is present, it is certainly much less than in prior studies. In fact, at some point, adding explanatory variables runs the risk of overcontrolling, which also could lead one to obtain biased estimates of the effects of smoking.

The process of adjusting for the other factors was embodied in the concept of the nonsmoking smoker. This type of smoker was similar to a smoker in many respects, except that the person did not smoke. Thus, the effects of smoking were computed as the differences between the predicted values for actual smokers and those for the nonsmoking smokers.

The surprising result is that controlling for these other factors embodied in the nonsmoking smoker calculations had such a large effect on the estimates, only partly supporting the critique of the tobacco manufacturers and their experts. Consider our mortality calculations (appendix to chapter 4). Of 100,000 men who smoked at age 24, we predicted that 74,618 men would be alive at age 65. Among 100,000 never male smokers at age 24, 87,480 would be alive at age 65. For 100,000 nonsmoking smokers—persons with the same characteristics as smokers except they never smoked, 84,908 men would be alive at age 65. Thus, the implication without adjusting for nonsmoking smokers is that the effect of smoking is to reduce the probability of survival by 0.13. Adjusting for other factors, the reduction is 0.10. By age 85, the effect of smoking is to reduce the probability of survival by 0.18 if the comparison is a never smoker and by 0.11 if the comparison is the nonsmoking smoker, implying that the bias from confounding is greater at higher ages. But the effect of smoking on survival remains appreciable, nevertheless. Virtually no one survives past 100. Our calculations of survival stopped at that age in any event. Between ages 85 and 100, differences in survival rates by smoking status narrow as one approaches this "terminal" age.[8] But with any positive discount rate, including the three percent rate we used in our analysis, outcomes at ages of eighty-five and above do not figure very much in the decisions of a 24-year-old.

Cost of Mortality and Disability as a Share of the Total Cost of Smoking

The notion of placing a dollar value on life years and on dimension of quality of life will be objectionable to some. But one indicator that life and quality of life has value is that societies devote resources to extending life and its quality, starting with public investments in biomedical research.

Somewhat less surprising, but surprising nevertheless, is the high private cost of smoking to young adults, especially to men. Our estimates are conservative in that we used a conservative value for a lost life year. Much higher estimates of life year value than we have used have been reported and values appear to have risen over time (Costa and Kahn 2002), implying that a cohort of persons turning twenty-four today would probably value life years gained in mid and late life much more highly than we did. Mortality cost was the largest single element of private cost, which is not a surprising finding (see e.g., Cutler et al. 2002). Although the effects of smoking in extending life years with disability were not as large as we anticipated, costs associated with earlier occurrence of disability and its modest extension were among the more important components of the total private cost of smoking.

Effects of Smoking on Medicaid and Medicaid Expenditures

The low values of Medicaid cost attributable to smoking and the negative values of smoking-attributable Medicare cost and Social Security are surprising for what they imply about the arguments on which federal and state governments have based demands for compensation from tobacco manufacturers. Smoking imposes a huge social cost, but the governments and taxpayers have not generally been the main victims. Nevertheless, the results are not surprising, given the method we used to compute such cost.

In any year, Medicaid or Medicare would save money if the programs did not cover the expense of smoking-related illnesses. If smoking would magically disappear, the programs would reap short-run savings as a result. But we have posed the question differently, and in our view, correctly. Smoking is not only a major lifestyle choice made during adolescence or early adulthood having implications over the whole life cycle. It is analogous to the decision to stay in high school or to attend college or to sink equity capital into a house. If the tobacco manufacturers are culpable of inducing people to smoke, they are culpable of inducing people to engage in a habit that often lasts for many years. For this reason, an incidence or life cycle approach that considers the effects of smoking on survival is appropriate. By contrast, the prevalence approaches takes a selected population as given and does not incorporate these survival effects.

For a program such as Medicare that mainly covers persons after age 65, it is of great consequence that of 100,000 men alive at age 24 who smoke, only 74,618 would be alive to receive Medicare benefits and Old Age Survivors Insurance (OASI) of Social Security at the normal retirement age of 65, as contrasted with 84,908 "nonsmoking smoking" men who would survive to age 65 if they did not smoke. The 10,290 men who smoke and do not survive to age 65 contribute to but do not receive full OSAI benefits on average and receive no Medicare benefits unless they are very disabled and receive Social Security Disability Insurance (SSDI), a small component of the Social Security program (chapter 6) or if they develop end-stage renal disease. SSDI beneficiaries are automatically entitled to Medicare benefits. Persons with ESRD do not receive income transfers unless they qualify for an income transfer program, but they are automatically entitled to Medicare.

If we were to base our estimates of smoking costs on data from persons alive in a particular year, the prevalence approach, in any year smoking would add to Medicare outlays. But the mortality effects are powerful and more than offset the higher cost to Medicare in any given year attributable to smoking. The implication is that, if anything, Medicare should compensate smokers and tobacco companies, not the reverse, based purely on cash receipts versus expenditures attributable to smoking. That smoking favorably affects Medicare and Social Security's cash flows is a fact. Of course, the notion of compensating the losers is a value judgment.

Premium Surcharges for the Cost of Smoking

For some forms of insurance, premium surcharges based on the insureds' behavior or prior experience are commonplace. The best example is automobile insurance, which bases premiums on prior accident records and traffic violations as well as on personal characteristics, such as the insured's age and gender and location of residence (Lemaire 1985). By contrast, surcharging is relatively rare in health insurance and not as widespread as we would have expected for life insurance. For health insurance, there is no surcharging on the basis of prior health experience or health-relevant behaviors by Medicare or private group insurance. Our results (chapter 8) suggest little or no surcharging based on smoking status by individual private health insurers as well. And for life insurance, surcharging has been insufficient, at least historically, to eliminate the financial transfer from nonsmokers to smokers. The result for life insurance is a surprising finding. Of course, the policies that respondents to the Health and Retirement Study had were probably purchased years ago, and life insurers may be surcharging more frequently at present. One might think that competitive forces in insurance markets would eliminate community-rated (age-, gender-based) premiums. But if such forces work toward this result, they do so quite slowly.

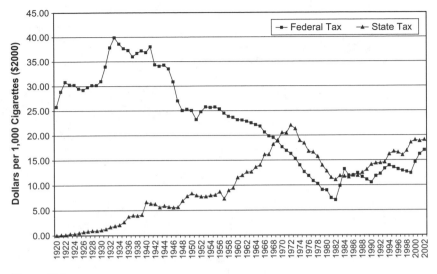

Figure 11.1
U.S. federal and state tax rates for cigarettes, 1920 to 2002.

Implications for Specific Programs

Cigarette Excise Taxes

Federal and state cigarette excise tax rates have varied dramatically over time (fig. 11.1). Real (in year 2000 dollars) federal tax rates (expressed in cents per pack) declined until 1983. Since then, in fits and starts, the trend in federal rates has been positive. Real state tax rates generally rose until the early 1970s, then declined for about a decade. Since then, the trend has been positive, especially since 2000 (Orzechowski and Walker 2002).

Using these tax rates, our life table, and, from the 1998 National Health Interview Survey, quit rates and smoking consumption levels by age and gender, we computed federal and state cigarette tax payments by birth year (fig. 11.2). These calculations neglect cohort effects in smoking patterns (see discussion below). We find that persons born in 1913 faced a higher cigarette tax burden than did persons born in 1973. To the extent that we underestimated smoking consumption of persons born in 1913 relative to their counterparts born sixty years later, this comparison is conservative. We have assumed that real tax rates will remain at their 2002 levels, and given recent trends, this assumption may be invalid. Although such real increases would decrease

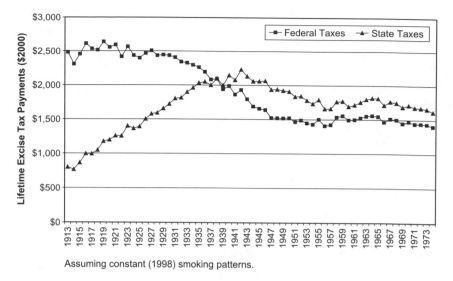

Assuming constant (1998) smoking patterns.

Figure 11.2
Estimated lifetime excise tax payments per smoker by birth year.

cigarette consumption, over the range of likely increases, tax payments would probably rise. This would have the effect of raising payments of the 1973 vintage persons relative to those born in 1913.

Are cigarette taxes too high or too low? It depends. If we employ the criteria used in the best known prior economic studies of the cost of smoking (Manning et al. 1989, 1991; Viscusi 1995, 1999, 2002), that is, to cover the external cost excluding the cost of secondary smoke to smokers' spouses/partners, we agree with their conclusion that excise taxes are set at about the right level. If we include secondary smoke losses to spouses/partners (quasi-external cost) as part of external cost, cigarette taxes are too low. If as Gruber and Köszegi (2001) and Gruber and Mullainathan (2002) have argued, cigarette excise taxes are a self-control device that makes smokers better off (see chapter 1 for a discussion of this issue), cigarette taxes are far too low. Private or internal cost of smoking far exceeds external cost, irrespective of how the latter is computed.

Whether smokers are time-inconsistent, requiring self-control devices, or time consistent, forward-looking, and rational, will continue to be debated. We have not attempted to resolve this dispute in our study. Similarly, whether quasi-external cost is really internal or external cannot be decided with evidence on spousal interactions available at this time. Rather we take an agnostic view, carefully separating it from internal and external cost, letting the users of our estimates place them into the category they deem to be appropriate.

At least for the present, we are inclined to conclude that cigarette excise taxes are not excessive. However, states may get a bigger bang for the buck if revenues from this source are tied to public expenditures on tobacco control, as such states as California have done.

Master Settlement Agreement

In November 1998, 46 state attorneys general and major tobacco manufacturers settled all litigation filed by the states. In return for an agreement not to sue, the states obtained a commitment from the companies to pay $206 billion over a period of 25 years, (Cutler et al. 2002; Viscusi 2002), which Cutler et al. (2002) estimated to be about $105 billion in present value. Although states receive a federal subsidy for part of the Medicaid expense, this was not considered in determining the amount of the settlement (Viscusi 2002).

The motive for filing suits on behalf of Medicaid seems to have been strategic at least in part, as described in box 11.3. Individuals who had smoked and suffered from smoking-related diseases had had difficulty in winning their cases against the tobacco companies since the companies were able to argue that the smokers knowingly engaged in an unhealthy behavior. By contrast, Medicaid (and other payers) were unwilling victims.

Based on our estimates of the impact of smoking on Medicaid expenditures, there is no way that a payment of $105 billion over 25 years

Box 11.3
Plaintiffs' Strategy for Defeating the Tobacco Companies

> "In the crowded motel room, Lewis (Michael, attorney) laid out his unorthodox and untried plan. He didn't have to work hard to convince the Mississippians.
>
> Scruggs (Richard, attorney) and Barrett (Don, attorney) had tried several times to get past the industry's defense of pinning individuals with the responsibility of choosing to smoke. The plan to take on Big Tobacco by suing the cigarette companies to pay for the medical costs of the state's 200,000 Medicaid smokers seemed perfect. The industry's argument that smoking was a personal decision couldn't be an issue here. 'Eureka!' said Barrett. 'The state of Mississippi has never smoked a cigarette'" (Mollenkamp et al. 1998, p. 29).

could be justified on this basis.[9] One problem in making a comparison is that we used a life cycle approach, whereas the settlement was probably based on a prevalence approach. Nevertheless, we make the following comparison. Each year, a new cohort of persons becomes 24-year-old smokers. We estimate that the gross cost to Medicaid of each new cohort attributable to smoking is $874 million. Considering 25 such cohorts raises the sum to $21.9 billion. Net of the extra taxes paid by smokers for the extra cost imposed on Medicaid, the amounts are substantially reduced to $442 million annually and $11.5 billion over 25 years.

Part of the reason for our lower estimates is that our calculations incorporated smoking cessation, premature deaths from smoking, and our estimates are discounted. For particular age cohorts, much, if not most, of the higher cost of personal services was born by Medicaid (and ultimately taxpayers).[10] Thus, the distinction lies not in any lack of evidence that smoking increased expenditures, but rather in use of our estimates of the effect of smoking on utilization of health care services.

There is another way to assess the impact of the settlement between the state attorneys general and the tobacco manufacturers. Since the settlement, the price of cigarettes has risen considerably, which is directly or indirectly related to the settlement. The direct effect is the pass-through settlement cost by the manufacturers in the price of cigarettes. The indirect effect is the effect of the settlement on the general political environment in the states, which made antismoking public policies more easily implemented.

Trogdon and Sloan (2003) estimated that the settlement through 2001 had saved 3.4 million life years among persons aged 18–24 alone. This is a one-time saving. Annually, the saving in life years would be about one-sixth as large. In this sense, the settlement was quite worthwhile. From our analysis, without taking a position on liability and rather focusing on damages, we only question whether the states were the correct recipient of funds from the settlement. Individual smokers and their families have suffered far more from smoking than have state taxpayers.

Federal Litigation Against the Tobacco Industry

In another suit, the U.S. government opposed the tobacco manufacturers. The complaint stated that "[d]efendants' tortuous and unlawful course of conduct has caused consumers of the defendants' products to suffer dangerous diseases and injuries. As a consequence of defendants' tortious and unlawful conduct, the Federal Government spends more than \$20 billion annually for the treatment of injuries and diseases caused by defendants' products" (*United States of America vs. Philip Morris* 1999, p. 4).[11] Although Medicare allegedly suffered the greatest share of the loss, the total reflected excess payments on all federal programs. As in the MSA, individual smokers covered by Medicare and other federal programs were free to sue the companies on their own, but the compensation sought by this lawsuit was not to be shared with individual smokers.

Clearly the above damage calculation does not consider the impact of smoking on survival. In any year, large numbers of people acquire such smoking-related diseases as lung cancer, chronic obstructive pulmonary disease (COPD), and cardiovascular disease and many other lower-incidence diseases. Federal programs cover the personal health services of many of these persons. However, smoking also kills, and the cost savings from the mortality effects exceed the cost increases attributable to care for persons with these smoking-related diseases.

In the end, the burden of financing Medicare falls on employed persons who pay Medicare premium taxes, Medicare beneficiaries who pay Part B premiums, and taxpayers who contribute to general revenue. In contrast to individual injury victims, the federal government is relatively efficient in pursuing claims for compensation from the tobacco manufacturers. In this sense, government is a proper agent for pursuing claims. However, because nonsmokers outnumber smokers, when governments are compensated for damages, there is a transfer from smokers to nonsmokers. To the extent that external costs net of cigarette excise taxes remain positive (as in table 11.2), such transfers are justified.

Limitations of Our Study

Although our study is comprehensive, we acknowledge several limitations.

Technological Change

Two forms of technological change are potentially important: change in medical technology and change in technology of cigarette manufacturing. Dramatic changes in medical technology have occurred, especially since World War II. Changes have occurred in disease prevention, diagnosis of disease, and in therapy. Deaths from cardiovascular disease have decreased because of better control of hypertension. Use of aspirin and introduction of beta blockers and ace inhibitors have been useful in at least secondary prevention of heart attacks. Changes in imaging technology have greatly improved diagnosis of heart disease and cancer, although using this technology as screening tools for such conditions as lung cancer remains controversial (see e.g., Patz, Black, and Goodman 2001). New drugs may prolong life with lung disease, although not cure it. Invasive cardiology and use of thrombolitics may save lives of smokers suffering from heart attacks and stroke.

Holding other factors constant, these changes should extend life and reduce some of the consequences of disability from smoking. The effect of medical technological change on the cost of smoking is affected by more than these changes alone. Persons who do not acquire smoking-related illness or are cured of it become exposed to the risk of non-smoking-related disease. Technological change also has occurred for diseases not directly linked to smoking, but for some diseases, such as Alzheimer's, clinically effective methods of prevention, diagnosis, and treatment have not yet been found.

Our analysis is static in that we did not account for such technological change in our calculations. Smokers, however, may reason that they have less to lose because they will eventually be rescued by technological change. If they are right, our estimates of cost will prove to have been too high.

There have also been changes in the cigarette, starting with filters and reductions in the tar context. However, there may be compensatory actions by companies (e.g., greater use of the tobacco stem with the more widespread use of filters [Kluger 1996]) and in smoking habits [Evans and Farrelly 1998]). Thus, we are reluctant to conclude that cigarette product changes have reduced the cost of smoking.

Cohort Effects

Because of data limitations, our analysis ignored cohort effects. The life table we developed is for the late 1990s. Quit rates came from cross-sectional evidence from the 1998 NHIS. Yet our estimates of contributions to Social Security and Medicare was for a cohort of individuals with birth years 1931–1941, as were our adjustments for the effects of other covariates (other health behaviors, risk preference, financial-planning horizon) underlying our estimates for nonsmoking smokers.

Over the course of the twentieth century, cigarette consumption increased until midcentury, declining thereafter (Sloan, Smith, and Taylor 2002). Women started smoking in greater numbers later in the twentieth century than did men. To the extent that there is a secular decline in the share of adults who smoke, quit rates can be expected to decline as well. A decline in quit rates would increase loss attributable to smoking.

Contributions to Social Security and Medicare have increased over time, measured in dollars with a constant purchasing power. Thus, our estimates of contributions to these programs understate the amounts that both smokers and nonsmokers who turned 24 during the late 1990s could have expected to contribute to these programs over their lifetimes. By contrast, Social Security benefits are linked to the consumer price index and therefore will not increase in real terms over time. To the extent that smokers are net losers from Social Security, we have probably underestimated the losses that 24-year-olds in the late 1990s could have expected. For Medicare, however, real outlays as well as contributions will increase, making the net effect of these changes more difficult to deduce.

Increases in the Real Price of Personal Health Care Services

In general, we assumed no real increase in the future prices of various personal health care services. Historically, such prices have increased faster than prices overall. In this sense, we have underestimated the loss attributable to a person who turned 24 during the late 1990s.

Lack of Panel Data for Persons Under Age 50

Much of the harm from smoking occurs among smokers over age 50. However, adverse health outcomes of all types, death, disability, and morbidity, also occur at much higher rates after age 50. Thus, a priori, it is not clear that the relative risks of adverse health outcomes are lower for smokers before age 50. With the life cycle approach we have used, it was critically important to have data for smokers and nonsmokers under age 50.

Unfortunately, although smoking questions are asked on surveys of younger persons, such as the National Longitudinal Survey of Youth, smoking questions have been asked irregularly. Also, the health questions are not nearly as good as those in the HRS. Data from the Rand Health Insurance Experiment cover persons under 50 (used by Manning et al. 1989, 1991), but the data are now old and the panel is for a shorter period than is the HRS. Thus, we used a single cross section, the 1998 National Health Interview Survey (NHIS). The NHIS is nationally representative, recent, and it contains detailed information on smoking, other health behaviors that may be correlated with smoking, utilization of personal health services, sick days, and health and functional status. But the NHIS is not a panel. One unfortunate consequence is that endogeneity problems loom larger than with the Health and Retirement Study panel. With the panel, we could evaluate the effects of smoking at the beginning of a two-year period on utilization and health outcomes reported two years subsequently. Adding questions on health utilization, health status, and on health behaviors to existing panels of young adults merits a high priority.

Potential Components of Smoking Costs Not Quantified

Although we quantified most of the important components of smoking costs, we did not consider them all. Among costs incurred by mature adults, we did not assess the cost of caregiving for spouses with diseases related to smoking. We performed no new analysis of environmental smoke outside the household or effects of smoking on health of infants and children. Results from past research are summarized in chapter 3.

Imprecise Estimates of Value of Life and Quality of Life

Many researchers and the vast majority of nonresearchers appear to be reluctant to place a dollar value on a life, a life year, and time spent with disease and disability. Yet values are implicit in decisions of people in their daily lives and as public citizens and of policymakers who act on their behalf. Estimates of the values of life and life years have been obtained by observing trade-offs that individuals really make (such as the wage premium required by workers to take jobs with higher risk to life) or from stated preferences. Progress has been made in valuation, although there is still room for progress.

We have been explicit about the values of life years and life years with particular forms of disability we have used. Readers who take issue with our assumed values can easily adjust our estimates of loss due to premature death and disability by plugging in alternative values. Or they can disregard these estimates entirely, focusing instead on effects of smoking on utilization of personal health services or on public programs, such as Medicare, Medicaid, and Social Security.

Complementarities: Smoking, Excessive Alcohol Consumption, and Obesity

Smoking and alcohol consumption are complements, and smoking reduces the probability of being overweight (see e.g., Picone and Sloan 2003). Eliminating or greatly reducing smoking would have important effects on health behaviors and on health more generally. In our study, we did not consider these potential effects. Our understanding of these interrelationships is still too superficial. More research on these topics is needed.

Final Word

Even with all of the publicity about the harmful effects of smoking, improving personal health habits receives insufficient attention in discussions of national health policy. Clearly, the private and social costs are huge. Perhaps further publicity of these costs will help to stimulate the interest among smokers, potential smokers, and the public at large in smoking issues.

Perhaps estimates of the high cost of smoking will influence policymakers. It is remarkable to us that in spite of all of the adverse publicity of the harmful effects of smoking, almost all of the proceeds from the MSA are not being spent on tobacco control (National Conference of State Legislatures 2002).

Tobacco control programs can help to curb the high costs of smoking as can increases in the cigarette excise tax rates. It seems unlikely, however, that these policies can fully succeed in reducing smoking rates on their own. It will be necessary for persons aged 24 and younger to face the fact that the decision to smoke is a very costly one—one of the most costly decisions they make. Estimating such cost is only a first step in delivering this message.

Notes

Chapter 1

1. A footnote in the latter advertisement reads: "Fully reported in authoritative medical journals."

2. See Warner et al. 1995; Chaloupka et al. 2000; and Cutler et al. 2002 for the most complete discussions.

3. The available evidence shows that federal taxes are more potent than state taxes in reducing consumption, in part because the effects of state tax increases are partially dissipated by increased bootlegging, but also because historically, federal taxes have tended to rise in large increments, whereas state taxes tend to go up in increments of a penny or two a pack, making these less noticeable to smokers (Meier and Licari 1997; Chaloupka et al. 2000). Public health advocates have long pressured government officials to increase the federal tax rate by sizable amounts. In the early 1990s, the American Heart Association, American Lung Association, and American Cancer Society all were on record as supporting an increase in the federal excise tax by $2 per pack. Likewise, prior to the emergence of the Clinton health reform plan, Senator Bill Bradley (D-NJ) and Representative Mike Andrews (D-Tex) had introduced legislation to increase the tax to $1.00 per pack (MacKensie, Bartecchi, and Schrier 1994). In the debate whether to rely on a 75 cent-per-pack increase in federal tobacco taxes to help fund the Clinton health reform plan, competing estimates of the external costs of smoking, including new estimates developed by the U.S. Department of Treasury (1998), played an important role in the policy debate in Congress (e.g., Harris 1993; Passell 1993; Gravelle and Zimmerman 1994; Tollison 1994). The general consensus at the time was that if anything, cigarette taxes already exceeded optimal levels. The current federal tax rose to 39 cents a pack in January 2002. The U.S. Public Health Service report *Healthy People 2000: National Health Promotion and Disease Prevention Objectives* included the objective of "increase the average (State and Federal combined) tobacco excise tax to at least 50 percent of the average retail price of all cigarettes and smokeless tobacco" (National Center for Health Statistics 2001). As of November 2001, this objective had not yet been achieved even in the state with the highest state cigarette tax in the nation: New York's combined taxes of $1.45 per pack amounted to only 34 percent of the average retail price (Orzechowski and Walker 2002). The latest surgeon general's report concluded "when recent estimates of the costs of ETS (including the long-term costs of fetal and perinatal exposure to ETS) are considered, and when the premature death of smokers is not considered an economic benefit, a tax that would generate sufficient revenues to cover the external costs of smoking is almost certainly well above current cigarette taxes" (U.S. Department of Health and Human Services 2000a, p. 19).

4. Also, PHS sympathized with the view that good science comes out of the laboratory, that is, it is not based on epidemiology.

5. To date, the U.S. Food and Drug Administration (FDA) has approved only the use of sustained-release buproprion (the active compound in Zyban and Wellbutrin) for smoking cessation, although nortriptyline and clonidine also have been found to be effective and are used by some physicians (Rigotti 2002). A recent metanalysis showed that after 6 months, smoking cessation rates are 1.73 times higher among those using NRT compared to controls (Silagy et al. 1998, cited in Ranson et al. 2000). In combination with behavioral support, current pharmacologic approaches to smoking cessation allow 20 to 25 percent of quitters to abstain for at least one year; even physician advice alone produces cessation rates of 5 to 10 percent (U.S. Department of Health and Human Services 2000a). As a consequence, NRT sales are estimated to be responsible for an 8.3 percent reduction in per capita cigarette consumption between 1984 and 1998 (Hu et al. 2000). The 2.5 percent of smokers who successfully quit includes many persons who do not obtain help in the form of therapy or use smoking cessation aids consistently for sufficient duration.

6. Many plans also cover smoking cessation drugs requiring a prescription; some also will cover nonprescription smoking cessation drugs as part of the lifetime benefit. In addition, the U.S. Office of Personnel Management supports and encourages federal-agency-authorized smoking cessation programs, and such programs are permitted to pay for pharmacologic treatments. Such services are covered for retired and active military personnel and their dependents through Tricare (formerly CHAMPUS) and to veterans through the Veterans Health Administration (VHA) system, yet smoking cessation drugs and products are explicitly not covered under CHAMPVA (a program for dependents of veterans).

7. A more recent study showed that even when taking into account productivity losses and medical costs, one cessation aid, buproprion, provided a net benefit of $338 per employee who attempts to quit, compared to $26 for a nicotine patch, and $258 for a placebo (Nielsen and Fiore 2000).

8. Evidence of harm from smoking comes from nonexperimental or observational data, not from controlled experiments. For example, to the extent that smokers have higher rates of lung cancer, are hospitalized more than nonsmokers, have more work loss days, or receive greater amounts of personal care from friends and relatives, one may infer that smoking is the culprit. In the past, the tobacco companies have objected to such inferences, noting that an association does not *prove* causation. Some third factor, not included in the analysis but correlated with both smoking and the adverse outcome of interest, indeed may be the true determinant of the adverse outcome. But one may also return the ball to the companies' court: if, for example, the probability of dying of lung cancer is elevated some 25 times among male smokers versus male never smokers, what is the omitted factor that might explain the observed relationship?

9. Tobacco litigation can be divided into: (1) individual cases and class actions brought on behalf of past and present users of tobacco products who have allegedly been harmed by its use, (2) class actions brought on behalf of persons allegedly harmed from exposure to secondhand smoke, and (3) civil actions brought by governmental entities to recover the cost of welfare and health care costs attributable to consumption of tobacco products. In the third category, all fifty states filed lawsuits against tobacco manufacturers. With the exception of four cases settled earlier (for a total of $36.8 billion over 25 years; see Viscusi 1999 for details), these cases all were settled in the MSA, representing the largest amount ever paid in civil litigation in U.S. history, $206 billion, $105 billion in present

value (Cutler et al. 2002). Terms of the settlement agreement fall into four categories: financial provisions, youth targeting, tobacco corporate culture, and attorneys' fees and enforcement (see, e.g., Price and Dake 1999; Wilson 1999; Cutler et al. 2002). In return, the agreement settles all state, city, and county claims against participating tobacco companies as civil or statutory claims for past or future acts pertaining to exposure to tobacco products. In financial terms, states will continue to receive tobacco payments in perpetuity.

10. Sims (1994) (Fla.); Watson et al. (1995) (Wis.); Oster (1996) (Miss.); Hopkins and T. A. Lynch (1997) (Fla.); Harris (1997b) (Fla.); Harris (1997a) (Wash.); Max (1997a) (Miss.); Max (1997b) (Texas); Max (1997c) (Wash.); Miller (1997a) (Fla.); Miller (1997b) (Texas); Oster (1997a) (Miss.); Oster (1997b) (Fla.); Schumacher (1996) (Alaska); Harrison (1998a) (Okla.); Harrison (1998b) (Okla.); and Harrison (1999) (Hawaii).

Chapter 2

1. Although principles underlying this method date back centuries (Petty 1699), more recent studies by Fein (1958) and Mushkin (1962) are generally credited with applying this approach to the health field.

2. The SAF concept can be applied to other metrics as well. For example, based on the relative risk of death from lung cancer among smokers compared to nonsmokers and the prevalence of smoking in the population, one can estimate the fraction of lung cancer deaths due to smoking (see e.g., Lightwood et al. 2000).

3. The *Federal Reference Manual on Scientific Evidence* uses as a threshold for legal significance a relative risk of two or higher, on grounds that below this value, results are considered to be insufficiently reliable to conclude that a particular agent caused a disease (Levy and Marimont 1998). Similarly, the National Cancer Institute guidelines state that "relative risks of less than 2 [that is, a 100 percent increase] are considered small ... Such increases may be due to chance, statistical bias, or effects of confounding factors that are sometimes not evident" (ibid., p. 24). Yet of the 418,690 average annual deaths attributed to smoking by the U.S. Centers for Disease Control and Prevention (CDC), 163,071 are based on relative risks ranging from 1.1 to 1.9 (table 1, ibid., p. 28).

4. The literature is discussed in considerable detail in chapter 3.

5. For more detailed information on this survey, see Soldo et al. 1997.

6. Also, see Taylor et al. 2002 for discussion of this point.

7. See also Buchsbaum et al. 1991; Chan, Pristach, and Welte 1994; Girela et al. 1994; Mayfield, McLeod, and Hall 1974; McIntosh, Leigh, and Baldwin 1994. A recent review of screening methods for alcohol abuse and dependence found that the sensitivity of the CAGE in older populations ranged from 63 to 70 percent, while the specificity ranged from 82 to 91 percent, when a score of two or higher was used to define alcohol abuse or dependence (Fiellin, Reid, and O'Connor 2000). In these terms, the CAGE compares well with other, generally lengthier, screens for alcohol abuse and/or dependence, such as the Alcohol Use Disorders Test (AUDIT), and the Michigan Alcoholism Screening Test (MAST).

8. See, e.g., Picone et al. 2004, who examined this question in the context of the decision to obtain mammography.

9. See Grossman and Kaestner 1997 and Kenkel 2000 for reviews of this literature.

10. Such factors as educational attainment are important determinants of smoking behavior (see e.g., Wray et al. 1998 and Wong et al. 2002).

11. To compute life expectancies from these data, one can use the life expectancy calculator at http://www.LifeExpectancy.com/asp/software. See Taylor et al. (2002) for a description of the data and how it has been used to assess effects of smoking.

Chapter 3

1. In a well-cited legal study, Hanson and Logue (1998) estimated cost at $7.00 per pack, but claimed that this was a lower bound on such cost. They modified estimates from economists.

2. "Incidence-based" in that they evaluate the cost of adding another case, in this context, another smoker. The cross-sectional is a prevalence approach in that it purports to capture cost attributable to a particular type of behavior at a point in time. The cross-sectional approach is often called the "cost-of-illness" approach, but this term reveals nothing about the underlying methodology. All approaches measure the cost of illness.

3. Hanson and Logue (1998) argue that only costs, not benefits, associated with death are relevant to policy decisions.

4. In much of the literature, productivity losses are called "indirect costs." These costs include lost earnings from death, disability, and morbidity as opposed to "direct costs," which include expenditures on medical care. The terms *direct* and *indirect* are not informative and therefore are not used in this book. When lost earnings are used, these represent lost productivity.

5. For example, Miller et al. (1998b,c) report smoking-related medical expenditures to be 15.8 percent of total medical costs measured, but this total constitutes only 12.6 percent of personal health expenditures overall.

6. These include psoriasis, osteoporosis and osteoarthritis, impotence, cataracts, macular degeneration, optic neuropathy, ulcers, Crohn's disease, hearing loss, and peridontal disease. See chapter 9 for further discussion.

7. See Warner, Hodgson, and Carroll 1999 and Lightwood et al. 2000 for further explanations of differences in these two studies.

8. The concept of the nonsmoking smoker was used earlier by Leu (1984) but made more well known after publication of the studies by Manning et al. (1989, 1991).

9. This is based on Rice's (1999) estimate of mortality losses in 1995, reported in table 3.1 divided by 430,700 estimated annual lives lost to smoking from 1990–1994 using the Smoking-Attributable Mortality, Morbidity, and Economic Costs (SAMMEC) II model on which Rice's estimates were based (Centers for Disease Control and Prevention 1997).

10. Fine-grained criticisms also may be leveled at individual components that have been estimated to date. For example, in relying on U.S. Office of Technology Assessment (OTA) estimates of the average incremental cost of LBW infants, the Marks et al. (1990) study might have overstated smoking-attributable costs. A more recent study found that, principally due to the difference in severity of LBW, the cost difference between the net incremental costs per LBW infant due to smoking may be up to 18 percent smaller than

the net incremental costs per LBW infant due to all causes (Li, Windsor, and Hassan 1994).

11. As we shall see in chapter 5, this assumption is not valid.

12. See Pauly 1997 for a detailed discussion of this issue and empirical evidence. Also, see our chapter 5.

13. They cited evidence from Van Nostrand et al. 1979 indicating that only 0.6 percent of nursing home residents had emphysema, a condition caused by smoking (see their p. 39).

14. According to Manning et al. (1991, p. 199), "The 38 percent value ... is one of our 'softest' numbers."

15. In a footnote, Manning et al. (1991) argued that "Although lower-income people pay a higher percentage of earnings than higher-income persons pay for private health insurance, they pay a lower percentage of earnings for nursing home care and they collect proportionately more in Social Security payments, so the error in assuming that overall financing is proportional to earnings should be small (Pechman 1977)" (p. 200).

16. The tar adjustment is controversial. For a critique, see Hanson and Logue 1998. Also, there are other qualitative characteristics of a cigarette that may matter (see Sloan, Smith, and Taylor 2003).

17. Warner, Hodgson, and Carroll (1999) argued that the relative risks for utilization should be lower than the relative risks linking smoking to mortality published in the peer-reviewed literature.

Chapter 5

1. The advantages of this approach are explained in chapter 2.

2. The definition of smoking differs among surveys. Fig. 5.1 is based on data from the NHIS. Using the behavioral risk factor surveillance system, we computed a 23 percent smoking rate for persons age 50 as of 2001.

3. In the HRS and AHEAD longitudinal analysis, we included explanatory variables that were both time invariant or time varying. Time-invariant variables, measured at wave one, were: gender; education; race; history of problem drinking (HRS only); a risk tolerance measure (Barsky et al. 1997); and two measures of the person's time horizon. Some of these variables, such as problem drinking and the person's time horizon, are logically time varying, but the HRS only collected such information at the baseline interview. Time-varying explanatory variables were: marital status; body mass index (BMI); current alcohol consumption; health insurance status; age; and survey wave.

4. Judging from the HRS, the cessation rate after age 55 is low (Sloan, Smith, and Taylor 2003).

5. As described in chapter 2, our method controlled for sample selection stemming from differential mortality over time in a reference population of 24-year-old smokers and nonsmokers prior to the age at which they are sampled for the NHIS, HRS, and AHEAD, respectively.

6. Centers for Medicare and Medicaid Services (2000).

7. U.S. Prospective Payment Assessment Commission (1995, p. 21).

8. U.S. Department of Commerce (2000, tables 172 and 191).

9. U.S. Physician Payment Review Commission (1995, pp. 77–84).

10. Jones (2002).

11. See Pauly 1997 for a detailed explanation of the conventional versus the economists' view.

12. See Ehrenberg and Smith 1988, p. 399.

13. See e.g., Phelps 1973.

14. See Barsky et al. 1997.

15. See chapter 2.

16. Age was specified as a series of splines, and a squared term for the last spline to allow for nonlinear age effects between the ages of 45 and 61 and for predictions through age 64. Time-invariant smoking and alcohol consumption variables were interacted with age splines, and the remaining variables were interacted with the spline interval.

17. Cigarette excise taxes represent a special and important case. We excluded such taxes from our calculations in this chapter because these taxes are only paid by smokers. With a few exceptions in which cigarette excise taxes have been earmarked for specific types of public expenditures, states spend such revenue on a variety of goods and services of which health care in general and Medicaid in particular are only one. We analyze the impact of excise taxes separately (see chapter 11).

18. But progressivity may be declining in the first decade of the twenty-first century.

19. Predicted probabilities for the two nonresponse categories were reallocated proportionately to the ten ordered categories.

Chapter 6

1. In addition to redistribution, other rationales for the existing Social Security program are: (1) "paternalism to counter life-cycle myopia" and (2) "avoidance of counterproductive 'gaming' of the welfare system by the aged" (Feldstein and Liebman 2002). Smokers' greater average myopia, if true, might rationalize Social Security on grounds of paternalism even in the presence of moral hazard from the redistributive dimension.

2. Furthermore, quantifying the differences in the value of Social Security benefits across individuals allows for an analysis of the extent to which the system's well-documented effects on retirement and savings decisions (e.g., Feldstein and Liebman 2002) may differ by smoking status and, on an aggregate basis, how these effects will change over time as the consequences of smoking cessation and greater rates of never smokers materialize. However, these indirect consequences of changes in smoking behavior on Social Security and retirement more generally, with potentially substantial macroeconomic impact, will not be analyzed in this chapter.

3. Although nonsmokers take breaks as well, it might be argued that smokers are less productive between breaks due to cravings.

4. See chapter 2 for a description of this data source.

5. As part of wave one, respondents were asked for permission for HRS to obtain their Social Security taxable earnings history and benefits data from SSA. In total, 9,539 respondents agreed to release their records. We restricted the sample to persons aged 51 to 62 in 1992. This screen resulted in a usable sample of 3,358 males and 3,948 females.

6. Income subject to Social Security taxation and tax rates have varied since the program's start. Initially, Social Security covered only earnings of workers in commerce and industry (except railroads) under age 65. In 1940, about 24 million persons were covered. By 1991, coverage had expanded to about 134 million persons, or about 96 percent of jobs and 88 percent of earnings (U.S. House of Representatives Committee on Ways and Means 1992). Earnings limits ranged from $3,600 in 1951 to $53,400 in 1991. Tax rates varied from 3 percent in 1951 to 11.2 percent in 1991.

7. Since earnings histories differ substantially by gender, particularly during the historical period, we estimated separate equations by gender.

8. To generate predictions of earnings, we used a fifth degree polynomial in age.

9. This would have necessitated inclusion of interactions of each characteristic with every smoking status/age spline, i.e., 45 additional variables per characteristic. Such a more general specification would have increased multicollinearity and resulted in a substantial loss of degrees of freedom. Our estimates represent the effects of smoking assuming age- and gender-specific mean returns to other characteristics.

Chapter 7

1. See, e.g.: Anderson, Gustman, and Steinmeier 1999; Brown 2001; Gustman and Steinmeier 2002; Hardy and Shuey 2000; and Lumsdaine, Stock, and Wise 1998.

2. See the studies cited in the previous footnote on retirement effects and research oriented toward measuring pension wealth such as Johnson, Samba Moorthis, and Crystal (2000).

3. A comparable assumption was made in our analysis of Social Security contributions and benefits (chapter 6).

4. Under Social Security, survivor benefits are only paid to the extent that they exceed the amount that the spouse would get if he or she were not married, or the other spouse is still alive. Here we assume that own earnings have no effect on survivor benefits from the spouse.

Chapter 8

1. See, e.g., Sloan, Bovbjerg, and Githens 1991.

2. See Rothschild and Stiglitz 1976 for the seminal article on adverse selection in insurance markets and the welfare implications of adverse selection. Bond and Crocker (1991) show that endogenous categorization of risks, e.g., on the basis of smoking status, may be welfare enhancing in the presence of adverse selection.

3. See, generally, Abraham 1986 and Sloan, Bovbjerg, and Githens 1991.

4. In the insurance field, "credibility" refers to the extent to which an insurer can rely on evidence, such as past claims, for purpose of setting premiums in relation to other factors, such as the person's age, location, etc.

5. Interestingly, a 1949 edition of the *Handbook of Insurance*, although lengthy (discussing such arcane subjects as hair plucking), contains no references to smoking, cigarettes, or tobacco. See Crobaugh 1949. By about 1980, smoking had begun to be used by life insurers in risk classification (see e.g. Crowne and Shapiro 1980).

6. Revenue from cigarette excise taxes accrues to governments and thus is only available to offset cross subsidies in the life insurance market very indirectly. That is, nonsmokers who purchase life insurance may pay lower taxes because of revenue generated by this excise tax.

7. See Brigham 1998.

8. Experience-rated premiums are common in automobile liability insurance (Lemaire 1985), but mechanisms generally exist so that drivers with bad driving records can at least obtain minimum liability limits coverage.

Chapter 9

1. See chapter 2 for a brief description of the NHIS.

2. Cutler and Richardson (1997), based on a review of the literature on value of life by Tolley, Kenkel, and Fabian (1994) concluding that life was worth from $70,000 to $175,000 per life year, assumed a life year in perfect health is worth $100,000 per year. If this is so, it does not seem far fetched that a year lived with at least one ADL limitation is worth $50,000.

3. Cutler and Richardson (1997) employed a novel method for valuing losses due to chronic conditions, relating specific conditions to a five-point self-reported health scale from which they computed quality-adjusted life years (QALYs). The QALYs for most chronic diseases related to smoking were estimated to be around 0.7 to less than 0.9. Although interesting, the estimates are probably illustrative at best. Our approach, which is roughly consistent with Cutler and Richardson's, was to take half of the value of loss for ADL limitations for limitations not involving ADLs, and round to the nearest thousand, nearly $25,000 per limitation per year.

4. This could be an underestimate of loss since some employers may hire temporary workers from an employment service at a premium to replace sick workers. Also, there may be training costs associated with hiring temporary or replacement workers.

Chapter 10

1. More formally, joint decision making via bargaining affects decisions primarily through the joint revenue constraint and the implied sharing rule. Changes in the allocation of good among spouses are thus driven by changes in reservation utilities or sharing rules.

2. These decisions can be analyzed as a noncooperative game, which is an extension of the simple one-person decision problem. The outcome of this game can be characterized as a Nash equilibrium. If choices are only observed in discrete intervals, one can charac-

terize this game using, for example, an endogenous probit model. To date, no one has conducted such analysis.

3. The authors of this review referred to a study by Wells (1998), who analyzed five studies that best controlled for other risk factors for heart disease. That author obtained an adjusted relative risk for passive smoking and heart disease mortality of 1.7, and a pooled risk from 11 studies of 1.3 for nonfatal cardiac events such as myocardial infarction, angina, or malignant electrocardiographic changes.

4. The authors suggested that researchers use subclinical measures, which due to their greater prevalence than clinical measures could yield more accurate measures of effects of ETS; moreover, the subclinical measures should require smaller sample sizes to detect statistically significant differences of a given magnitude.

5. Risk factors for SIDS include such diverse characteristics as younger mothers, LBW, prone sleep position, male sex, and late birth order (Anderson and Cook 1997). Its occurrence is often linked to low socioeconomic status, which further confounds analyses of cause due to its association with many of the risk factors.

6. See chapter 2 for a description of the HRS.

7. These estimates were based on rates of ever smokers in the 1998 NHIS cohort of 40.8 percent among females and 59.2 percent among males. Smoking rates for persons aged 24 in the 1998 NHIS were 28.8 percent and 36.6 percent, respectively. Using these smoking rates would yield a lower unconditional expected value of the life years lost due to reduced exposure to ETS, but this value would be divided by a smaller share of smokers, resulting in comparable values of the lost life years per smoker. We will use the latter shares in projecting lifetime losses in the next chapter.

Chapter 11

1. See, e.g., ⟨http://www.philipmorrisinternational.com⟩.

2. Of course, practice may fall short of the ideal. For example, the recently concluded Master Settlement Agreement (MSA) gave major tobacco companies limited immunity against lawsuits in return for substantial payments to the states. The feature of the MSA does not offer *ex ante* incentives to exercise due care. However, to the extent that the companies raised cigarette prices to cover the payments to states, the settlement had the effect of imposing an excise tax on cigarette consumption.

3. One possible objection to the use of values based on labor market decisions is that they do not generalize to nonemployed persons such as the elderly. However, we are looking at cost from the perspective of 24-year-olds. At this age virtually all persons expect to participate in some labor market activity over their life cycle. Admittedly, the life years lost from smoking may come out of nonworking years, but assigning different values over the life cycle would have added too much complexity.

4. ⟨http://jama.ama-assn.org/cgi/content/full/289/14/1785/TABLEJOC22407T1⟩.

5. Admittedly, this line of reasoning runs the risk of leading to a circular argument. That is, if the government has intervened, this must be because of a major externality in consumption. Yet consumption externalities provide plausible justifications for many public programs ranging from food stamps to Medicaid.

6. See the citation in this chapter's footnote 1.

7. See Bound, Jaeger, and Baker 1995, Nelson and Startz 1990, and Staiger and Stock 1997.

8. We assumed 100 to be the terminal age.

9. This estimate is discounted to present value. The undiscounted value is over twice this.

10. In particular, see table 5.10.

11. This suit had opposition from the right side of the political spectrum at the time it was proposed. For example, Gaziano (1999) argued that "[t]he planned federal suit against the tobacco industry is not really about recovering Medicare costs or vindicating legal rights; it is best explained as an attempt to use the majesty and might of the federal government to force an unjust settlement with no basis in law. Regardless of the merits of the legislative options available to Congress, everyone should oppose a naked attempt to misuse the courts in order to impose industry-wide regulation by litigation" (p. 2).

References

Abraham, K. S. (1986). *Distributing Risk: Insurance, Legal Theory, and Public Policy*. New Haven: Yale University Press.

Adams, E. K., Cathy Melvin, Rob Merritt, and Brenda Worrall (1999). *Costs of Environmental Tobacco Smoke: An International Review*. Atlanta: Rollins School of Public Health Emory University.

Adams, E. Kathleen, G. Solanski, and L. S. Miller (1997). Medical-care Expenditures Attributable to Cigarette Smoking during Pregnancy—United States, 1995. *Morbidity and Mortality Weekly Report* 46(44): 1048–1050.

Aligne, C. A., and Jeffrey J. Stoddard (1997). Tobacco and Children. *An Economic Evaluation of the Medical Effects of Parental Smoking* 151: 648–653.

American SIDS Institute (2001). U.S. Annual SIDS Rate per 1000 Live Births. Marietta, Georgia: American SIDS Institute. Accessed at http://www.sids.org/nannualrates.htm.

Anderson, H. R., and Derek G. Cook (1997). Passive Smoking and Sudden Infant Death Syndrome: Review of the Epidemiological Evidence. *Thorax* 52: 1003–1009.

Anderson, P. M., Alan L. Gustman, and Thomas L. Steinmeier (1999). Trends in Male Labor Force Participation and Retirement: Some Evidence on the Role of Pensions and Social Security in the 1970s and 1980s. *Journal of Labor Economics* 17: 757–783.

Arthur D. Little International, I. (2001). *Public Finance Balance of Smoking in the Czech Republic*. Prague: Philip Morris.

Athanasou, J. A. (1975). Sickness Absence and Smoking Behavior and Its Consequences: A Review. *Journal of Occupational Medicine* 17: 441–445.

Atkinson, A. B., and Joy L. Townsend (1977). Economic Aspects of Reduced Smoking. *Lancet* 2: 492–495.

Barendregt, J. J., L. Bonneux, and P. J. Van der Maas (1997). Health Care Costs of Smoking. *New England Journal of Medicine* 337 (15): 1052–1057.

Barnes, D. E., and L. A. Bero (1998). Why Review Articles on the Health Effects of Passive Smoking Reach Different Conclusions. *Journal of the American Medical Association* 279: 1566–1570.

Barsky, R. B., F. Thomas Juster, Miles S. Kimball, and Matthew D. Shapiro (1997). Preference Parameters and Behavioral Heterogeneity: An Experimental Approach in the Health and Retirement Study. *Quarterly Journal of Economics* 112: 537–579.

Bartlett, J. C., D. P. Rice, and W. B. Max (1994). Medical-care Expenditures Attributable to Cigarette Smoking—United States 1993. *Morbidity and Mortality Weekly Report* 43: 469–472.

Becker, G., and K. Murphy (1988). A Theory of Rational Addiction. *Journal of Political Economy* 96: 675–700.

Becker, G. S., Michael Grossman, and Kevin M. Murphy (1994). An Empirical Analysis of Cigarette Addiction. *American Economic Review* 84: 396–418.

Becker, G. S., and Mulligan, C. B. (1997). The Endogenous Determination of Time Preference. *Quarterly Journal of Economics* 112: 729–758.

Behrman, J. R., and M. R. Rosenzweig (2003). Returns to Birthweight. Unpublished paper. Philadelphia, Penn.: University of Pennsylvania.

Bell, C. (1996). *Cigarette Smoking and the Insurance Industry: A Bibliographic Review*. Berkeley, Calif.: Berkeley Economic Research Associates.

Berkey, C. S., J. H. Ware, F. E. Speizer, and B. G. Ferris, Jr. (1984). Passive Smoking and Height Growth of Preadolescent Children. *International Journal of Epidemiology* 13: 454–458.

Bertera, R. L. (1991). The Effects of Behavioral Risks on Absenteeism and Health-care Costs in the Workplace. *Journal of Occupational and Environmental Medicine* 33: 1119–1124.

Biering-Sorensen, F., J. Lund, O. J. Hoydalsmo, E. M. Darre, A. Deis, P. Kryger, and C. F. Muller (1999). Risk Indicators of Disability Pension: A 15 Year Follow-up Study. *Danish Medical Bulletin* 46: 258–262.

Blair, P. S., P. J. Fleming, D. Bensley, I. Smith, C. Bacon, E. Taylor, J. Berry, J. Golding, and J. Tripp (1996). Smoking and the Sudden Infant Death Syndrome: Results from 1993–5 Case-control study for confidential Inquiry into Stillbirths and Deaths in Infancy Confidential Enquiry into Stillbirths and Deaths Regional Coordinators and Researchers. *British Medical Journal* 313: 195–198.

Bond, E. W., and Keith J. Crocker (1991). Smoking, Skydiving, and Knitting: The Endogenous Categorization of Risks in Insurance Markets with Asymmetric Information. *Journal of Political Economy* 99: 177–200.

Bound, J., D. Jaeger, and R. Baker (1995). Problems with Instrumental Variables Estimation When the Correlation between the Instruments and the Endogenous Explanatory Variables Is Weak. *Journal of the American Statistical Association* 90: 443–450.

Branch, L. G. (1985). Health Practices and Incident Disability among the Elderly. *American Journal of Public Health* 75: 1436–1439.

Breyer, S. (1982). *Regulation and Its Reform*. Cambridge, Mass.: Harvard University Press.

Brigham, J. (1998). *Dying to Quit: Why We Smoke and How We Stop*. Washington, D.C.: John Henry Press.

Brown, J. R. (2001). Private Pensions, Mortality Risk, and the Decision to Annuitize. *Journal of Public Economics* 82: 29–62.

Brown, K. G. (1999). Lung Cancer and Environmental Tobacco Smoke: Occupational Risk to Nonsmokers. *Environmental Health Perspectives* 107: 885–890.

Buchsbaum, D. G., R. G. Buchanan, R. M. Centor, S. H. Schnoll, and M. J. Lawton (1991). Screening for alcohol abuse using CAGE scores and likelihood ratios. *Annals of Internal Medicine* 115: 774–777.

Bulow, J., and Paul Klemperer (1998). The Tobacco Deal. Washington, D.C.: Brookings Papers on Economic Activity, Microeconomics.

Bush, R., and M. Wooden (1995). Smoking and Absence from Work—Australian Evidence. *Social Science and Medicine* 41: 437–446.

Califano, Joseph A. (1979). The Secretary's Foreword. In *Smoking and Health: A Report of the Surgeon General*, Education and Welfare Office on Smoking and Health, U.S. Department of Health. Washington, D.C.: U.S. Government Printing Office.

Centers for Disease Control and Prevention (1994). Cigarette Smoking among Adults—United States 1993. *Morbidity and Mortality Weekly Report* 43: 925–930.

Centers for Disease Control and Prevention (1993). Cigarette Smoking-Attributable Mortality and Years of Potential Life Lost—United States, 1990. *Morbidity and Mortality Weekly Report* 42: 645–649.

Centers for Disease Control and Prevention (2001a). *Investment in Tobacco Control: State Highlights 2001*. Atlanta: U.S. Department of Health and Human Services, Centers for Disease Control and Prevention, National Center for Chronic Disease Prevention and Health Promotion, Office on Smoking and Health.

Centers for Disease Control and Prevention (1997). *Smoking-Attributable Mortality and Years of Potential Life Lost—United States, 1984. Morbidity and Mortality Weekly Report* 46: 444–451.

Centers for Disease Control and Prevention (2001b). State Medicaid Coverage for Tobacco-dependence Treatments—United States, 1998 and 2000. *Morbidity and Mortality Weekly Report* 50: 979–982.

Centers for Medicare and Medicaid Services (2000). Table 25. *Health Care Financing Review* 22: 138.

Chaloupka, F. J., and K. E. Warner (2000). The Economics of Smoking. In J. Newhouse and A. Culyer (eds.), *Handbook of Health Economics*, pp. 1539–1627. New York: Elsevier.

Chaloupka, F. J., Teh-Wei Hu, Kenneth E. Warner, Rowena Jacobs, and Ayda Yurekli (2000). The Taxation of Tobacco Products. In P. Jha and Frank Chaloupka (eds.), *Tobacco Control in Developing Countries*, pp. 237–272. Oxford: Oxford University Press.

Chan, A. W., E. A. Pristach, and J. W. Welte (1994). Detection by the CAGE of Alcoholism or Heavy Drinking in Primary Care Outpatients and the General Population. *Journal of Substance Abuse* 6: 123–135.

Charlton, A. (1994). Children and Passive Smoking—A Review. *Journal of Family Practice* 38: 267–277.

Chen, Y., W. Li, and S. Yu (1986). Influence of Passive Smoking on Admissions for Respiratory Illness in Early Childhood. *British Medical Journal* 293: 303–306.

Chiappori, P. A., B. Fortin, and G. Lacroix (2002). Marriage Market, Divorce Legislation, and Household Labor Supply. *Journal of Political Economy* 110: 37–72.

Chilmonczyk, B. A., G. J. Knight, G. E. Palomaki, A. J. Pulkkinen, J. Williams, and J. E. Haddow (1990). Environmental Tobacco Smoke Exposure During Infancy. *American Journal of Public Health* 80: 1205–1208.

Chiriboga, C. A. (1993). Fetal Effects. *Neurologic Clinics* 11: 707–728.

Chudy, N., P. L. Remington, and R. Yoast (1992). The Increasing Health and Economic Burden from Cigarette Smoking in Wisconsin. *Wisconsin Medical Journal* 91: 633–636.

Coates, E. O., G. C. Bower, and N. Reinstein (1965). Chronic Respiratory Disease in Postal Employees. *Journal of the American Medical Association* 191: 95–100.

Collins, D. J., and H. M. Lapsley (1991). *Estimating the Economic Costs of Drug Abuse in Australia.* Canberra, Australia: Department of Community Services and Health.

Concord Coalition (2001). *Testimony of Robert Bixby, Executive Director of the Concord Coalition, at a Public Hearing of President's Commission to Save Social Security.* San Diego: Concord Coalition.

Cooke, R. W. (1998). Smoking, Intra-uterine Growth Retardation and Sudden Infant Death Syndrome. *International Journal of Epidemiology* 27: 238–241.

Costa, D. L., and M. E. Kahn (2002). Changes in the Value of Life, 1940–1980. Cambridge, Mass.: National Bureau of Economic Research Working Paper 9396.

Crobaugh, C. J. (1949). *Handbook of Insurance*, vol. I: *Life Insurance and Annuities, Accident and Health Insurance.* New York: Prentice-Hall.

Crowne, J. E., and Robert D. Shapiro (1980). The Nonsmoker as a Preferred Risk. *National Underwriter* 84: 13.

Csonka, P., M. Kaila, P. Laippala, A. L. Kuusela, and P. Ashorn (2000). Wheezing in Early Life and Asthma at School Age: Predictors of Symptom Persistence. *Pediatric Allergy and Immunology* 11: 225–229.

Cunningham, J., G. T. O'Connor, D. W. Dockery, and F. E. Speizer (1996). Environmental Tobacco Smoke, Wheezing, and Asthma in Children in 24 Communities. *American Journal of Respiratory and Critical Care Medicine* 153: 218–224.

Cutler, D. (2002). Health Care and the Public Sector. Cambridge, Mass.: National Bureau of Economic Research, Working Paper 8802.

Cutler, D., A. M. Epstein, R. G. Frank, R. S. Hatman, C. King, J. P. Newhouse, M. B. Rosenthal, and E. R. Bigdor (2000). How Good a Deal was the Tobacco Settlement? Assessing Payments to Massachusetts. Cambridge, Mass.: National Bureau of Economic Research Working Paper W7747.

Cutler, D., Jonathan Gruber, Mary Beth Landrum, Joseph P. Newhouse, and Meredith B. Rosenthal (2002). The Economic Impacts of the Tobacco Settlement. *Journal of Policy Analysis and Management* 21: 1–19.

Cutler, D. A., and Elizabeth Richardson (1997). Measuring the Health of the U.S. Population. Washington, D.C.: Brookings Papers on Economic Activity.

Daviglus, M. L., K. Liu, P. Greenland, A. R. Dyer, D. B. Garside, L. Manheim, L. P. Lowe, M. Rodin, J. Lubitz, and J. Stamler (1998). Benefit of a Favorable Cardiovascular Risk-factor Profile in Middle Age with Respect to Medicare Costs. *New England Journal of Medicine* 339: 1122–1129.

DeCicca, P., D. Kenkel, and A. Mathios (2002). Putting Out the Fires: Will Higher Taxes Reduce the Onset of Youth Smoking? *Journal of Political Economy* 110: 144–169.

Dejin-Karlsson, E., B. S. Hanson, P. O. Ostergren, N. O. Sjoberg, and K. Marsal (1998). Does Passive Smoking in Early Pregnancy Increase the Risk of Small-for-gestational-age Infants? *American Journal of Public Health* 88: 1523–1527.

Diamond, P. A., and J. A. Hausman (1994). Contingent Valuation: Is Some Number Better than No Number? *Journal of Economic Perspectives* 8: 45–64.

DiFranza, J. R., and R. A. Lew (1995). Effect of Maternal Cigarette Smoking on Pregnancy Complications and Sudden Infant Death Syndrome. *Journal of Family Practice* 40: 385–394.

Doll, R., R. Peto, and K. Wheatley, R. G. I. S. (1994). Mortality in Relation to Smoking: 40 Years' Observations on Male British Doctors. *British Medical Journal* 309: 901–911.

Douglas, S. (1998). The Duration of the Smoking Habit. *Economic Inquiry* 36: 49–64.

Duan, N. (1983). Smearing Estimate: A Nonparametric Retransformation Method. *Journal of the American Statistical Association* 78: 605–610.

Dunn, H. G., A. K. McBurney, S. Ingram, and C. M. Hunter (1976). Maternal Cigarette Smoking During Pregnancy and the Child's Subsequent Development: I. Physical Growth to the Age of 6 1/2 Years. *Canadian Journal of Public Health* 67: 499–505.

Edwards, G., E. J. Marshall, and C. C. H. Cook (1997). *The Treatment of Drinking Problems: A Guide for the Helping Professions*. Cambridge: Cambridge University Press.

Ehrenberg, R. G., and R. S. Smith (1988). *Modern Labor Economics. Theory and Public Policy*, third edition. Glenview, Ill.: Scott, Foresman.

Elster, J. (1999). *Alchemies of the Mind: Rationality and Emotion*. New York: Cambridge University Press.

Estimates of Smoking-attributable Medicaid Expenditures in Florida (1997). Senate Judiciary Committee Hearings on the "Proposed Global Settlement: Who Benefits?" July 30, 1997.

Etzel, R. A., E. N. Pattishall, N. J. Haley, R. H. Fletcher, and F. W. Henderson (1992). Passive Smoking and Middle Ear Effusion among Children in Day Care. *Pediatrics* 90: 228–232.

Evans, W. N., and M. C. Farrelly (1998). The Compensating Behavior of Smokers and Taxes, Tar, and Nicotine. *Rand Journal of Economics* 29: 578–595.

Evans, W. N., J. S. Ringel, and D. Stech (1999). Tobacco Taxes and Public Policy to Discourage Smoking. In James M. Poterba (ed.), *Tax Policy and the Economy*, pp. 1–55. Cambridge, Mass.: The MIT Press for the National Bureau of Economic Research.

Farrell, P., and V. R. Fuchs (1982). Schooling and Health: The Cigarette Connection. *Journal of Health Economics* 1: 217–230.

Federal Trade Commission (1997). *Competition and the Financial Impact of the Proposed Tobacco Industry Settlement*. Washington, D.C.: Bureau of Economics, Competition, and Consumer Protection.

Feenberg, D. R., and J. M. Poterba (1993). Income Inequality and the Incomes of High-income Taxpayers: Evidence From Tax Returns. In Anonymous *Tax Policy and the Economy*. Cambridge, Mass.: The MIT Press.

Fein, R. (1958). *The Economics of Mental Illness: A Report to the Staff Director, Jack R. Ewalt*. New York: Basic Books.

Feldstein M., and J. B. Liebman (2002). Social Security. In A. J. Auerbach and M. Feldstein (eds.), *Handbook of Public Economics*, pp. 2245–2324. Amsterdam: Elsevier.

Ferguson, D. (1973). Smoking, Drinking, and Non-narcotic Analgesic Habits in the Occupational Group. *Medical Journal of Australia* 1: 1271–1274.

Ferrucci, L., G. Izmirlian, S. Leveille, C. Phillips, M. Corti, D. Brock, and J. Guralnik (1999). Smoking, Physical Activity, and Active Life Expectancy. *American Journal of Epidemiology* 149: 645–653.

Fiellin, D. A., M. C. Reid, and P. G. O'Connor (2000). Outpatient Management of Patients with Alcohol Problems. *Annals of Internal Medicine* 133: 815–827.

Fink, A., M. C. Tsai, R. D. Hayes, A. A. Moore, S. C. Morton, K. Spritzer, and J. C. Beck (2002). Comparing the Alcohol-related Problems Survey (ARPS) to Traditional Alcohol Screening Measures in Elderly Outpatients. *Archives of Gerontology and Geriatrics* 34: 55–78.

Fortier, I., S. Marcoux, and J. Brisson (1994). Passive Smoking during Pregnancy and the Risk of Delivering a Small-for-gestational-age Infant. *American Journal of Epidemiology* 139: 294–301.

Freeman, A. M. I. (2003). *The Measurement of Environmental and Resource Values: Theory and Methods*, second edition. Washington, D.C.: Resources for the Future.

Fry, W. A., J. L. Phillips, and H. R. Menck (1999). Ten-year Survey of Lung Cancer Treatment and Survival in Hospitals in the United States: A National Cancer Data Base Report. *Cancer* 86: 1867–1876.

Gaziano, T. F. (1999). *Federal Litigation Against the Tobacco Industry: Elevating Politics Over Law*. Washington, D.C.: The Heritage Foundation.

Girela, E., E. Villanueva, C. Hernandez-Cueto, and J. D. Luna (1994). Comparison of the CAGE Questionnaire versus Some Biochemical Markers in the Diagnosis of Alcoholism. *Alcohol and Alcoholism* 29: 337–343.

Glantz, S. A., and W. W. Parmley (1995). Passive Smoking and Heart Disease: Mechanisms and Risk. *Journal of the American Medical Association* 273: 1047–1053.

Gold, M. R., J. E. Siegel, L. B. Russell, and M. C. Weinstein (eds.) (1996). *Cost-Effectiveness in Health and Medicine*. New York: Oxford Press.

Gori, G. B., and B. J. Richter (1978). Macroeconomics of Disease Prevention in the United States. *Science* 200(4346): 1124–1130.

Gori G. B., B. J. Richter, and W. K. Yu (1984). Economics and Extended Longevity: A Case Study. *Preventive Medicine* 13: 396–410.

Gravelle, J. (1998). The Proposed Tobacco Settlement: Who Pays for the Health Costs of Smoking? Washington, D.C.: Library of Congress, Congressional Research Service. No. 97–1053 E.

Gravelle, J. G., and Dennis Zimmerman (1994). Cigarette Taxes to Fund Health 7Care Reform: An Economic Analysis. Washington, D.C.: U.S. Government Printing Office.

Grossman, M., and R. Kaestner (1997). Effects of Education on Health. In J. R. Behrman and Stacy Nevzer (eds.), *The Social Benefits of Education*. Ann Arbor, Mich.: University of Michigan Press.

Gruber, J. (2001). Tobacco at the Crossroads: The Past and Future of Smoking Regulation in the United States. *Journal of Economic Perspectives* 15: 193–212.

Gruber, J., and B. Koszegi (2001). Is Addiction "Rational"? Theory and Evidence. *Quarterly Journal of Economics* 116: 1261–1303.

Gruber, J., and S. Mullainathan (2002). Do Cigarette Taxes Make Smokers Happier? Cambridge, Mass.: National Bureau of Economic Research Working Paper #8872.

Gruber, J., and Jonathan Zinman (2000). Youth Smoking in the U.S.: Evidence and Implications. Cambridge, Mass.: National Bureau of Economic Research Working Paper #7780.

Gruber, J., and Jonathan Zinman (2001). Youth Smoking in the U.S.: Evidence and Implications. In Jonathan Gruber (ed.), *Risky Behavior among Youth: An Economic Analysis*, pp. 69–120. Chicago: University of Chicago Press.

Gustman, A. L., Olivia S. Mitchell, and Thomas L. Steinmeier (1994). The Role of Pensions in the Labor Market: A Survey of the Literature. *Industrial and Labor Relations Review* 47: 417–438.

Gustman, A. L., Olivia S. Mitchell, and Thomas L. Steinmeier (1995). Retirement Measures in the Health and Retirement Study. *Journal of Human Resources* 30: S57–S83.

Gustman, A. L., and Rhomas L. Steinmeier (1999a). Employer Provided Pension Data in the NLS Mature Women's Survey and in the Health and Retirement Study. Cambridge, Mass.: National Bureau of Economic Research Working Paper #7174.

Gustman, A. L., and Thomas L. Steinmeier (1999b). What People Don't Know About their Pensions and Social Security: An Analysis Using Linked Data from the Health and Retirement Study. Cambridge, Mass.: National Bureau of Economic Research Working Paper #7368.

Gustman, A. L., and Thomas L. Steinmeier (2000). Pensions and Retiree Health Benefits in Household Wealth: Changes from 1969–92. *Journal of Human Resources* 35: 30–50.

Gustman, A. L., and Thomas L. Steinmeier (2002). Social Security, Pensions, and Retirement Behavior Within the Family. Cambridge, Mass.: National Bureau of Economic Research Working Paper #8772.

Hackshaw, A. K., M. R. Law, and N. J. Wald (1997). The Accumulated Evidence on Lung Cancer and Environmental Tobacco Smoke. *British Medical Journal* 315: 980–988.

Hanson, J. D., and Kyle D. Logue (1998). The Costs of Cigarettes: The Economic Case for Ex Post Incentive-based Regulation. *Yale Law Review* 107: 1163–1262.

Hanson, J. D., Kyle D. Logue, and Michael S. Zamore (1998). Smokers' Compensation: Toward a Blueprint for Federal Regulation of Cigarette Manufacturers (Symposium: Ending the Tobacco Wars). *Southern Illinois University Law Journal* 22: 519–600.

Hardy, M. A., and Kim Shuey (2000). Pension Decisions in a Changing Economy: Gender, Structure, and Choice. *Journal of Gerontology: Social Sciences* 55B: S271–S277.

Harlap, S., and A. M. Davies (1974). Infant Admissions to Hospital and Maternal Smoking. *The Lancet* 1: 529–532.

Harrington, S. E., and Helen I. Doerpinghaus (1993). The Economics and Politics of Automobile Insurance Rate Classification. *Journal of Risk and Insurance* 60: 59–84.

Harris, J. E. (1993). The Health-care Costs of Cigarette Smoking. November 18, 1993. Testimony before the Committee on Ways and Means, U.S. House of Representatives. Public Hearings on the Financing Provisions of the Admisitration's Health Security Act. Washington, D.C.

Harris, J. E. (1997). Health-care Spending Attributable to Cigarette Smoking and to Cigarette Manufacturers' Anti-competitive Conduct: State of Washington Medicaid Program, 1970–2001. Damage expert's disclosure in *State of Washington v. American Tobacco, Inc., et al.* November 3, 1997, Seattle, Washington.

Harrison, G. W. (1999). Damages to Medicaid from Smoking. Columbia, S.C.: Darla Moore School of Business.

Harrison, G. W. (1998a). Health Care Expenditures Attributable to Smoking in Oklahoma. Columbia, S.C.: Darla Moore School of Business, University of South Carolina.

Harrison, G. W. (1998b). Medicaid Expenditures Attributable to Smoking in Oklahoma. Columbia, S.C.: Darla Moore School of Business, University of South Carolina.

Harrison, G. W., I. M. Lau, and M. B. Williams (2002). Estimating Individual Discount Rates in Demark: A Field Experiment. *American Economic Review* 92: 1606–1617.

Hartunian, N. S., C. L. Smart, and M. S. Thompson (1980). The Incidence and Economic Costs of Cancer, Motor Vehicle Injuries, Coronary Heart Disease, and Stroke: A Comparative Analysis. *American Journal of Public Health* 70: 1249–1260.

Hasdai, D., Amir Lerman, Charanjit S. Rihal, Douglas A. Criger, Kirk N. Garratt, Amadeo Betriu, Harvey D. White, Eric J. Topol, Christopher B. Granger, Stephen G. Ellis, Robert M. Califf, and David R. Holmes, Jr. (1999). Smoking Status and outcome After Primary Coronary Angioplasty for Acute Myocardial Infarction. *American Heart Journal* 137: 612–620.

Hasselblad, V., M. Thun, D. H. Taylor, Jr., J. Henley, and F. A. Sloan (2003). The Effect of Smoking Cessation on the Time Course and Cause of Death. Unpublished paper. Durham, N.C.: Duke University.

Hausman, J., Bronwin H. Hall, and Zvi Griliches (1984). Econometric Models for Count Data with an Application to the Patent–R&D Relationship. *Econometrica* 52: 202–227.

Hay, J. W. (1991). The Harm They Do to Others: A Primer on the External Costs of Drug Abuse. In M. B. Krauss and E. P. Lazear (eds.), *Searching for Alternatives: Drug Control Policy in the United States*. Stanford, Calif.: Hoover Institution Press.

He, J., S. Vupputuri, K. Allen, M. R. Prerost, J. Hughes, and P. K. Whelton (1999). Passive Smoking and the Risk of coronary Heart Disease—A Meta-analysis of Epidemiologic Studies. *New England Journal of Medicine* 340: 920–926.

Hearne, R., A. Connolly, and J. Sheehan (2002). Alcohol Abuse: Prevalence and Detection in a General Hospital. *Journal of the Royal Society of Medicine* 95: 84–87.

Hedrick, J. L. (1971). The Economic Costs of Cigarette Smoking. *HSMHA Health Reports* 86(2): 179–182.

Hersch, J., and W. K. Viscusi (1998). Smoking and Other Risky Behaviors. *Journal of Drug Issues* 28: 645–661.

Hinton, A. E. (1989). Surgery for Otitis Media with Effusion in Children and Its Relationship to Parental Smoking. *Journal of Laryngology and Otology* 103: 559–561.

Hirschhorn, N. (2000). Shameful Science: Four Decades of the German Tobacco Industry's Hidden Research on Smoking and Health. *Tobacco Control* 9: 242–248.

Ho, R. (1998). The Intention to Give Up Smoking: Disease versus Social Dimensions. *Journal of Social Psychology* 138: 368–380.

Hocking, B., H. Grain, and I. Gordon (1994). Cost to Industry of Illness Related to Alcohol and Smoking: A Study of Telecom Australia Employees. *Medical Journal of Australia* 161: 407–412.

Hodgson, T. A. (1992). Cigarette Smoking and Lifetime Medical Expenditure. *Milbank Quarterly* 70: 81–125.

Holcomb, H. S., and J. W. Meigs (1972). Medical Absenteeism among Cigarette, Cigar, and Pipe Smokers. *Archives of Environmental Health* 21: 670–677.

Hopkins, R. S., and T. Lynch (1997). Smoking-attributable Medicaid Expenditures in Florida, 1994–1996. Expert report filed in *The State of Florida et al. v. The American Tobacco Company, Inc., et al.* April 15, 1997, Tallahassee, Florida.

House, J. S., J. M. Lepkowski, A. M. Kinney, R. P. Mero, R. C. Kessler, and A. R. Herzog (1994). The Social Stratification of Aging and Health. *Journal of Health and Social Behavior* 35: 213–234.

Howard, G., and L. E. Wagenknecht (1999). Environmental Tobacco Smoke and Measures of Subclinical Vascular Disease. *Environmental Health Perspectives* 107: 837–840.

Howard, G., and M. J. Thun (1999). Why Is Environmental Tobacco Smoke More Strongly associated with Coronary Heart Disease than Expected? A Review of Potential Biases and Experimental Data. *Environmental Health Perspectives* 107: 853–858.

Hu, T., Hai-Yen Sung, Theodore E. Keeler, and Martin Marciniak (2000). Cigarette Consumption and Sales of Nicotine Replacement Products. *Tobacco Control* 9: ii60–ii63.

Hunink, M. G., L. Goldman, A. N. Tosteson, M. A. Mittleman, P. A. Goldman, L. W. Williams, J. Tsevat, and M. C. Weinstein (1997). The Recent Decline in Mortality from Coronary Heart Disease 1980–1990: The Effect of Secular Trends in Risk Factors and Treatment. *Journal of the American Medication Association* 277: 535–542.

Hurd, M., Lee Lillard, and Constantijn Panis (1998). An Analysis of the Choice to Cash Out Pension Rights at Job Change or Retirement. Santa Monica, Calif.: Rand Corporation (DRU-1979–DOL).

Ibbotson, R., and Rex Sinquefeld (1976). Stocks, Bonds, Bills, and Inflation: Year-by-year Historical Returns (1926–1974). *Journal of Business* 49: 11–47.

Idler, E. L. S. V. K. (1995). Self-Reatings of Health: Do They also Predict Change in Functional Ability? *Journal of Gerontology* 50B: S344–S353.

Institute of Medicine (1994). *Growing Up Tobacco Free*. Washington, D.C.: National Academy Press.

Jaakola, M. S., and J. M. Samet (1999). Occupational Exposure to Environmental Tobacco Smoke and Health Risk Assessment. *Environmental Health Perspectives* 107: 829–835.

Jacobs, D. R., Jr., H. Adachi, I. Mulder, D. Kromhout, A. Menotti, A. Nissinen, and H. Blackburn (1999). Cigarette Smoking and Mortality Risk. *Archives of Internal Medicine* 159: 733–734.

Jha, P., Fred Paccaud, and Son Nguyen (2000a). Strategic Priorities in Tobacco Control for Governments and International Agencies. In P. Jha and Frank J. Chaloupka (eds.), *Tobacco Control in Developing Countries*. Oxford: Oxford University Press.

Jha, P., Philip Musgrove, Frank J. Chaloupka, and Ayda Yurekli (2000b). The Economic Rationale for Intervention in the Tobacco Market. In P. Jha and Frank Chaloupka (eds.), *Tobacco Control in Developing Countries*. Oxford: Oxford University Press.

Johnson, R. W., Usha Sambamoorthis, and Stephen Crystal (2000). Pension Wealth at Midlife: Comparing Self-reports with Provider Data. *Review of Income and Wealth* 36: 59–83.

Jones, A. (2002). The National Nursing Home Survey: 1999 Summary. Washington, D.C.: National Center for Health Statistics. Vital Health Statistics Series 13: No. 152.

Jones, A. M. (1996). Smoking Cessation and Health: A Response. *Journal of Health Economics* 15: 755–759.

Juster, F. T., and R. Suzman (1995). An Overview of the Health and Retirement Study. *Journal of Human Resources* 30: S7–S56.

Kasten, R., F. Sammartino, and E. Toder (1994). Trends in Federal Tax Progressivity, 1980–93. In Joel Slemrod (ed.), *Tax Progressivity and Income Inequality*. New York: Cambridge University Press.

Kawachi, I., and G. A. Colditz (1999). Workplace Exposure to Passive Smoking and Risk of Cardiovascular Disease: Summary of Epidemiologic Studies. *Environmental Health Perspectives* 107: 847–851.

Kenkel, D. E. (2000). Prevention. In A. J. Culyer and J. P. Newhouse (eds.), *Handbook of Health Economics*, pp. 1676–1714. Amsterdam: North Holland Press.

Kessler, D. (2001). *A Question of Intent: A Great Battle with a Deadly Industry*. New York: Public Affairs.

Klesges, R. C., C. K. Hancock, C. F. Chang, G. W. Talcott, and H. A. Lando (2001). The Association of Smoking and the Cost of Military Training. *Tobacco Control* 10: 43–47.

Klonhoff-Cohen, H. S., S. L. Edelstein, E. S. Lefkowitz, I. P. Srinivasan, D. Kaegi, J. C. Chang, and K. J. Wiley (1995). The Effect of Passive Smoking and Tobacco Exposure through Breast Milk on Sudden Infant Death Syndrome. *Journal of the American Medical Association* 273: 795–798.

Kluger, R. (1996). *Ashes to Ashes: America's Hundred-year Cigarette War, the Public Health, and the Unabashed Triumph of Philip Morris*. New York: Alfred P. Knopf.

Kopp, P., and P. Fenoglio (2000). Social Costs of Alcohol and Tobacco in France [Le cout social des drogues licities (alcool et tabac) et illicites en France]. Unpublished research.

Kristein, Marvin M. (1983). How Much Can Business Expect to Profit from Smoking Cessation? *Preventive Medicine* 12: 358–381.

Krupnick, A. (2002). Commentary On: What Determines the Values of Life? A Meta-analysis. *Journal of Policy Analysis and Management* 21: 275–282.

Krupnick, A., Anna Alberini, Maureen Cropper, Nathalie Simon, Bernie O'Brien, Ron Goeree, and Martin Heintzelman (2002). Age, Health, and the Willingness to Pay for Mortality Risk Reductions: A Contingent Valuation Survey of Ontario Residents. *Jouranl of Risk and Uncertainty* 24: 161–186.

Kubik, J. D., and J. R. Moran (2001). Can Policy Changes Be Treated as Natural Experiments? Evidence from State Excise Taxes. Syracuse, N.Y.: Working paper.

Kunreuther, H., N. Novemsky, and D. Kahneman (2001). Making Low Probabilities Useful. *Journal of Risk and Uncertainty* 23: 103–120.

Lacroix, A. Z., J. M. Guralnik, L. F. Berkman, R. B. Wallace, and S. Scatterfield (1993). Smoking and the Compression of Morbidity in Late Life. II. Smoking, Alcohol Consumption, Physical Activity, and Body Mass Index. *American Journal of Epidemiology* 137: 858–869.

Lannerstad, O. (1980). Morbidity Related to Smoking and Other Risk Factors. *Scandinavian Journal of Social Sciences* 8: 25–31.

Law, M. R., J. K. Morris, and N. J. Wald (1997). Environmental Tobacco Smoke Exposure and Ischaemic Heart Disease: An Evaluation of the Evidence. *British Medical Journal* 315: 973–980.

Leigh, J. P. (1995). Smoking, Self-selection, and Absenteeism. *Quarterly Review of Economics and Finance* 35: 365–386.

Leistikow, B. N. (2000). The Human and Financial Costs of Smoking. *Clinics in Chest Medicine* 21: 189–197.

Leistikow, B. N., D. C. Martin, and C. E. Milano (2000a). Estimates of Smoking-Attributable Deaths at Ages 15–54: Motherless or Fatherless Youths, and Resulting Social Security Costs in the United States in 1994. *Preventive Medicine* 30(5): 353–360.

Leistikow, B. N., D. C. Martin, and C. E. Milano (2000b). Fire Injuries, Disasters, and Costs from Cigarettes and Cigarette Lights: a Global Overview. *Prevention* 31(2): 91–99.

Lemaire, J. (1985). *Automobile Insurance.* Boston: Kluwer.

Leu, R. E. (1984). Anti-smoking Publicity, Taxation, and the Demand for Cigarettes. *Journal of Health Economics* 3: 101–116.

Leu, R. E., and Thomas Schaub (1985). More on the Impact of Smoking on Medical Care Expenditures. *Social Science and Medicine* 7: 825–827.

Levine, P. B., Tara A. Gustafson, and Ann D. Velenchik (1997). More Bad News for Smokers: The Effects of Cigarette Smoking on Wages. *Industrial and Labor Relations Review* 50: 493–509.

Levy, R. A. (1998a). Tobacco Medicaid Litigation: Snuffing Out the Rule of Law. *Southern Illinois Law Journal* 22: 601–647.

Levy, R. A. (1998b). Tobacco Wars: Will the Rule of Law Survive? *Journal of Health Care Law and Policy* 2(1): 45–78.

Levy, R. A., and Rosalind Marimont (1998). Lies, Damned Lies, and 400,000 Smoking-related Deaths. *Regulation* 21: 24–29.

Lewitt, E. M. (1984). Estimated Cost of Illness Attributable to Cigarette Smoking, 1964–1983. Report prepared for the American Council on Science and Health (unpublished).

Li, C. Q., R. A. Windsor, and M. Hassart (1994). Cost Differences between Low Birthweight Attributable to Smoking and Low Birthweight for All Causes. *Preventive Medicine* 23(1): 28–34.

Lightwood, J. M., D. Collins, H. Lapsley, and T. Novotny (2000). Estimating the Costs of Tobacco Use. In P. Jha and F. Chaloupka (eds.), *Tobacco Control in Developing Countries*. Oxford: Oxford University Press.

Lightwood, J. M., C. S. Phibbs, and S. A. Glantz (1999). Short-term Health and Economic Benefits of Smoking Cessation: Low Birth Weight. *Pediatrics* 104: 1312–1320.

Liu, X., J. Liang, N. Muramatsu, and H. Sigosawa (1995). Transitions in Functional Status and Active Life Expectancy among Older People in Japan. *Journal of Gerontology and Social Sciences* 50(6): S383–S394.

Lowe, C. R. (1960). Smoking Habits Related to Injury and Absenteeism in Industry. *British Journal of Preventive Social Medicine* 14: 57.

Luce, Bryan R., and S. O. Schweitzer (1978). Smoking and Alcohol Abuse: A Comparison of Their Economic Consequences. *New England Journal of Medicine* 298(10): 569–571.

Lumsdaine, R., James Stock, and David Wise (1998). Why Are Retirement Rates So High at Age 56? In David A. Wise (ed.), *Advances in the Economics of Aging*, pp. 11–82. Chicago: University of Chicago Press.

Lye, J., and J. Hirschberg (2000). Alcohol Consumption, Smoking, and Wages. Melbourne: University of Melbourne Department of Economics Paper No. 764.

MacKensie, T. D., Carl E. Bartecchi, and Robert W. Schrier (1994). The Human Costs of Tobacco Use. *New England Journal of Medicine* 330: 975–980.

Manning, W. G., Emmett B. Keeler, Joseph P. Newhouse, Elizabeth M. Sloss, and Jeffrey Wasserman (1989). The Taxes of Sin: Do Smokers and Drinkers Pay Their Way? *Journal of the American Medical Association* 261: 1604–1609.

Manning, W. G., Emmett B. Keeler, Joseph P. Newhouse, Elizabeth M. Sloss, and Jeffrey Wasserman (1991). *The Costs of Poor Health Habits*. Cambridge, Mass.: Harvard University Press.

Mannino, D. M., J. E. Moorman, B. Kingsley, D. Rose, and J. Repace (2001). Health Effects Related to Environmental Tobacco Smoke Exposure in Children in the United States: Data from the Third National Health and Nutrition Examination Survey. *Archives of Pediatrics and Adolescent Medicine* 155: 36–41.

Manser, M., and M. Brown (1980). Marriage and Household Decision-making: A Bargaining Analysis. *International Economic Review* 21: 31–44.

Marks, J. S., J. P. Koplan, C. H. Hogue, and M. E. Dalmat (1990). A Cost-benefit/cost-effectiveness Analysis of Smoking Cessation for Pregnant Women. *American Journal of Preventive Medicine* 6: 282–289.

Martinez, F. D., A. L. Wright, and L. M. Taussig (1994). The Effect of Paternal Smoking on the Birth Weight of Newborns Whose Mothers Did Not Smoke. *American Journal of Public Health* 84: 1489–1491.

Martinez, F. D., M. Cline, and B. Burrows (1992). Increased Incidence of Asthma in Children of Smoking Mothers. *Pediatrics* 89: 21–26.

Max, W. (1997a). Estimation of Smoking-attributable Public Expenditures for the State of Mississippi, 1970–2000. Unpublished manuscript.

Max, W. (1997b). Estimation of Smoking-attributable Public Expenditures for the State of Texas, 1968–2007. Unpublished manuscript.

Max, W. (1997c). Estimation of Smoking-attributable Public Expenditures for the State of Washington, 1970–2001. Unpublished manuscript.

Mayfield, D., G. McLeod, and P. Hall (1974). The CAGE Questionnaire: Validation of a New Alcoholism Screening Instrument. *American Journal of Psychiatry* 131: 1121–1123.

McElroy, M. B., and M. J. Horney (1981). Nash-bargained Household Decisions—Toward a Generalization of the Theory of Demand. *International Economic Review* 22: 333–349.

McGinnis, J. M., and W. H. Foege (1993). Actual Causes of Death in the United States. *Journal of the American Medical Association* 270(18): 2207–2212.

McIntosh, M. C., G. Leigh, and N. J. Baldwin (1994). Screening for Hazardous Drinking: Using the CAGE and Measures of Alcohol Consumption in Family Practice. *Canadian Family Physician* 40: 1546–1553.

Meier, K., and Michael J. Licari (1997). The Effect of Cigarette Taxes on Cigarette Consumption, 1955 through 1994. *American Journal of Public Health* 87(7): 1126–1130.

Miller, L. S., X. Zhang, T. Novotny, D. P. Rice, and W. Max (1998b). State Estimates of Medicaid Expenditures Attributable to Cigarette Smoking, Fiscal Year 1993. *Public Health Reports* 113: 140–151.

Miller, L. S., Ziulan Zhang, Dorothy P. Rice, and Wendy Max (1998c). State Estimates of Total Medical Expenditures Attributable to Cigarette Smoking, 1993. *Public Health Reports* 113: 140–151.

Miller, V. P. (1997a). A Preliminary Estimate of Cigarette Smoking-attributable Medical Care Expenditures Incurred by the State of Florida, Fiscal Years 1994/1995–1996/1997. Oakland, Calif.: Miller and Associates.

Miller, V. P. (1997b). Cigarette Smoking-attributable Medical Care Costs Incurred by the State of Texas, 1967–2007. Berkeley, Calif.: Berkeley Economic Research Associates.

Miller, V. P., Carla Ernst, and Francois Collin (1999). Smoking-attributable Medical Care Costs in the USA. *Social Science and Medicine* 48: 375–391.

Miller, V. P., Caroline R. James, Carla Ernst, and Francois Collin (1997). Smoking Attributable Medical Care Costs: Models and Results. Berkeley, Calif.: Berkeley Economic Research Associates.

Mishan, E. J. (1971). Evaluation of Life and Limb: A Theoretical Approach. *Journal of Poliitical Economy* 79: 687–705.

Mitchell, E. A., R. P. Ford, A. W. Stewart, B. J. Taylor, D. M. Becroft, J. M. Thompson, R. Scragg, I. B. Hassall, D. M. Barry, and E. M. Allen (1993). Smoking and the Sudden Infant Death Syndrome. *Pediatrics* 91: 893–896.

Mollenkamp, C., A. Levy, J. Menn, and J. Rothfelder (1998). *The People vs. Big Tobacco: How the States Took on the Cigarette Giants*. Princeton, N.J.: Bloomberg Press.

Moore, M. J., and James W. Hughes (2001). The Health Care Consequences of Smoking and Its Regulation: Working Paper 7979. *Research Briefs: SAMHSA*.

Moore, M. J., and W. K. Viscusi (1990a). Discounting Environmental Health Risks: New Evidence and Policy Implications. *Journal of Environmental Economics and Management* 18: S51–62.

Moore, M. J., and W. K. Viscusi (1990b). Models for Estimating Discount Rates for Long-term Health Risks Using Labor Market Data. *Journal of Risk and Uncertainty* 3: 381–401.

Mrozek, J. R., and Laura O. Taylor (2002). What Determines the Value of Life? A Meta Analysis. *Journal of Policy Analysis and Management* 21: 243–270.

Mudarri, D. (1994). The Costs and Benefits of Smoking Restrictions: An Assessment of the Smoke-free Environment Act of 1993 (H.R. 3434). Washington, D.C.: Indoor Air Division, U.S. Environmental Protection Agency.

Mushkin, S. J. (1962). Investment in Human Beings. *Journal of Political Economy* 70: 129–157.

National Center for Health Statistics (1967). Current Estimates from the Health Interview Survey: United States, 1966. Hyattsville, Md.: Dept. of Health, Education, and Welfare, Public Health Service, Health Resources Administration, National Center for Health Statistics.

National Center for Health Statistics (2001). Healthy People 2000 Final Review (Healthy People 2000: National Health Promotion and Disease Prevention Objectives). Hyattsville, Md.: Public Health Service.

National Center for Health Statistics (2003). Asthma Prevalence, Health Care Use and Mortality, 2000–2001. Hyattsville, Md.: Center for Disease Control.

National Conference of State Legislatures (2002). *Analysis of States' Allocations of Tobacco Settlement Revenues.* Denver: National Conference of State Legislatures, Health.

National Governors Association and National Association of State Budget Officers (2002). The Fiscal Survey of States. Washington, D.C.: National Governors Association and National Association of State Budget Officers.

National Research Council, C.o.P.S.B.o.E.S.a.T. (1986). Environmental Tobacco Smoke: Measuring Exposures and Assessing Health Effects. Washington, D.C.: National Academies Press.

Nelson, C. R., and R. Startz (1990). The Distribution of the Instrumental Variables Estimator and t-Ratio When the Instrument is a Poor One. *Journal of Business* 63: S125–S140.

Neuspiel, D. R., D. Rush, N. R. Butler, J. Golding, P. E. Bijur, and M. Kurzon (1989). Parental Smoking and Post-infancy Wheezing in Children—A Prospective Cohort Study. *American Journal of Public Health* 79: 168–171.

Ney, T., and A. Gale (eds.) (1989). *Smoking and Human Behavior.* Chichester: Wiley.

Nicholl, J. P., and A. O'Cathain (1992). Epidemiology of Babies Dying at Different Ages from the Sudden Infant Death Syndrome. *Journal of Epidemiology and Community Health* 43: 133–139.

Nielsen, K., and M. C. Fiore (2000). Cost Benefit Analysis of Sustained Release Bupropion Patch for Smoking Cessation. *Preventive Medicine* 30: 209–216.

Nusselder, W. J., C. W. Looman, P. J. Marang-van de Mheen, H. van de Mheen, and J. P. Mackenbach (2000). Smoking and the Compression of Morbidity. *Journal of Epidemiology and Community Health* 54: 566–574.

Office of Technology Assessment (OTA), U.S. Congress (1985). Smoking-related Deaths and Financial Costs (OTA-H-181). Washington, D.C.: U.S. Government Printing Office.

Office of Technology Assessment (OTA), U.S. Congress (1993). Smoking-related Deaths and Financial Costs: Office of Technology Assessment Estimates for 1990. U.S. Senate Special Committee on Aging. Serial no. 103-7. Washington, D.C.: U.S. Government Printing Office.

Ohsfeldt, R. L., R. G. Boyle, and E. I. Capilouto (1998). Tobacco Taxes, Smoking Restrictions, and Tobacco Use. Cambridge, Mass.: National Bureau of Economic Research Working Paper #6486.

Olshan, A. F., and D. A. Savitz (1995). Paternal Smoking and Low Birthweight: The Routes of Exposure. *American Journal of Public Health* 85: 1169–1170.

Orzechowski, W., and R. C. Walker (2002). *The Tax Burden on Tobacco: Historical Compilation 2002*, vol. 37. Arlington, Va.: Orzechowski and Walker.

Oster, G. (1996). Letter to Richard F. Scruggs (personal communication).

Oster, G. (1997a). Letter to Richard F. Scruggs (personal communication).

Oster, G. (1997b). Letter to William Michael Gruenloh (personal communication).

Oster, G., Graham Colditz, and Nancy Kelly (1984a). *The Economic Costs of Smoking and Benefits of Quitting*. Lexington, Mass.: Lexington Books.

Ostro, B. D. (1989). Estimating the Risks of Smoking, Air Pollution, and Passive Smoke on Acute Respiratory Conditions. *Risk Analysis* 9: 189–196.

Parascandola, M. (2001). Cigarettes and the U.S. Public Health Service in the 1950s. *American Journal of Public Health* 91: 196–206.

Parkes, K. R. (1987). Relative Weight, Smoking, and Mental Health as Predictors of Sickness and Absence from Work. *Journal of Applied Psychology* 72: 275–286.

Parkes, K. R. (1983). Smoking as a Moderator of the Relationship between Affective State and Absence from Work. *Journal of Applied Psychology* 68: 698–704.

Parrott, S., C. Godfrey, and M. Raw (2000). Costs of Employee Smoking in the Workplace in Scotland. *Tobacco Control* 9: 187–192.

Passell, P. (1993). Experts Wavering on Steep Rise in Cigarette Tax. *New York Times*, June 7, A ed., 1 18 A.

Patz, E. F., W. C. Black, and P. C. Goodman (2001). CT Screening for Lung Cancer: Not Ready for Routine Practice. *Radiology* 221: 587–591.

Pauly, M. V. (1995). Valuing Health Care Benefits in Monetary Terms. In Frank A. Sloan (ed.), *Valuing Health Care: Costs, Benefits, and Effectiveness of Pharmaceuticals, and Other Medical Technologies*, pp. 99–124. New York: Cambridge University Press.

Pauly, M. V. (1997). *Health Benefits at Work: An Economic and Political Analysis of Employment-based Health Insurance*, Ann Arbor: University of Michigan Press.

Pechman, J. A. (1977). *Federal Tax Policy*, third edition. Washington, D.C.: The Brookings Institution.

Petska, T., and M. Strudler (2002). *Income, Taxes, and Tax Progressivity: An Examination of Recent Trends in the Distribution of Individual Income and Taxes*. Washington, D.C.: Internal Revenue Service.

Petty, S. W. (1699). *Several Essays in Political Arithmetics: The Titles of Which Follow in the Ensuing Pages*. London: Robert Clavel.

Phelps, C. E. (1973). *Demand for Health Insurance: A Theoretical and Empirical Investigation*. Santa Monica, Calif.: Rand Corporation (R-1054–OEO).

Picone, G., and F. Sloan (2003). Smoking Cessation and Lifestyle Changes. In Alan Garber (ed.), *Frontiers in Health Policy Research*. Cambridge, Mass.: The MIT Press.

Picone, G., F. Sloan, and D. Taylor (2004). Effect of Risk and Time Preference and Expected Longevity on Demand for Medical Tests. *Journal of Risk and Uncertainty* 28(1): 39–53.

Pirkle, J. L., K. M. Flegal, J. T. Bernert, D. J. Brody, R. A. Etzel, and K. R. Maurer (1996). Exposure of the U.S. Population to Environmental Tobacco Smoke—The Third National Health and Nutrition Examination Survey, 1988 to 1991. *Journal of the American Medical Association* 275: 1233–1240.

Price, J. H., and Joseph A. Dake (1999). An Analysis of the Tobacco Settlement in Relation to Adolescent Tobacco Use. *Journal of Health Education* 30: 345–351.

Puelz, R., and Arthur Snow (1994). Evidence on Adverse Selection: Equilibrium Signaling and Cross-subsidization in the Insurance Market. *Journal of Political Economy* 102: 236–257.

Pukander, J., J. Lustonen, M. Timore, and P. Karma (1985). Risk Factors Affecting the Occurrence of Acute Otitis Media among Two and Three Year Old Urban Children. *Acta Otolaryngol* 100: 260–265.

Rabin, R. L., and S. Sugarman (2001). *Regulating Tobacco*. New York: Oxford.

Ramalingam, S., K. Pawlish, S. Gadgeel, R. Demers, and G. P. Kalemkerian (1998). Lung Cancer in Young Patients: Analysis of a Surveillance, Epidemiology, and End Results. *Journal of Clinical Oncology* 16: 651–657.

Ranson, K., Prabhat Jha, Frank J. Chaloupka, and S. Nguyen (2000). The Effectiveness and Cost-effectiveness of Price Increases and Other Tobacco-control Policies. In: P. Jha and Frank Chaloupka (eds.), *Tobacco Control in Developing Countries*. Oxford: Oxford University Press.

Rebagliato, M., C. D. V. Florey, and F. Bolumar (1995). Exposure to Environmental Tobacco Smoke in Nonsmoking Pregnant Women in Relation to Birth Weight. *American Journal of Epidemiology* 142: 531–537.

Reed, D. M., Daniel J. Foley, Lon R. White, Harley Heimovitz, Cecil M. Burchfiel, and Kamal Masaki (1998). Predictors to Healthy Aging in Men with High Life Expectancies. *American Journal of Public Health* 88: 1463–1468.

Rice, D. P., S. Kelman, and S. Durmeyer (1990). The Economic Costs of Alcohol and Drug Abuse, and Mental Illness: 1985. Report submitted to the Office of Financing and Coverage Policy of the Alcohol, Drug Abuse, and Mental Health Administration, U.S. Department of Health and Human Services. DHHS Publication No. (ADM) 90-1694.

Rice, D. P., T. A. Hodgson, P. Sinsheimer, W. Browner, and A. N. Kopstein (1986). The Economic Costs of the Health Effects of Smoking. *Milbank Quarterly* 64: 489–547.

Rice, D. P. (1999). Economic Costs of Substance Abuse, 1995. *Proceedings of the Association of American Physicians* 111: 119–125.

Rice, D. P., S. R. Kaufman, E. McLoughlin, W. Max, E. J. MacKenzie, G. S. Smith, D. S. Salkever, G. V. deLissovoy, A. S. Jones, T. R. Miller, L. S. Robertson, and B. M. Faigin (1989). Cost of Injury—United States: A Report to Congress, 1989. *Morbidity and Mortality Weekly Report* 38: 743–746.

Richards, H., and J. R. Abele (1999). Life and Worklife Expectancies. Tucson: Lawyers and Judges.

Rigotti, N. A. (2002). Treatment of Tobacco Use and Dependence. *New England Journal of Medicine* 346: 506–507.

Rona, R. J., C. D. Florey, G. C. Clarke, and S. Chinn (1981). Parental Smoking at Home and Height of Children. *British Medical Journal Clinical Research Ed.* 283: 1363.

Rona, R. J., S. Chinn, and C. D. Florey (1985). Exposure to Cigarette Smoking and Children's Growth. *International Journal of Epidemiology* 14: 402–409.

Rosenbaum, D. E. (2002). Hard Truths Are Avoided on Social Security. *New York Times*, Dec. 22, Money and Business ed., 4.

Rothschild, M., and Joseph E. Stiglitz (1976). Equilibrium in competitive Insurance Markets: The Economics of Markets with Imperfect Information. *Quarterly Journal of Economics* 90: 629–649.

Rubin, B. K. (1990). Exposure of Children with Cystic Fibrosis to Environmental Tobacco Smoke. *New England Journal of Medicine* 323: 782–788.

Rubin, Donald B. (1997). Texas Tobacco Litigation: Report of Professor Donald Rubin. Cambridge, Mass.: Harvard University Department of Statistics.

Rush, D., J. Orme, J. King, J. R. Eiser, and N. R. Butler (1992). A Trial of Health Education Aimed to Reduce Cigarette Smoking among Pregnant Women. *Pediatric and Perinatal Epidemiology* 6: 285–297.

Ryan, J., C. Zwerling, and E. J. Orav (1992). Occupational Risks Associated with Cigarette Smoking: A Prospective Study. *American Journal of Public Health* 82: 29–32.

Schelling, T. C. (1968). The Life You Save May Be Your Own. In Samuel B. Chase, Jr. (ed.), *Problems in Public Expenditure Analysis*, pp. 127–162. Washington, D.C.: Brookings Institution.

Schmidt, F. (1972). Smoking and the Federal Armed Forces. *Medizinische Welt* 23: 921–924.

Schneider Institute for Health Policy, B.U. (2001). Substance Abuse: The Nation's Number One health Problem. Princeton, N.J.: Robert Wood Johnson Foundation.

Schumacher, C. (1996). Smoking Attributable Mortality and Economic Costs in Alaska 1992–94. *Alaska Medicine* 38: 13–17.

Schwartz, M. (1992). Insurers are Reclassifying Definition of Smoking. *National Underwriter, Life and Health-Financial Services Edition* 96: 16–21.

Seeman, T. E., L. F. Berkman, P. A. Charpentier, D. G. Blazer, M. S. Albert, and M. E. Tinetti (1995). Behavioral and Psychosocial Predictors of Physical Performance:

MacArthur Studies of Successful Aging. *Journal of Gerontology: Medical Sciences* 50A: 177–183M.

Seeman, T. E., L. G. Berkman, P. A. Charpentier, M. E. Tinetti, J. M. Garlanik, and M. S. Albert, et al. (1994). Predicting Changes in Physical Performances in a High-functioning Elderly Cohort: MacArthur Studies of Successful Aging. *Journal of Gerontology: Medical Sciences* 49: 97–108M.

Shoven, J. B., J. O. Sundberg, and J. P. Bunker (1989). The social security cost of smoking. In D. A. Wise (ed.), *The Economics of Aging*. Chicago: University of Chicago Press.

Silagy, C., T. Lancaster, G. Fowler, et al. (1998). Effectiveness of Training Health Professionals to Provide Smoking Cessation Interventions. *Cochrane Review (in The Cochrane Library—Update Software)*.

Sims, J. (1994). Tobacco Use in Florida: Consequences and Costs. *Cancer* 1: 441–445.

Singer, R. B. (1972). To Smoke or Not to Smoke. *Best's Review, Life/Health Insurance edition* 72: 50.

Sloan, F. A., R. Randall Bovbjerg, and Penny B. Githens (1991). *Insuring Medical Malpractice*. New York: Oxford University Press.

Sloan, F. A., V. K. Smith, and D. H. Taylor, Jr. (2002). Information, Addiction, and "Bad Choices": Lessons from Century of Cigarettes. *Economics Letters* 77: 147–515.

Sloan, F. A., V. Kerry Smith, and Donald H. Taylor, Jr. (2003). *Parsing the Smoking Puzzle: Information, Risk Perception, and Choice*. Cambridge, Mass.: Harvard University Press.

Smith, D. J. (1970). Absenteeism and "Presenteeism" in Industry. *Archives of Environmental Health* 21: 670–677.

Smoking and Health Action Foundation (2002). Global Cigarette Taxes and Prices. Accessed at http://www.nsra-adnf.ca/english/staxratesus.html.

Soldo, B. J., M. D. Hurd, W. L. Rodgers, and R. B. Wallace (1997). Asset and Health Dynamics among the Oldest Old: An Overview of the AHEAD Study. *Journal of Gerontology* Special Issue 52B: 1–20.

Soyseth, V., J. Kongerud, and J. Boe (1995). Postnatal Maternal Smoking Increases the Prevalence of Asthma but not of Brochial Hyperresponsiveness of Atopy in their Children. *Chest* 107: 389–394.

Staiger, D., and J. Stock (1997). Instrumental Variable Regressions with Weak Instruments. *Econometrica* 65(3): 557–586.

Steenland, K. (1999). Risk Assessment for Heart Disease and Workplace ETS Exposure among Nonsmokers. *Environmental Health Perspectives* 107: 859–863.

Sterling, T. D., W. L. Rosenbaum, and J. J. Weinkam (1993). Risk Attribution and Tobacco-related Deaths. *American Journal of Epidemiology* 138: 128–139.

Stickels, G. (1994). Lost Output on the Smoke Threshold. *Business Review Weekly* (September 26): 85–86.

Stoddard, Jeffrey J., and Bradley Gray (1997). Maternal Smoking and Medical Expenditures for Childhood Respiratory Illness. *American Journal of Public Health* 87(2): 205–209.

Stratton, K., P. Shetty, R. Wallace, and S. Bondurant (2001). *Clearing the Smoke: The Science Base for Tobacco Harm Reduction*. Washington, D.C.: National Academy Press.

Strauss, David, and Robert Shavelle (2002). The Life Table. Accessed at http://www.lifeexpectancy.com.

Strawbridge, W. J., R. D. Cohen, S. J. Shema, and G. A. Kaplan (1996). Successful Aging: Predictors and Associated Activities. *American Journal of Epidemiology* 144: 135–141.

Strnad, L., A. Fingerland, and J. Mericka (1969). Economic and Medical Consequences of Smoking. *Sborn ved Praci lek Fak Hradci Kralove (Collection of Scientific Works of the Charles University Faculty of medicine in Hradec Kralove)* 12: 401–414.

Stuck, A. E., J. M. Walthert, T. Mikolaus, C. J. Bula, C. Hohmann, and J. C. Beck (1999). Risk Factors for Functional Status Decline in Community Living Elderly People: A Systematic Literature Review. *Social Sciences and Medicine* 48: 444–469.

Tate, C. (2000). *Cigarette Wars: The Triumph of the Little White Slaver*. New York: Oxford Press.

Taurus, J. A., and F. J. Chaloupka (2001). The Demand for Nicotine Replacement Therapies. Cambridge, Mass.: National Bureau of Economic Research Working Paper 8332.

Taylor, D. H., Jr., V. Hasselblad, S. J. Henley, M. J. Thun, and F. A. Sloan (2002). Benefits of Smoking Cessation for Longevity. *American Journal of Public Health* 92: 990–996.

Tengs, T.O., M. Adams, J. Pilskin, D. Safran, J. Siegel, M. Weinstein, and J. Graham (1995). Five-Hundred Life Saving Interventions and Their Cost-Effectiveness. *Risk Analysis* 15(3): 369–389.

Thorndike, A. N., L. Biener, and N. A. Rigotti (2002). Effect on Smoking Cessation of Switching Nicotine Replacement Therapy to Over-the-counter Status. *American Journal of Public Health* 92: 437–442.

Thun, M., J. Henley, and L. Apicella (1999). Epidemiologic Studies of Fatal and Nonfatal Cardiovascular Disease and ETS Exposure from Spousal Smoking. *Environmental Health Perspectives* 107: 841–846.

Tolley, G. S., D. Kenkel, and R. Fabian, eds. (1994). *Valuing Health for Policy: An Economic Approach*. Chicago: University of Chicago Press.

Tollison, Robert D. (1994). Tax Treatment of Organizations Providing Health Care Services, and Excise Taxes on Tobacco, Guns and Ammunition Testimony before the Senate Committee on Finance, Subcommittee on Health. April 28.

Trogdon, J., and F. Sloan (2003). Effects of the Master Settlement Agreement on Tobacco Consumption. Unpublished paper. Duke University, Durham, N.C.

Trupin, L., D. Rice, and W. Max (1996). Who Pays for the Medical Care of People with Disabilities? Washington, D.C.: U.S. Department of Education, National Institute for Disability and Rehabilitation Research. Abstract No. 16.

Tsevat, J. (1992). Impact and Cost-effectiveness of Smoking Interventions. *American Journal of Medicine* 93: 43S–47S.

U.S. Department of Commerce (2000). Statistical Abstract of the United States, 1999. Washington, D.C.: U.S. Government Printing Office.

U.S. Department of Commerce (2001). Statistical Abstract of the United States, 2001. Washington, D.C.: U.S. Department of Commerce, Bureau of the Census.

U.S. Department of Commerce (2002). Statistical Abstract of the United States, 2002. Washington, D.C.: U.S. Department of Commerce, Bureau of the Census.

U.S. Department of Health and Human Services (1991). Current Intelligence Bulletin 54: Environmental Tobacco Smoke in the Workplace. Washington, D.C.: U.S. Department of Health and Human Services, Public Health Service, Centers for Disease Control, National Institute of Occupational Safety and Health.

U.S. Department of Health and Human Services (1990). The Health Benefits of Smoking Cessation: A Report of the Surgeon General. Atlanta: U.S. Department of Health and Human Services, Public Health Service, Centers for Disease Control, Center for Chronic Disease Prevention and Health Promotion, Office on Smoking and Health, DHHS Pub. No. (CDC) 90-8416.

U.S. Department of Health and Human Services (1986). The Health Consequences of Involuntary Smoking. A Report of the Surgeon General. Bethesda, MD: U.S. Department of Health and Human Services, Public Health Service, Centers for Disease Control, Center for Health Promotion and Education, Office on Smoking and Health. DHHS Publication No. (CDC) 86-2874.

U.S. Department of Health and Human Services (2000a). Reducing Tobacco Use: A Report of the Surgeon General. Atlanta: U.S. Department of Health and Human Services, Centers for Disease Control and Prevention, National Center for Chronic Disease Prevention and Health Promotion, Office on Smoking and Health.

U.S. Department of Health and Human Services (2000b). *Healthy People 2010: Understanding and Improving Health*, second edition, Washington, D.C.: U.S. Government Printing Office.

U.S. Department of Health and Human Services (2001). Women and Smoking: A Report of the Surgeon General. Atlanta: U.S. Department of Health and Human Services, Centers for Disease Control and Prevention, National Center for Chronic Disease Prevention and Health Promotion, Office on Smoking and Health.

U.S. Department of Health, E.a.W. (1972). The Health Consequences of Smoking: A Report of the Surgeon General. Washington, D.C.: U.S. Department of Health, Education, and Welfare, Public Health Services and Mental Health Administration. DHEW Publication No. (HSM) 72-7516.

U.S. Department of Health, E.a.W. (1964). Smoking and Health. Report of the Advisory Committee to the Surgeon General of the Public Health Service. Washington, D.C.: U.S. Department of Health, Education, and Welfare, Public Health Service, Communicable Disease Center. DHEW Publication no. 1103.

U.S. Department of Treasury, O.o.E.P. (1998). *The Economic Costs of Smoking in the United States and the Benefits of Comprehensive Tobacco Legislation*. Washington, D.C.: Government Printing Office.

U.S. Environmental Protection Agency (1992). *Respiratory Health Effects of Passive Smoking: Lung Cancer and Other Disorders*. EPA 600/6-90/00F. Washington, D.C.: U.S. Environmental Protection Agency, Office of Research and Development.

U.S. Environmental Protection Agency (1994). *The Costs and Benefits of Smoking Restrictions: An Assessment of the Smoke-free Environment Act of 1993 (H.R. 3434)*. Washington, D.C.: U.S. Environmental Protection Agency.

U.S. House of Representatives Committee on Ways and Means (1992). 1992 Green Book. Washingon, D.C.: U.S. Government Printing Office.

U.S. House of Representatives Committee on Ways and Means (1998). 1998 Green Book. Washingon, D.C.: U.S. Government Printing Office.

U.S. Physician Payment Review Commission (1995). Annual Report to Congress. Washington, D.C.: Physician Payment Review Commission.

U.S. Prospective Payment Assessment Commission (1995). Medicare and the American Health Care system—Report to Congress. Washington, D.C.: Prospective Payment Assessment Commission.

U.S. Public Health Service (National Center for Health Statistics). (1967). The Health Consequences of Smoking: A Public Service Health Review. *Public Health Service Publication* no. 1696.

U.S. Social Security Administration (1999). Social Security Programs Throughout the World, 1999. Washington, D.C.: U.S. Social Security Administration.

U.S. Social Security Administration (2001). The 2001 Annual Report of the Board of Trustees of the Federal Old-age and Survivors Insurance and Disability Insurance Trust Funds. Washington, D.C.: U.S. Social Security Administration.

United States of America vs. Philip Morris, Inc., et al. (1999). United States District Court, District of Columbia, Civil Action No. 99-CV-02496(GK).

van de Mheen, P. J., and L. J. Gunning-Schepers (1996). Differences between Studies in Reported Relative Risks Associated with Smoking: An Overview. *Public Health Reports* 111: 420–426.

Van Nostrand, J. F., A. Zappolo, E. Hing, B. Bloom, B. Hirsch, and D. J. Foley (1979). The National Nursing Home Survey: 1977 Summary for the United States. National Center for Health Statistics. Series 13: No. 43. (PHS) 79-1794.

van Walbeek, C. P. (1996). Excise Taxes on Tobacco: How Much Scope Does the Government Have? *South African Journal of Economics* 64: 20–42.

van Walbeek, C. P. (2002). The Distributional Impact of Tobacco Excise Increases. *South African Journal of Economics* 70: 560–578.

Viscusi, W. K. (1992). *Smoking: Making the Risky Decision*. Oxford: Oxford University Press.

Viscusi, W. K. (1993). The Value of Risks to Life and Health. *Journal of Economic Literature* 31: 1912–1946.

Viscusi, W. K. (1995). Cigarette Taxation and the Social Consequences of Smoking. In James Poterba (ed.), *Tax Policy and the Economy*. Cambridge, Mass.: The MIT Press.

Viscusi, W. K. (1999). The Governmental Composition of the Insurance Costs of Smoking. *Journal of Law and Economics* 42: 574–609.

Viscusi, W. K. (2002). *Smoke Filled Rooms: A Post Mortem on the Tobacco Deal*. Chicago: University of Chicago Press.

Viscusi, W. K., and J. E. Aldy (2003). The Value of a Statistical Life: A Critical Review of Market Estimates Throughout the World. National Bureau of Economic Research, Working Paper 9647.

Viscusi, W. K., and J. Hersch (2001). Cigarette Smokers as Job Risk Takers. *Review of Economics and Statistics* 83: 269–280.

Vistnes, J. P. (1997). Gender Differences in Days Lost from Work Due to Illness. *Industrial and Labor Relations Review* 50: 304–323.

Warner, K. E., Frank J. Chaloupka, Philip J. Cook , Willard G. Manning, Joseph P. Newhouse, Thomas E. Novtny, Thomas C. Schelling, and Joy Townsend (1995). Criteria for Determining an Optimal Cigarette Tax: The Economist's Perspective. *Tobacco Control* 4: 380–386.

Warner, K. E., Richard Smith, Dean G. Smith, and Brant E. Fires (1996). Health and Economic Implications of a Work-site Smoking-cessation Program: A Simulation Analysis. *Journal of Occupational and Environmental Medicine* 38: 981–992.

Warner, K. E., Thomas A. Hodgson, and Caitlin E. Carroll (1999). Medical Costs of Smoking in the United States: Estimates, Their Validity, and Their Implications. *Tobacco Control* 8: 290–300.

Wasserman, J., W. G. Manning, J. P. Newhouse, J. D. Winkler, and M. Grossman (1991). The Effects of Excise Taxes and Regulations on Cigarette Smoking: The Demand for Cigarettes. *Journal of Health Economics* 10: 43–67.

Watson, L., R. Yoast, S. Wood, and P. L. Remington (1995). The Costs of Cigarette Smoking to Wisconsin's Medicaid Program. *Wisconsin Medical Journal* 94: 263–265.

Weiss, S. T., I. B. Tager, F. E. Speizer, and B. Rosner (1980). Persistent Wheze: Its Relation to Respiratory Illness, Cigarette Smoking, and Level of Pulmonary Function in a Population Sample of Children. *American Review of Respiratory Disease* 122: 697–707.

Weitzman, M. S. G., and A. Sobol (1990). Racial, Social, and Environmental Risks for Childhood Asthma. *American Journal of Diseases of Children* 144: 1189–1194.

Wells, A. J. (1998). Lung Cancer from Passive Smoking at Work. *American Journal of Public Health* 88: 1025–1029.

Wilson, J. J. (1999). Summary of the Attorneys General Master Tobacco Settlement Agreement. *National Conference of State Legislatures*.

Wilson, R. W. (1973). Cigarette Smoking, Disability Days, and Respiratory Conditions. *Journal of Occupational Medicine* 15: 236–240.

Wingerd, J., and E. J. Schoen (1974). Factors Influencing Length at Birth and Height at Five Years. *Pediatrics* 53: 737–741.

Wisborg, K., U. Kesmodel, T. B. Henriksen, S. F. Olsen, and N. J. Secher (2000). A Prospective Study of Smoking During Pregnancy and SIDS. *Archives of Disease in Childhood* 83: 203–206.

Wolfe, Sidney M. (1977). *Economic Costs of Smoking*. Washington, D.C.: Public Citizen's Health Research Group.

Wolfson, M. (2000). *The Fight against Big Tobacco*. Hawthorne, N.Y.: Aldine de Gruyter.

Wong, M. D., M. F. Shapiro, W. J. Boscardin, and S. L. Ettner (2002). Contribution of Major Diseases to Disparities in Mortality. *New England Journal of Medicine* 347: 1585–1592.

Wooden, M., and R. Bush (1995). Smoking Cessation and Absence from Work. *Preventive Medicine* 24: 535–540.

World Health Organization (1997). Tobacco or Health: A Global Status Report. Geneva: World Health Organization.

World Health Organization (2002). *The Tobacco Atlas*. London: Hanway Press.

World Health Organization (2003). Tobacco Free Initiative: Health Impact: Cancer. Accessed January 30, 2003, at http://www.who.int/tobacco/health_impact/cancer/en/.

Wray, L. A., A. Regula Herzon, Robert J. Willis, and Robert B. Wallace (1998). The Impact of Education and Heart Attack on Smoking Cessation among Middle-aged Adults. *Journal of Health and Social Behavior* 39: 271–294.

Wright, V. B. (1986). Will Quitting Smoking Help Medicare Solve Its Financial Problems? *Inquiry* 23: 76–82.

You, R. X., A. G. Thrift, J. J. McNeil, S. M. Davis, and G. A. Donnan (1999). Ischemic Stroke Risk and Passive Exposure to Spouses' Cigarette Smoking: Melbourne Stroke Risk Factor Study (MERFS) Group. *American Journal of Public Health* 89: 572–575.

Zhang, J., and J. M. Ratcliffe (1993). Paternal Smoking and Birthweight in Shanghai. *American Journal of Public Health* 83: 207–210.

Index